We Fought the Navy and Won

We Fought the Navy

and Won A PERSONAL MEMOIR

Guam's Quest for Democracy

Doloris Coulter Cogan

A Latitude 20 Book | University of Hawai'i Press | Honolulu

Library of Congress Cataloging in Publication Data
Cogan, Doloris Coulter.
We fought the Navy and won : Guam's quest for
democracy / Doloris Coulter Cogan.
    p. cm.
"A Latitude 20 book."
Includes bibliographical references and index.
ISBN 978-0-8248-3089-2 (hardcover : alk. paper)
ISBN 978-0-8248-3216-2 (pbk. : alk. paper)
    1. Guam — Relations — United States.   2. United
States — Relations — Guam.   3. Guam — History —
Autonomy and independence movements.   4. Guam —
Politics and government — 20th century.   5. Democracy
— Guam — History — 20th century.   6. Representative
government and representation — Guam — History
— 20th century.   7. United States. Navy — History —
20th century.   8. Collier, John, 1884–1968.   9. Cogan,
Doloris Coulter.   10. Journalists — United States —
Biography.   I. Title.
E183.8.G86C64   2008
327.967073 — dc22   2008001823

Designed by April Leidig-Higgins

Printed by The Maple-Vail Book Manufacturing Group

Dedicated to the memory
of John Collier and the brave Chamorros
who stood up to the United States Navy
in Guam's quest for self-government

Contents

Guam.

Acknowledgments

If it were not for Betty Winquest Cooper, I would not be the one telling this story. A college friend of mine from Nebraska Wesleyan University, Betty was employed by John Collier as executive secretary of the new Institute of Ethnic Affairs in 1946, and it was she who recommended that I be hired as editor of publications. Upon graduating from Wesleyan in 1945, Betty had gone directly to Washington, D.C., for management training in the federal government by the National Institute of Public Affairs. Part of her internship had included working with Collier in the Bureau of Indian Affairs. I had gone to New York City and was getting my master's degree from the Graduate School of Journalism at Columbia University in June of 1946. We were the Institute's only paid staff members throughout the most critical four years when the action of this book was taking place. We shared an office; we shared an appreciation for cultures other than our own; we shared an understanding of democratic government; and we became lifelong friends. Betty has participated in dozens of ways in the creation of this book.

I am also indebted to Carlos Taitano, who read the first draft of my manuscript and encouraged me to include more about the cultural history of Guam. He also made other worthwhile suggestions. Carlos was the young Guam Assemblyman who notified the press in Hawai'i when the lower house of the Guam Congress walked out in protest against continued United States Navy rule in 1949. He later became known to some as "Mr. Organic Act." Carlos, at eighty-eight, and I, at eighty-one, were lucky to be alive in 2005 when the manuscript was being revised.

I am particularly grateful to Dr. Lee D. Carter, coeditor of *Guam History: Perspectives, Vol. 1,* whom I met on Guam in the year 2000 and who asked me for a chapter for the intended *Perspectives, Vol. 2.* While preparing to write a chapter, I discovered I had a whole book.

It was Robert F. Rogers, author of *Destiny's Landfall,* the comprehensive history of Guam first published in 1995, who read and did the first cutting of my overlong manuscript and who constantly encouraged me to be patient about the publishing process, as this was my first book.

Others who read and commented on my first draft included Dirk Ballendorf, director of the Micronesian Area Research Center and professor of History and Micronesian Studies at the University of Guam; Marjorie G. Driver, curator of the Spanish Documents Collection at the Micronesian Area Research Center; Arnold Liebowitz, author of *Defining Status;* Byron B. Bender, editor, *Oceanic Linguistics,* who spent several years in Micronesia as an administrator; Alfred Laureta, retired judge of the U.S. District Court, Saipan, N.M.I., Joseph Lehman, former attorney in the Marshall Islands; Retired Navy Commander Richard Takahashi, who spent years on Guam and in the Pentagon during the Vietnam War; John Fisher, retired English professor at Goshen College and a peace activist who wrote the first favorable review; and Virginia Manley, retired Assistant Superintendent Concord Community Schools, a close friend who was the first to wade through my long manuscript and recognize its historical significance.

Archivists who went the extra mile in helping me obtain historical photos included Lewis Wyman and Kenneth Johnson at the U.S. Library of Congress; Pauline Testerman at the Harry S. Truman Library; Kim Robinson at the Interior Museum; an unnamed staff at the National Archives and Records Administration; and Monica Storie, Lou Nededog, John Sablan, and Perry Pangelinan at the Micronesian Area Research Center, who spent hours finding suitable photos.

Rod Liechty, a retired teacher of both art and history at Elkhart Central High School, suggested cover designs for the book. Julie Barth, president of Pearl Design, gave me constant encouragement as well as tutorials on the use of my new IMac G-5 computer. Jeff Hudson, a history buff at Express Press in Elkhart, expedited multitudinous copies of the manuscript every time I ordered them.

Most of all, I want to thank Bill Hamilton, director of the University of Hawaiʻi Press, who believed enough in what I was writing to take the manuscript to his editorial board for approval and was supportive all the rest of the way; Ann Ludeman, managing editor, who actually had lived on Guam in the 1970s and could closely relate to what she was reading; and Barbara Folsom, manuscript editor, whose refinement of what I had written was beautifully done and mutually agreeable in every respect.

To my grown sons, Tom, Richard and Doug Cogan, who have interesting careers of their own, just let me say thanks for making suggestions and standing by as the months grew into years while I worked on the book.

Introduction

This book is about the five-year struggle, between 1945 and 1950, leading up to the Organic Act of Guam. It is about the Chamorros who defied the U.S. Navy in their determination to achieve the civil rights that they correctly believed were promised them when Guam was taken from Spain in 1898. It is also about the Institute of Ethnic Affairs and John Collier, its founder, his anthropologist wife, Laura Thompson, its scholarly directors, and the small staff, who worked tirelessly in support of the Guamanians.

This is the *detailed* story of how the Chamorros achieved United States citizenship and civilian government shortly after the end of World War II. Much of it is from the Washington perspective. While the Guam Assembly walkout in 1949 and its significance are well known to those interested in Guam's history, this is the first time the full five-year story has been told.

I am in the fortunate position of being able to tell it because I lived it. I was editor of publications for the Institute of Ethnic Affairs from June 1946 through December 1949, when most of the action took place. Located in Washington, D.C., the Institute published a total of thirty monthly *News Letters* devoted to articles about dependent peoples worldwide. To some extent, those newsletters chronicled the end of twentieth-century colonialism. I was there to help write and edit all but the first three and last three issues. Beginning in February 1946, the Institute published thirty-seven monthly *Guam Echos*, a kind of newspaper for the people of Guam. I wrote and edited all but the last three of those as well.

In writing this book, I had the yellowed copies of those publications by my side. I hadn't read them in more than fifty years. And when I began reading them in 2004, I found they held the suspense of a mystery story. They told how the advocates of self-determination for Guam introduced the final campaign for civilian administration in the spring of 1946 and how proponents of continued military occupancy staunchly defended navy rule during the next four years.

At the invitation of Collier and Dr. Thompson, former Interior Secretary Harold L. Ickes launched the campaign with a hard-hitting speech against continued naval administration at the first annual meeting of the Institute of Ethnic Affairs in Washington, D.C., on May 29, 1946. Taken by surprise, Navy Secretary James V. Forrestal found himself in the position of having to defend half a century of naval neglect of both Guam and American Samoa. Collier and Dr. Thompson corroborated Ickes' adverse facts, prompting Forrestal to send news reporters to the field in a doomed effort to refute them. The Hopkins Committee, the United States Congress, the United Nations, newspapers, and a few national magazines got into the act. Meanwhile, Forrestal attempted to throttle Collier with an adverse ruling from the IRS preventing the Institute from receiving tax-free contributions.

Part of the story centers around a young Chamorro named Carlos Taitano who came back to Guam in 1948 after serving with the U.S. Army in the Pacific under General MacArthur during World War II, imbued with the determination to see that his people obtained the civil rights promised when the United States took the Philippines, Cuba, and Guam from Spain at the turn of the twentieth century. Taitano was elected to the advisory Guam Assembly, the lower house of the Guam Congress; and on March 5, 1949, when that body walked out because the naval governor wouldn't let them subpoena a stateside man perhaps illegally involved in Guam business, Taitano quietly telegraphed the AP and UPI in Hawai'i, which spread the word to the *Washington Post* and other American publications. Collier and I wrote a widely distributed press release stating the significance of the walkout, and as editor of the *Guam Echo* I further publicized the situation through an op-ed to the *Post* and a letter to the *New York Times*. The walkout was the catalyst that finally brought the U.S. Congress around to passing the Organic Act of Guam, but the process still dragged on for seventeen months and required constant surveillance.

This was a seesaw battle fought at the very top of our government. It was a David and Goliath struggle between the military and civilian forces that President Harry Truman finally ended by signing the Organic Act of Guam on August 1, 1950. Taitano and key stateside officials were present at the signing, as is shown on this book's cover.

The timing of the campaign was right. Hundreds of thousands of young American men (and some women) had enlisted in the armed services in the early 1940s to save democracy from the totalitarian regimes of Germany, Russia, and Japan. In 1946 they were returning home. That helped. When the plight of the Guamanians became known through the national media, the leaders of the campaign for civilian government had support from these young veterans. For example, 200,000 American servicemen were stationed on Guam in 1944 and 1945 as the United States prepared for the final battles against Japan in World War II. When they came back to the United States they did not forget Guam. Some servicemen, like Roy James and Dick Wels, both attorneys, gave voice to the rights of the islanders they had come to know. I am hopeful this book will be of interest to anyone who has ever been to Guam — or to their descendants.

Unlike the battles those servicemen fought with their lives, this was a philosophical war in which not one bullet was fired. Instead, verbal volleys were launched and public relations strategies were employed. This battle was publicly discussed and argued out in the halls of the United States Congress. It holds lessons for the Middle and Far East conflicts in which our government finds itself in the twenty-first century. One retired naval officer who read the manuscript has suggested that this book should be in the library of every college and university that has an ROTC office.

Guamanian leaders who fought for the changes included B. J. Bordallo, F. B. Leon Guerrero, Antonio Won Pat, and Concepcion Barrett — all of whom were members of the Guam Congress — as well as Agueda Johnston, assistant superintendent of Guam schools. All visited Washington, D.C., at different times and did their part in persuading Congress that an organic act should be passed. Simon A. Sanchez, superintendent of Guam schools, well understood democracy and was a civil rights activist who encouraged Guamanians to become informed by joining the Institute of Ethnic Affairs and reading our publications. These leaders were backed by the twenty-one thousand other indigenous inhabitants. The battle could not have been won without them.

Credit for the results of this campaign must also be given Julius A. Krug, who succeeded Harold L. Ickes as Secretary of the Interior. Oscar L. Chapman followed Mr. Krug as secretary and brought the campaign to its conclusion. Roy E. James, an attorney who had spent time with the military government on Guam during the war, was their point man in the Office of Territorial Affairs at Interior. Emil J. Sady, a protégé of John Collier and a student of military government, was assigned to the Pacific Islands desk at the State Department and got the Organic Act ball rolling. Philleo Nash, a member of the board of the Institute of Ethnic Affairs, was the White House staff member in charge of issues involving minorities; he provided inestimable help. The names of many United States Congressmen appear throughout this book and in the appendixes. I have included photographs of those my memory tells me were the most important. I apologize if I have missed some.

Eventually, even the Navy came around to supporting the necessary legislation, particularly Navy Secretary John L. Sullivan, Under Secretary W. John Kenney, and Captain Peter G. Hale, Chief of the Office of Island Governments, Navy Department, 1948–1950.

Guam's campaign for civil rights was led by a handful of dedicated people at a cost so small it can hardly be figured. Over the five years from 1945 to 1950, many people joined in, but the hard work was done by only a few. I learned then what the anthropologist Margaret Mead has often been quoted as saying: "Never doubt that a small group of thoughtful committed citizens can change the world. Indeed, it is the only thing that ever has."

I have written this book mostly for the children and grandchildren of the people of Guam who populated the island at the end of World War II. More than five hundred Guamanians were members of the Institute of Ethnic Affairs, and consequently subscribers to the *Guam Echo* when the Organic Act of Guam was finally passed. They included members of the Guam Congress, leaders of the local village councils, Catholic priests and lay leaders, business men and women, doctors, teachers, and ordinary residents of Guam. They were solidly behind the change and let the movers and shakers in Washington know that.

Washington readers of the *Guam Echo* included Navy, Interior, and State Department officials; members of the U.S. Congress; a few White House staff members; veterans of the armed services formerly stationed on Guam; magazine and newspaper reporters and editors; the board and membership of the Institute of Ethnic Affairs. This book is for them and their descendants, too.

To a lesser extent, I have written this book for the sons and daughters living in American Samoa and the former Trust Territory of the Pacific Islands. One future governor of American Samoa, Peter Coleman, while a law school student at George Washington University, shared an office with me at Interior in 1951 and became my lifelong friend.

Last but not least, I have written this memoir to supplement other histories of those postwar years and document the end of one phase of American colonialism. I hope it will be used in high schools and colleges wherever history and government are taught. Perhaps the most important lesson of this book is that democracy must always come from the people to be governed; it can never be imposed from the outside. A secondary lesson is that freedom of the press plays an important part in achieving and sustaining true democracy. When discourse and legislation supplant guns and missiles, humankind will have learned these lessons well.

* * *

Full sets of both the *News Letter* and the *Guam Echo* are in the collections of the Library of Congress in Washington, D.C.; Hamilton Library at the University of Hawai'i at Mānoa; and the Micronesian Area Research Center at the University of Guam.

Chapter 1

Welcome to Guam

"Welcome home," he said, standing there at the end of the ramp as I descended from Pan-American's Strato Clipper that had brought me to Guam.

It was B. J. Bordallo, longtime leader in the Guam Congress, speaking. He, along with Simon Sanchez, superintendent of schools, and Agueda Iglesias Johnston, assistant superintendent, had come as a welcoming committee. It was late afternoon on a beautiful day early in June 1951.

That was a moment I will never forget. Here I was, a young woman from Nebraska, then twenty-six, who had traveled alone halfway around the world to visit the far-flung Pacific islands. I had never been to Guam before. And yet these islanders were welcoming me "home" like a long-lost daughter. I was there in my capacity as Pacific Island Assistant in the Office of Territories at the United States Department of the Interior.

The weekend before, for the first time in our eight-month marriage, I had left Tom, my husband, alone in Washington, D.C., working in the State Department. He was proud that I had been asked by the Departments of the Navy and Interior to make this orientation trip to Guam and the Trust Territory of the Pacific Islands. A Navy man himself, his ship had stopped at Eniwetok and Okinawa en route to China, where he had served as an epidemiologist at the hospital in Peking (now Beijing) at the end of World War II. He knew quite a bit about where I was going.

I had already worked more than four years in Washington for the new Institute of Ethnic Affairs. That job had taken me to Latin America for three weeks in 1949 to an Inter-American Indian Conference. More important, it had given me an in-depth introduction to the Pacific islands. For more than four years, I had been writer/editor of a monthly "newspaper" for the people of Guam, named by them the *Guam Echo*. A long weekend in Honolulu en route to Micronesia had given me plenty of time to think about Guam. If Hawai'i is "paradise," what would Guam be like?

I knew I would be housed in a Quonset hut. There were no hotels on

Guam in 1951. It was still suffering from the ravages of World War II. But I didn't care. What I cared about was the indigenous people I would meet and what I could learn of their needs. I was an idealist when it came to democracy and self-government. Along with others connected with the Institute of Ethnic Affairs, I had worked hard for the Organic Act of Guam — a constitution, in effect, establishing separate executive, legislative, and judiciary branches of Guam's local government. And here were three political and educational leaders of Guam who had been directly involved — Mr. Bordallo, Mr. Sanchez, and Mrs. Johnston. They had actually come to the airport to meet me. I hadn't expected that.

I knew Mrs. Johnston best. A Chamorro married to an American citizen shipped to Japan as a prisoner of war early in 1942 and left to die there, Mrs. Johnston was the beloved principal of the high school on Guam before becoming assistant superintendent of schools. She and Mr. Sanchez were civic leaders. In the late summer of 1949 she had come to the United States to visit some of her children then in college on the West Coast. In October she had visited John Collier, president of the Institute of Ethnic Affairs, and his wife, Laura Thompson, author of *Guam and Its People,* in New York City. They had encouraged her to go on to Washington and see members of Congress about the proposed Organic Act of Guam then awaiting debate. I met her in Washington and got to know her fairly well.

I knew B. J. Bordallo less well. His family in Guam had been prominent for perhaps centuries, even when the island was under Spanish rule. I knew him as a leader of the Guam Congress and one of the island's strongest advocates of American citizenship for his people and civilian government for Guam. He had gone to Washington twice, once in 1937 and again in 1949, to lobby for those civil rights. I had met him briefly in 1949.

I had never before met Mr. Sanchez, superintendent of Guam schools. Well-educated and politically savvy, he was another active proponent of civilian government. One of the very first Guam members of the Institute of Ethnic Affairs, he had voluntarily collected the $5.00-a-year memberships from other indigenous residents of the island, known as Chamorros, and mailed them to us in Washington, D.C.

But before I go further, let me tell you a little about the geography, history, and culture of Guam. To really appreciate what transpired between 1945 and 1950, one must be aware of the five millennia of discovery and cultural isolation followed by the five centuries of foreign domination that preceded the five short years of my story.

The first habitation of Micronesia, of which Guam is a part, goes back to about 4,000 B.C., when daring seafarers in small boats sailed north from Southeast Asia. By 1,500 B.C. these explorers are thought to have reached what is now the Mariana Islands.[1]

Guam is the southernmost and largest of the fifteen islands in the Marianas archipelago. These islands are actually the peaks of a huge undersea mountain range that rises more than six miles off the bottom of the Mariana Trench, the deepest known spot in the world's oceans. Other well-known islands in the Mariana chain are Saipan, Tinian, and Rota.

With 209 square miles of landmass, Guam constitutes 20 percent of the entire dry land of Micronesia and is the most useful for shipping, communications, and military purposes. A peanut-shaped island thirty miles long and four to ten miles wide, Guam's southern bulge is volcanic and valued for its mountains, streams, lush vegetation, and picturesque villages. The northern half is volcanic, topped with a broad-reef limestone plateau and tropical growth, much of which has been cleared for large airfields. The temperature is warm and humid, averaging over 80° F. At the narrowest part of Guam, about at the middle of the island, are two fine boat harbors at Agana Bay and Tumon Bay. Closer to the southern end of the island, just before Orote Peninsula that juts five miles out into the Philippine Sea, is an even larger harbor for large ships, called Apra Harbor. All have figured prominently in the island's history.

Guam's time zone is fifteen hours ahead of the U.S. East Coast. Located just west of the International Date Line, Guam claims the right to be called, "Where America's Day Begins." It lies about 3,500 miles from Hawai'i, 1,500 miles from the Philippines, and 1,300 miles from Japan. Because Guam is in the path of the northeast winds and astride the ocean current that flows northwestward across the Pacific, it has been on trade routes and of strategic interest to the Great Powers for the last five hundred years.

Guam's first contact with the West occurred about thirty years after Columbus discovered America in 1492. In 1517, a Portuguese navigator named Ferdinand Magellan asked King Charles I of Spain to sponsor a voyage to Asia by way of South America. The king agreed because the Portuguese controlled the seas around the Horn of Africa, and if this Portuguese sea captain were to be successful, Spain would have its own route to Asia in search of spices.

Much of what follows I learned from *Destiny's Landfall,* the comprehensive history of Guam delightfully written by Robert F. Rogers and published

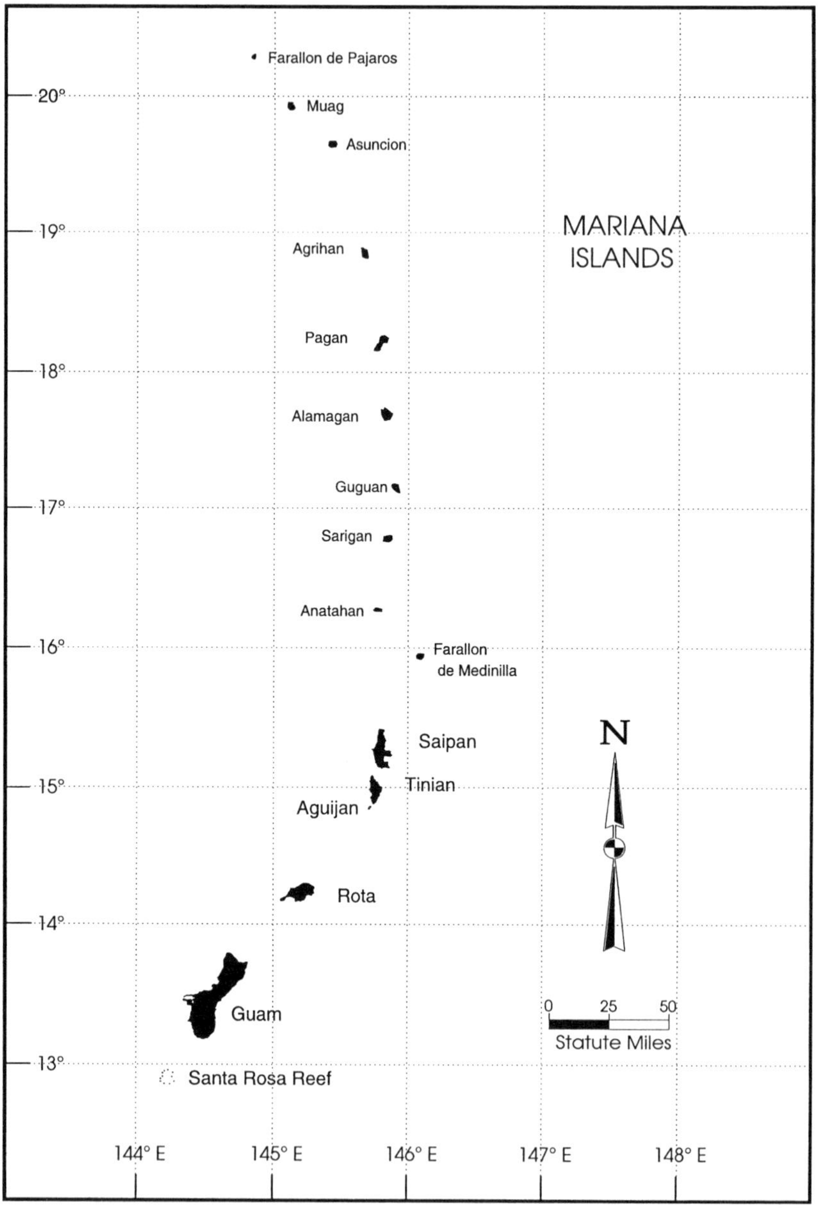

The Mariana Islands.

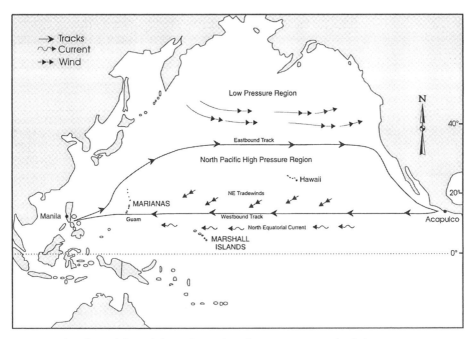

Spanish galleons followed the trade winds and ocean currents in both directions, making the 3,000-mile, one-way trip in about six months.

by the University of Hawai'i Press in 1995. He was then a professor at the University of Guam.

On September 20, 1519, Magellan sailed forth from Spain with five ships and a crew of about 240 men. On March 6, 1521, a much smaller, tired and hungry crew in only three ships spotted land that would later come to be known as Rota and Guam.[2] As the *Trinidad,* the *Concepcion,* and the *Victoria* sailed toward Guam, they were surrounded by proas (outrigger canoes) coming toward them. Pigafetta wrote in the ships' chronicle that the islanders in the boats were darkly tawny, taller than the Spaniards, had straight black hair, and wore no clothes. These were the Chamorros of the 1500s.

The first clash of cultures took place immediately. The islanders, out of curiosity, began swarming over Magellan's ships and carrying away whatever they could lay their hands on. The Europeans were unaware of a traditional custom whereby new arrivals on a Pacific island were expected to present gifts to their hosts and allow those same hosts to take anything they wished. The surprised Spaniards, filled with rage and too tired from

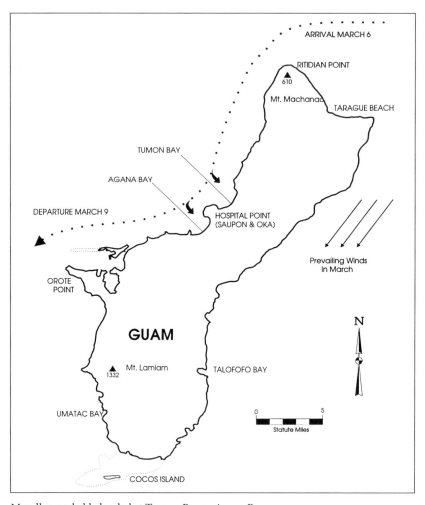

Magellan probably landed at Tumon Bay or Agana Bay.

the long trip to fight hand-to-hand, began firing crossbows at the invaders. The shocked islanders had never before seen such weapons, so after a few deadly encounters they hurriedly left the scene, but not before making off with a small rowboat being towed behind the *Trinidad*. The skiff was important to Magellan, as his crew used it to sound ocean depths with a weighted line ahead of the main ship. Consequently, the very next day, the sailors lowered two frigates so their captain and about forty men in full armor could go ashore and recover the boat. Angry and intent on imposing their will, when they reached land the Spaniards proceeded to burn at least forty huts and several proas. They killed eight Chamorros in the process, but suffered no casualties themselves. This episode left a bad taste in Magellan's mouth and caused him to name the islands the Islas de los Ladrones (Islands of the Thieves), an epithet that stuck for three centuries. Magellan's bad beginning with the islanders set a precedent for future relations with invaders who did not understand or respect the local customs.

It was almost 150 years after the arrival of Magellan that Spain laid claim to the Mariana Islands in 1665. Serious colonizing began in 1668, and then it was Father Diego Luis de San Vitores, a zealous Jesuit missionary with powerful connections to both church and state, who asserted authority. He had with him four other priests, some Filipino catechists, and a complement of soldiers—a little band of fifty foreigners expecting to convert to Christianity 12,000 Chamorros on Guam and an estimated 12,000 to 18,000 Chamorros on the other Mariana Islands. The Spanish Conquest took the next thirty years, and it was brutal.

This period was marked by the Chamorros' growing resentment of the Jesuits' unknowing erosion of the islanders' traditions. It began soon after his arrival in 1668 when San Vitores tried to convert hundreds of adults at once, promising them baptism after doctrinal instruction. The *chamorri* nobles of Agana insisted that baptism be restricted to them alone and not be granted to commoners. Tolerance ebbed when San Vitores further insisted on the destruction of ancestor skulls and other idols before he would baptize Quipuha, the highest-ranking *chamorri* of Agana. Confidence disappeared when some newborn infants died soon after baptism and the Chamorros began telling each other that the baptismal water must be poisonous. Within three years, the resentment grew into actual warfare. On September 11, 1671, two thousand *chamorri* warriors attacked the little group of Spaniards holed up in the Agana church and residence. The end came on April 2, 1672, when Father San Vitores asked permission to baptize the newborn daughter of Mata'pang, the headman of Tumon. Mata'pang refused and threatened to kill the priest. When Mata'pang and another villager went to search for lances, Father San Vitores stole into the house and performed the ceremony anyway. Enraged by the priest's arrogance, Mata'pang and his companion killed San Vitores and Pedro Calonsor, his aide, slashed open their heads with machetes, stripped their bodies naked, dragged them down to the shore, placed them in a boat, tied stones to their feet, paddled over the Tumon reef, and tossed the bodies overboard.

After the murder of San Vitores, the *chamorri* no longer had a choice.

Father San Vitores brought to Guam both an intolerable
military and a forgiving church.

Either they accepted Christianity or they were killed by the Spanish soldiers whose numbers increased when news of the priest's death reached
Manila, and later Spain. The Spanish nobles reacted with force to retrieve
a failing religious mission, especially since it was one in which their queen,
Mariana, had a personal and financial interest.

During the succeeding years, things went from bad to worse. In 1672,
Mata'pang and his accomplice fled to Rota to escape retribution. Small-
scale clashes between the *chamorri* and Spanish soldiers in Guam took
place in village after village, causing hundreds of Chamorro deaths. Seeking relief, whole villages sometimes moved to other islands. The islanders
on Guam were scattered, and by 1676 the Spanish soldiers began to take

away small children who had been orphaned or temporarily abandoned and gave them to priests to be raised in mission schools.

Pestilence took its toll in 1688 when supply ships from Acapulco reached Guam. The crew or passengers infected the island with diseases to which the islanders had no immunity, perhaps influenza or smallpox. Eighty people died within three months — 5 percent of the population. Venereal and other infections introduced earlier by the Spanish caused infertility, which also became a cause of depopulation. Disintegration of life patterns led to suicides, fewer marriages, and fewer births. Women purposely sterilized themselves or, if they conceived, found ways to abort or even kill their babies after birth in order to save them from subjugation to the Spaniards.

Large-scale clashes resulting in higher numbers of deaths revolved around three unsuccessful sieges of the Agana forts in 1671–1672, in 1676–1677, and in 1684. The Chamorro warriors attacked repeatedly despite being overpowered by Spanish firepower. In all instances, the Spaniards had the advantage of muskets and small cannons, while the *chamorri* were still fighting with sling-stones, lances, and machetes. Many return punitive sweeps by the Spanish soldiers killed hundreds of the islanders outright. Others died from disease, food shortages, other deprivations, and stress.

Although the Spanish soldiers seldom killed Chamorros except in combat and the missionaries tried to protect the islanders from harm, the historian Robert F. Rogers concluded in *Destiny's Landfall* that the Spanish colonial system was responsible for the decimation of the very people it sought to save. By 1689, Father José Hernandez of the Umatac church stated that the entire population of Guam, including Spaniards and Filipinos, was only 1,800 people. This was an enormous decline from the estimated 12,000 who populated Guam when Father San Vitores had arrived twenty-one years before. The total population of all the Marianas other than Guam was thought to be only 7,000, down from the 12,000 to 18,000 who were there in 1668.

It became imperative for the Spaniards to move all the remaining Chamorros in the northern islands to Guam, not only to cultivate crops and grow livestock to supply the visiting galleons and the Spanish garrison but to complete the religious conversion of the islanders, which was the basic purpose of the Spanish presence in the Marianas from the beginning. When the Chamorros of Tinian saw the Spanish fleet coming, they sent their women and children to the small, rugged island of Aguijan. That island has no beaches. It rises directly out of the sea and has steep cliffs crowned by a flat top. Joining their families later, the Tinian warriors dug trenches at the top from which to ward off the invading Spanish warriors. Finally overwhelmed after several of their men were killed, some Chamorros committed suicide by jumping off the cliffs. That scene has become a symbol of the Chamorros' defiance against Spanish rule.

In 1698, the new governor, José Madrazo, sent a final expedition of Spanish and Chamorro troops to the far northern islands of the Marianas, where about 1,000 people were rounded up and taken to Guam. Many died en route when some of the boats were swamped in a typhoon. From then on, the Spaniards required that all Chamorros reside only on Guam, Saipan, or Rota. The northern islands remained uninhabited for the next hundred years.

So ended the blood-drenched years of the Spanish Conquest.

For two hundred more years, Spain governed the Marianas. More than fifty different governors were assigned to Guam from 1668 to 1898. Much of what follows here I learned from the splendid new book, *The Spanish Governors of the Mariana Islands and the Saga of the Palacio,* written by Marjorie G. Driver and published by the University of Guam in 2005. She teaches at the University of Guam and serves as curator of the Spanish Documents Collection at the Micronesian Area Research Center.[3]

Most Spanish governors brought families with them to Agana. A great deal of time was spent building, maintaining, and rebuilding the Palacio (official residence) and the presidio (military garrison). Labor was supplied by the Spanish soldiers and the Chamorros, who, rather than being taxed, were required to work a given number of days each year on the royal farms or other public projects. A seminary for boys, the Colegio de san Juan de Letran, had been established by Father San Vitores in 1679 and endowed by Queen Mariana. In tribute to her support and generosity, the priest had changed the name of the archipelago from Las Islas de los Ladrones to the Mariana Islands. An attractive warehouse, the Almacen, for both local and foreign products, was built in the 1700s. Trade proved a temptation too difficult for several governors to resist, and they sometimes profited personally from illicit sales. Other governors strongly objected to commercial abuses and tried to open up economic opportunities that rightly belonged to the islanders. The population of Guam increased during the last third of Spanish rule. At the end of the Spanish administration in 1898, Agana was described as having a population of slightly more than 6,000, and there may have been almost 9,000 on all of Guam.

Spanish coat of arms.

During the Spanish period, the brave Chamorros adapted to whatever came across the waves, whether from Spain, Mexico, or the Philippines. The islanders crossed with so many other peoples that after two centuries there were almost no Chamorros left who had bloodlines unmixed with people of other cultures.

The extreme isolation of the Mariana Islands presented a difficult situation for the Spanish authorities from a communications and shipping standpoint. Galleons from Mexico would make the round-trip voyage through Guam and on to the Philippines about once a year. Letters would take at least that long to get delivered, and building supplies ordered in one year often would not arrive until the next. The indigenous inhabitants under Spain's control everywhere became rebellious, and her great empire began to shrink. Mexico and Peru broke away and became independent. Other countries then saw their chance to acquire what was left of Spain's outlying possessions. This brings us to the Spanish-American War in 1898, when the United States wrested Cuba, Puerto Rico, the Philippines, and Guam from Spain.

The Spanish-American War has been said to have grown out of the expansionist ambitions of Theodore (Teddy) Roosevelt when he was Assistant Secretary of the Navy in the 1890s. He was aided and abetted by Massachusetts Senator Henry Cabot Lodge and the naval strategist Alfred Thayer Mahon. Mahon, in particular, preached that in order for the United States to become a great nation it must extend its sea power into the Pacific and Caribbean (leaving the Atlantic to be controlled by the friendly British navy), and that trade would follow the flag. According to Rogers, by 1898 the United States had already tiptoed into Oceania as a hesitant colonial power with claims of sovereignty over several tiny unclaimed islands: Jarvis, Baker, and Howland in 1856 and Midway in 1867.[4]

Twenty years later, in 1887, the United States obtained exclusive use of Pearl Harbor as a naval station in return for allowing the Kingdom of Hawai'i to export sugar duty-free to the United States. A treaty of annexation was signed in 1898. Having previously entered into a protectorate over Samoa in the South Pacific with Germany and Great Britain, in 1899 the United States acquired American Samoa with its strategic Pago Pago Harbor.

Cuba became the center of attention in the late 1890s when William Randolph Hearst's newspaper, the *New York Journal,* and others like it criticized the autocratic military rule of Spain there. On February 15, 1898, the American battleship *Maine* mysteriously blew up on a visit to Havana. Teddy Roosevelt then proclaimed, "The *Maine* was sunk by an act of dirty treachery on the part of the Spaniards." Although no proof was ever presented, on April 15, 1898, the United States Congress declared war on Spain.

In fulfillment of Roosevelt's dream of expansion, Navy Captain Henry Glass was ordered to sail west out of Hawai'i en route to Manila on June 4, 1898. As soon as he was clear of land, he opened his sealed orders and found to his surprise that he was first "to capture the port of Guam, and to make prisoners of the governor and other officials and any armed forces that may be there" before proceeding on to the Philippines. This was to be done in no more than two days. Mahon and the U.S. Naval War Board in Washington saw Guam as a future coaling station to support the campaign in the Philippines. Arriving at Agana on June 20, Glass fired shells at Fort Santa Cruz expecting to draw fire, but no shots were returned. Not knowing that Spain and the United States were at war, the Spanish garrison on Guam mistook the U.S. gunfire for a salute! It was all too easy for Glass to ask for and accept their surrender. Two days later the cruiser embarked

Captain Henry Glass, U.S.N., in command of the USS *Charleston,* was ordered to capture Guam for the United States en route to the Philippines in 1898.

for Manila with Guam's Spanish governor and the entire Spanish garrison aboard.

Impatient to get to the Philippines, Glass sailed forth leaving no U.S. officers or enlisted men on Guam to oversee America's newest possession. He had, however, become acquainted with Francisco (Frank) Portusach, a Chamorro mestizo who spoke English. Notably entrepreneurial, Frank had offered his boats to load coal onto the *Charleston* while Glass was deciding what to do. When departing, Glass apparently told Portusach to take care of the island until some other naval officers might reach there. Portusach took the command literally.

During his second day on Guam, Glass had personally inspected Fort Santa Cruz and ordered his men to raise an American flag while a twenty-one-gun salute boomed out from the *Charleston* and the "Star Spangled

Banner" was played by bands on the troop ships. Three war correspondents aboard ship later reported that this had been accomplished at 2:45 p.m. on June 21, 1898. Later in the afternoon, however, the flag was lowered and taken back to the *Charleston,* since Glass did not know whether the United States intended to retain Guam permanently.

One Spanish official on Guam, José Sixto Rodriguez, administrator of the treasury, was not taken prisoner, apparently because he was a civilian. In the absence of American military authority on the island, Sixto claimed Spanish sovereignty over Guam and for months continued Spanish rule. He gathered a pro-Spanish group and a small Chamorro militia around himself. Having control of the government money, he liberally paid himself a salary as acting governor and, to assure their loyalty, paid his advisers and the Chamorro militamen as well. By Christmas 1898, the treasury was about empty. Law and order were breaking down.

Meanwhile, Frank Portusach and several prominent Chamorros, including Father José Bernardo Palomo, had formed a pro-American group. They had not attempted to occupy the governor's residence. Not yet.

Halfway around the world, on June 22, 1898, as the American convoy was departing from Guam, an American army of 17,000 enthusiastic soldiers was invading Cuba. By August 12, fighting ceased in Cuba and Puerto Rico under an armistice, as it did the next day in the Philippines. Spanish soldiers in the "Battle of Manila" surrendered after a mock show of resistance. The fighting had lasted less than four months. Theodore Roosevelt called it "a splendid little war." A protocol signed on August 12, 1898, outlined the terms of the peace. Spain agreed to give up Cuba, cede Puerto Rico and Guam to the United States, and permit the United States to occupy the city, bay, and harbor at Manila pending a peace treaty to determine the control, disposition, and government of the Philippines.

As Spain moved out of the western Pacific, Germany and Japan moved in. Germany wanted part of the Philippines and Micronesia, as did the United States and Japan, but was rebuffed. Germany then negotiated secretly with Spain, and on September 10, 1898, an agreement was signed allowing Germany to purchase the Marshalls and Carolines, including Palau and all the Marianas except Guam, for the equivalent of 4.2 million American dollars at that time. Spain would continue to govern those islands until its separate treaty with the United States was concluded. The Japanese were left out of the agreement.

In September 1889, the *Literary Digest* took a poll of 192 newspaper editors and found that the majority favored U.S. annexation of the conquered Spanish areas for U.S. naval bases. President William McKinley, a religious man educated in a seminary, later wrote, "The truth is I didn't want the Philippines and when they came to us as a gift from the gods, I did not know what to do with them. . . ."[5] So when the U.S. peace commissioners cabled from Paris for instructions, McKinley replied that the United States was prepared to offer $20 million to Spain for all the Philippines, including Guam. Of course, Guam was not part of the Philippines; McKinley obviously did not know that. His response seemed like an ultimatum, so Spain accepted it. The incorrect wording tied Guam's future destiny to the Philippines, just as it had been tied for most of the past three centuries.

The Treaty of Paris between Her Majesty Maria Cristina, queen regent of Spain, and the United States of America was signed on December 10, 1898. It was ratified by both governments in early 1899 and proclaimed law on April 11, 1899. The debate over the treaty was historic in that it made the United States a colonial nation and a major Pacific power.

Article IX of the Treaty of Paris is of particular importance to Guam and to this book. It states, "The civil rights and political status of the native inhabitants of the territories hereby ceded to the United States shall be determined by Congress." Rogers, in his *Destiny's Landfall,* summarizes the significance of the Treaty of Paris in this way:

> At no time in the transfer of sovereignty did American or Spanish officials consult with the inhabitants of Guam. And nowhere in the treaty did the United States explicitly obligate itself to bring the people of Guam to self-government or to improve their political, social, or economic well-being. There is no stipulation in the treaty that sovereignty remain in the hands of the indigenous people, and there is no acknowledgment of indigenous rights in the treaty other than what the U.S. Congress decides them to be.[6]

Scholars on Guam and elsewhere have gone back over Article IX time after time and acknowledged that the language is clear. The political destiny of the island was left in the hands of the United States Congress. No other. That is what this book is about: the effort it took after World War II to persuade the Congress—finally—to determine the political status of Guam and grant some civil rights.

Because it is important for students and other readers to know something of what went on between 1898 and 1945, I ask your indulgence as I repeat more of the history before getting into my own story.

As described by Rogers in *Destiny's Landfall*, the United States Navy was preparing to occupy Guam even before the Treaty of Paris was signed. On December 9, 1898, one day before the signing, a gunboat named the *Bennington* was ordered to visit Guam and conduct a hydrographic survey of Apra Harbor for the purpose of establishing the coaling and watering station envisioned by Mahon and the Naval War Board. On December 12, 1898, the Navy Bureau of Navigation, then in charge of all islands, recommended to President McKinley that Guam be placed under naval administration. On December 23, 1898, McKinley issued the official directive, known as Executive Order 108-A:

> The Island of Guam in the Ladrones is hereby placed under the control of the Department of the Navy. The Secretary of the Navy will take such steps as may be necessary to establish the authority of the United States and to give it the necessary protection and government.[7]

Less than a month later, on January 12, 1899, Navy Secretary John D. Long selected Captain Richard Phillips Leary to be the first U.S. naval governor of Guam and sent him a letter of instructions containing the following paragraph:

> Within the absolute domain of naval authority, which necessarily is and must remain supreme in the ceded territory until the legislation of the U.S. shall otherwise provide, the municipal [i.e., Spanish] laws of the territory . . . are to be considered as continuing in force . . . the mission of the United States is one of benevolent assimilation, substituting the mild sway of justice and right for arbitrary rule. In fulfillment of this high mission . . . there must be sedulously maintained the strong arm of authority, to repress disturbance and to overcome all obstacles to the bestowal of the blessings of good government upon the people of the Island of Guam under the green flag of the United States.[8]

Despite the rhetoric having to do with substituting "the mild sway of justice and right for arbitrary rule," this put the Navy solely in charge of Guam and gave any naval governor supreme authority until such time as the U.S. Congress might provide otherwise.

Oblivious to all of the above, on New Year's Day 1899, Frank Portusach, Father Palomo, and other pro-American leaders gathered at the Agana Tribunal y Carcel building and signed a document dismissing Sixto as governor and appointing Venancio Roberto in his place. Just as they were about to deliver the missive and confront Sixto at the Palacio, they were stopped by the tolling of signal bells on the hill behind Agana. An American naval vessel was arriving. Action was postponed until they could present their case to the American captain of the ship.

The ship was the collier *Brutus,* sent to recoal the *Bennington,* which was scheduled to arrive later in the month. Vincendon L. Cottman, captain of the *Brutus,* knew nothing of the outcome of the Paris peace talks, so when the two local factions came aboard his ship, he left Sixto in charge until the political status of Guam could become known. Cottman and his officers then undertook reconnaissance of the Agana and Apra areas to locate a coaling site. When received by the Secretary of the Navy in March, their observations in a twenty-eight-page handwritten report became the first detailed and current information about Guam that the United States government had received.

The *Bennington* arrived on January 23, 1899, under the command of Captain Edward D. Taussig, who brought news that the Treaty of Paris had been signed and that Guam was now a U.S. possession. After being briefed by Captain Cottman on the local situation, Captain Taussig issued the first two general orders by an American official. The first continued the Spanish laws in force and instructed the *Bennington*'s assistant paymaster to audit the treasury books. The second general order enabled the United States to take possession of all public lands that had been the property of the Spanish government, bordering on the port of San Luis d'Apra. This was to be the coaling site and navy yard. Its seizure was the first of many controversial actions through which the United States acquired much of the land on Guam.

In going through the books, the naval paymaster discovered that Sixto had paid himself and other employees eighteen months' advance pay, leaving the treasury nearly empty. Taussig relieved Sixto of his position and appointed Joaquin Perez y Cruz as acting governor, Vicente Perez as secretary, and Vicente Herrero in charge of finances. Taussig also approved of an advisory council of six prominent Chamorros, including Perez y Cruz as chair, but without Frank Portusach. Perez was from a *manak'kilo* family, was the *gobernadorcillo* (justice of the peace) of Agana, and thus more highly regarded.

On February 1, 1899, the Americans once more raised the U.S. flag over Fort Santa Cruz, but this time they simultaneously raised the flag over the Palacio in Agana with a detachment of the U.S. Marines in attendance and the *Bennington* band playing patriotic music. Spanish priests and Jose Sixto

This house at the mouth of the Agana River was typical of thatched-roof and masonry-wall homes of ordinary Chamorros in the early part of the twentieth century.

were invited to the event, but they refused to come because they saw nothing pleasant about Guam passing into the hands of another nation. Only two Spaniards witnessed the raising of the American flag — Vicente Perez, the lawyer, and Jose Munoz, a desperado. The *Bennington* and the *Brutus* sailed away on February 15, 1899. Captain Taussig, like Captain Glass, felt no need to leave officers or troops on Guam.

With a new government in place but still no American officials assigned to Guam, the Chamorros settled down to await their new masters. Acting Governor Joaquin Perez arrested Jose Sixto for misappropriation of funds and ordered that they be repaid. By May of that year, 1,875 Mexican dollars were refunded — with money borrowed in part from Father Palomo — and the troublesome Sixto sailed away on the *Elcano*.

It was August 7, 1899, when the USS *Yosemite* steamed into Apra Harbor with the stern Captain Richard Philips Leary aboard and Guam officially became a U.S. naval station. From then on, there was no doubt about who was the real governor of Guam. Within three days after his arrival, Leary issued his first proclamation, abolishing all political rights formerly exercised by the clergy "in dominating the people of the Island." Freedom of worship and full protection in the lawful pursuits of life were guaranteed as long as there was submission to American authority.

An Annapolis graduate, a Civil War veteran, and a Protestant with long service as a line officer, Leary spoke no Spanish and had little experience in civil government affairs. After receiving his commission from McKinley in January 1899, he had spent four months elaborately outfitting the *Yosemite* as a station ship for Guam. He spent the next three months leisurely cruising across the Atlantic and Mediterranean, through the Suez Canal to Ceylon (now Sri Lanka), on to Singapore and finally Manila before reaching Guam. Then he lived on the ship for three months while the Palacio (his residence) was being remodeled to suit his convenience. Leary was single, so he lived alone.

On August 16, 1899, Leary issued his first two executive orders, the first prohibiting the sale "of any intoxicating spirituous liquors . . . to any person who was not a resident of this island," and the second forbidding residents or visitors (meaning American marines and sailors) from obtaining *tuba* or *aguardiente* from the locals, because fights often broke out as a consequence. The third order halted all land sales until a new registry system could be established, and the fourth prohibited celebrations and processions in villages on patron-saint feast days. He even stopped the tolling of church bells in the morning and evening. Another order suppressed "the existing system of concubinage" and required that all couples be married "in order that their children may become legitimate." When a contingent of U.S. Marines trained for combat refused work detail around the Palacio, Leary threatened to shoot them, stating: "I have the law. I am supreme." The Marines went back to work.

Leary reported to the Navy Department that he had "disposed of the priests who were ringleaders in encouraging vicious and demoralizing habits and customs." What he didn't know was that the Navy was releasing his reports to the American press. Reaction among stateside Catholics was immediate and nationwide. As a result, Major General Elwell Otis in the Philippines ordered Major General Joseph Wheeler to inspect conditions on Guam and report back to the mainland. A crony of Teddy Roosevelt, Wheeler made a perfunctory inspection. Of social conditions the report remarked only that "the orders with regard to religion are evidently considered as a hardship and are distasteful to a majority of the people." Leary was allowed to stay on until he got bored with the job and asked for reassignment. He left Guam on August 1, 1900, and died in 1901 of heart disease.[9]

To his credit, Leary set up a public education system and considerably improved health conditions on Guam. Like many governors to come, he suffered from inadequate funding for Guam's civil government. Never mind that he used a good part of what he did receive to refurbish the Palacio and equip it with fine table linen, silver, porcelain, and glassware. He also bought a pair of white stallions in the Philippines and brought along a Filipino coachman to drive them. His steward and house servants were enlisted mess-Japanese.

This was the beginning of naval administration, described by Ruth G. Van Cleve in *The Office of Territorial Affairs* as one "characterized largely by somnolence, with occasional dashes of active political repression. Throughout the period, and until 1950, the U.S. Congress was silent on the subject of Guam's government. Almost unfettered power resided in the President, delegated by him to the Secretary of the Navy, and by him to the naval governor."[10]

Leary's administration was typical of many naval governments to come. The officers assigned to Guam had little or no training in civil administration. Assignment often came at the end of their careers and lasted for two years or less. Personal comfort and prestige outweighed concern for the local inhabitants. There was little continuity from one administration to another.

In December 1901, thirty-two prominent Chamorros sent the first of many petitions asking Washington to send a commission to Guam to study ways of creating a permanent civilian government there. The islanders described navy rule as "a military government of occupation." The petition stated, "It is not an exaggeration to say that fewer permanent guarantees of liberty and property rights exist now than under Spanish domain." Governor Seaton Schroeder, the naval officer who replaced Leary, endorsed the petition. Partly in response to it, the U.S. Senate passed a bill for a new government on Guam in 1903, but the House of Representatives let the matter die, mainly because of objections from the Navy in Washington. This was to become the Navy's pattern. It consistently opposed every Chamorro proposal that worked its way to the nation's capital. Breaking of that opposition between 1945 and 1950 is what my book is about. Understanding the importance of maintaining civilian authority over military power is critical to the survival of democracy.

Robert F. Rogers points out in *Destiny's Landfall* that "the Navy's absolute authority on Guam was confirmed indirectly but definitively in 1901 by the U.S. Supreme Court in four cases that concerned the newly acquired insular territories. Collectively referred to as the *Insular Cases,* these arose over the Foracker Act of 1900, which established new tariff laws and a civil government for Puerto Rico." These cases (1) confirmed that the U.S. Constitution does not apply to the insular territories as it does to the states, leaving plenary power (unlimited authority) to the U.S. Congress; (2) made a distinction between "incorporated" and "unincorporated" territories in that the former might sometime become states but the latter were not intended to become states; and (3) clarified the distinction between "organized" and "unorganized" territories in that the latter had not received an "organic act" from the U.S. Congress establishing local government. All of these determinations are addressed in Chapter 15 of this book.[11]

After 1901, periodic pleas from the Chamorros requesting more self-government went unheeded until 1917, when Captain Roy C. Smith appointed the First Guam Congress. It had advisory power only, and not much of that since most of its advice was ignored. Gradually, that legislative body fell into disuse. In 1931, Captain Willis W. Bradley, Jr., a more enlightened naval governor than most, dissolved it and issued a proclamation establishing the Second Guam Congress in which members were to be elected. He also proclaimed a bill of rights for the people of Guam, but it was later revoked by the Secretary of the Navy.

In 1936 the elected Guam Congress unanimously petitioned for United States citizenship and even sent B. J. Bordallo and F. B. Leon Guerrero to Washington to lobby for it in 1937. But the Navy Department told the U.S. Congress that "these people have not yet reached a state of development commensurate with the personal independence, obligations, and responsibility of United States citizenship." So the bill that had been proposed failed.

One can only marvel at the Guamanians' loyalty to the United States in the face of so many disappointments. Perhaps it was the hardships imposed by Japan during World War II that proved the clincher.

The same day on which it attacked Pearl Harbor, the Japanese Navy bombarded Guam. The island fell in three days. For three and a half years, from December 10, 1941, until July 21, 1944, the Japanese occupied the island. Theirs was a brutal occupation, under Japanese Lieutenant General Takeshi Takashina. All American citizens (including Agueda Iglesias Johnston's

Captain Willis W. Bradley, Governor of Guam from June 1929 to May 1931, proclaimed Guam's first Bill of Rights (which the Navy revoked) and reorganized the advisory Guam Congress. As a congressman (R., Calif.), 1946–1948, he introduced an organic act for Guam.

husband) were immediately shipped to Japan, where most died in prison camps. Hundreds of others were interned when 6,000 Japanese troops occupied Guam. There was forced labor for all Chamorro males over twelve as the Japanese built airstrips and planted rice. Severe beatings, sometimes rapes, and often the beheading of males characterized the Japanese treatment. As food became scarce, the Chamorros resorted to eating seeds of *fadang*, as they had learned to do centuries before. When it became clear that U.S. forces would launch an attack to reclaim the island, beginning on July 10, 1945, all eighteen thousand Chamorros were forced by the Japanese to march to concentration camps in the hills, where they waited for twenty days in squalid conditions without buildings, latrines, food, or medicine. When rescue came, the Chamorros welcomed the United States with open arms, even though the rescue brought with it devastation of the land.

In preparation for what was to be the largest invasion of the war in the

U.S. Marines storm the Asan beachhead on the morning of July 21, 1944, to reclaim Guam.

Pacific up until that time, American submarines and seaplanes began photographing the Marianas including Guam for targets in early April 1944. Those islands were to be taken by the United States armed forces in order to pursue the war in the Pacific from bases closer to Japan. The closing in began with a tight blockade around all the Marianas to choke off supplies to the Japanese. On April 8, 1944, the first U.S. attack was launched when the USS *Seahorse* torpedoed a 6,780-ton Japanese submarine tender and a 1,915-ton cargo ship near Guam. Early in May, B-24s began to bomb Saipan and Guam. On June 15, intensive aerial attacks on Guam were followed by three hours of massive naval gunfire. Planned landings were postponed because of the unexpected approach of the Japanese Combined Fleet from the Philippines on June 16. In a titanic Battle of the Philippine Sea to the west of the Marianas, the Japanese lost three aircraft carriers and 476 planes. This left General Takashina and his Japanese forces stranded on Guam to face the coming invasion alone.

According to Robert F. Rogers, the United States had a three-to-one superiority in numbers over the Japanese. Takashina's forces on Guam numbered about 20,500, but over 3,000 were in construction, not combat units, and hundreds of Japanese men had died or suffered wounds in the preinvasion bombardment since April. By comparison, the American forces totaled 54,891 Marines, Army, Coast Guard, and other military men.

In final preparation for the Guam invasion, an enormous fleet of 11 battleships, 24 aircraft carriers, and 390 other ships were massed off Guam's western shore. American aircraft and ships attacked the island for thirteen straight days beginning on July 8. For three nights, beginning July 17, demolition teams blew up reef and lagoon obstacles off the Agat and Asan beaches. On the morning of the invasion, July 21, 1944, before dawn a crescendo of loud firepower lasted for three hours as air and sea vessels bombed the island. In early morning, the first armored landing craft crossed the line of departure a thousand yards offshore of Asan as U.S. Marines in amphibious vehicles prepared to hit the beaches in four different places. Despite the bombardment, which was shifted inland as Americans were coming to shore, the Japanese emerged from their bunkers to fight. According to one eyewitness, all over, bodies were being blown up as the cannon shells fell. The earth and sand buried the soldiers. There was a lack of Japanese manpower, weapon power, and a weak first-line defense. On the opposite side, the Americans were landing on the beach and they were equipped to annihilate their opponents completely. By nightfall that first day, the Americans had secured the beachheads and over 25,000 U.S. troops were digging in and preparing for Japanese counterattacks.

By July 23, the fighting had assumed a pattern in which the Americans attacked in daylight hours behind massive artillery and air support and the Japanese counterattacked under the cover of night with weak artillery and no support. Takashina planned a major counterattack for the night of July 25–26 that he hoped would throw the Americans into the sea at the beachheads. This was to be mounted by the nearly 3,000 Japanese troops on Orote. In response, the Americans shot hundreds of flares into the cloudy night sky to illuminate the Japanese warriors. Fire from American artillery, mortars, and automatic weapons slaughtered most of the attackers. Those Japanese who reached the marine foxholes died in bloody man-to-man combat. In the final close-in murderous combat that took place, neither side was inclined to take prisoners. Over 3,500 Japanese men died in courageous but useless combat that night.

From July 26 to 29, battles along the shore continued. General Takashina was killed by tank machine-gun fire at Fonte on July 28, shortly after he had ordered a retreat. Shelling and air strikes against the Japanese went on from north to south until most of the largest communities were razed. Fearing a costly house-to-house defense of Agana by the Japanese, the Americans continued bombarding until the last of the town was destroyed on July 29. Formerly a capital city of 12,000 inhabitants, Agana was left a rubble. The prewar Guam Museum was smashed, as was the governor's residence, the Naval Hospital, and the Tribunal y Carcel, along with the residences. Of the 3,286 dwellings on Guam, more than 2,500 were destroyed. Late on the afternoon of July 30, U.S. Army patrols reached the edge of the concentration camps where the Chamorros were being held and rescue began. A group of Chamorros, including B. J. Bordallo and his family, followed a patrol back to the mountains above Agat. On July 31, the U.S. troops overran the main camps. Some Japanese guards were killed, and the rest fled. The Americans handed out C-rations, candy, and cigarettes to the hungry refugees, many of whom promptly suffered diarrhea from gorging on chocolate. Thousands in the camps then trekked westward across the center of the island to American refugee camps at Finile and Asan for food and help. By mid-August, all 18,000 Chamorros were housed behind U.S. lines in three main refugee camps. They were fed from caches of Japanese food until the U.S. military logistical system could be established. Once an area was cleared of Japanese stragglers, the Chamorros were encouraged to return to their homes and farms. But the tremendous war damage and the seizing of large amounts of land by the military for future operations against Japan meant that most Chamorros had no place to go. On August 11, 1944, Tokyo acknowledged the fall of Guam. The indigenous people of the island were at last liberated. But the fighting was not over. Many defiant Japanese soldiers remained in the island's jungles. Many committed suicide.

The number of U.S. servicemen reported killed in action on Guam as of August 11, 1944, totaled 1,747. Of these, 1,520 were U.S. Marines who died mostly in the beachhead battles. An additional 22 men were missing in action. American wounded totaled 6,053, again mostly U.S. Marines. The number of Chamorros killed as a consequence of the war is not precisely known, but formal claims submitted to the U.S. Congress came to 578, of which 320 were for deaths and 258 for injuries. The number of Japanese killed by American forces was 10,071 as of August 11, but by September 30, some 4,926 holdouts would be killed despite U.S. leaflets and broadcasts that induced a few to surrender. The number killed increased to 18,377 by August 31. At least 1,250 Japanese had surrendered and Guam was liberated.

Marines raise the U.S. flag on Guam as men and equipment come ashore at Asan beachhead on July 21, 1944.

On July 21, 1944, the first day of the American invasion of Guam, Admiral Chester W. Nimitz had issued a proclamation reestablishing the Navy's authority on Guam, but no Chamorros knew of his edict until Nimitz himself arrived on Guam on August 10. In the same vein as Captain Richard Leary back in 1899, Nimitz issued an order that set the stage for continued autocratic government until 1950. It declared:

> All powers of government and jurisdiction in Guam and adjacent waters, and over the inhabitants thereof, and final administrative responsibility are vested in me as Admiral United States Navy, commanding the forces of occupation and as Military Governor, and will be exercised through subordinate commanders by my direction. . . . No political activity will be permitted other than that authorized by me or under my authority.[12]

Admiral Chester W. Nimitz *(left),* Commander-in-chief, Pacific, discusses strategy with James V. Forrestal, Secretary of the Navy, in 1944.

Major General Henry (Hank) L. Larsen, U.S.M.C. was named island commander by Nimitz on August 15. Larsen's deputy chief for civil affairs, Marine Colonel Charles I. Murray, handled civilian administration. It was Murray's staff of 186 officers and men that administered the refugee camps for the Chamorros. Other deputies began transforming Guam into a military bastion by confiscating land for airfields. The invasion of Japan was yet to come.

Airfield construction was difficult and behind schedule. But on February 25, 1945, the first B-29 bombing mission destined for Japan took off from the still incomplete Northwest Field. That same month, Washington instructed Admiral Nimitz to have some of his Marines seize Iwo Jima, halfway between the Marianas and Japan. On the night of March 9, three hundred B-29s under the command of Major General Curtis LeMay took off from Guam, Tinian, and Saipan on the first mass incendiary bomb missions to Japan. They departed in waves over a three-hour period. Eight hours later, nearly 100,000 Japanese lay incinerated among the fires that consumed sixteen square miles of Tokyo. In the weeks that followed, more waves of B-29s from the Mariana Islands firebombed the great cities of Japan into ruins. It took a grueling fifteen hours to fly to and from Tokyo, but additional incendiary missions were planned.

Then, in mid-July, three special aircraft landed on Guam with components for secret new bombs. On July 26, 1945, the cruiser USS *Indianapolis* delivered to Tinian material for the warheads of the new weapons. When assembled, these were, of course, the atomic weapons developed by the Manhattan Project. On August 6, 1945, with Air Force Colonel Paul Tibbets at the controls of a B-29 named the *Enola Gay*, the first fission bomb, Little Boy, was dropped on the city of Hiroshima. When the Japanese did not immediately surrender, on August 9 the plutonium fusion bomb, Fat Man, was dropped on Nagasaki. More than 78,000 people were killed instantly at Hiroshima and 35,000 at Nagasaki. Thousands more soon died from radiation and other effects. On August 15, Emperor Hirohito broadcast Japan's surrender. Thus, the B-29s from bases in the Marianas did end the war without the need to invade Japan. But the annihilation of those two cities ushered in a whole new level of warfare, the morality of which has remained in constant debate. Probably not fully comprehending the implications of the dawn of nuclear warfare, most Americans breathed a sigh of relief. The long-lasting, disastrous war in the Pacific was over! August 21, 1945, was declared V-J Day, and on September 2, 1945, final terms of the Japanese surrender were signed in Tokyo Bay aboard the battleship USS *Missouri*.

Admiral Nimitz and his CINCPAC staff departed Guam for Hawai'i in late August 1945, leaving General Larsen as island commander. For anyone not there at the time, it is hard to comprehend that the military population on the island was then 201,718 trained fighters and auxiliary personnel. Chamorros numbered 21,838, bringing the total to 223,556. With a density of 1,045 persons per square mile, this was the largest number of people ever to inhabit Guam. Swift demobilization took place, and ten months later, by mid-June 1946, military personnel numbered only 36,923.

Five years later, when I went to Guam as an employee of the Interior Department, the indigenous population had grown to about 23,000. The number of military personnel was still around 30,000. Thousands of foreign laborers, mostly from the Philippines, also lived there. They were employed under Navy contract to help rebuild the island.

It was a long-suffering but hopeful Guam that I visited in June 1951. With a history of isolation in the vast Pacific Ocean going back to 1,500 B.C., a Spanish colonial administration from 1521 to 1898 that had nearly deci-mated the population, then forty-three years of autocratic United States naval rule from 1898 to 1941 followed by three years of brutal Japanese oc-cupation ended by U.S. military strafing of the island in 1944, the brave Chamorros had withstood unspeakable hardship. Through it all they had preserved their language, their culture, and their humanity.

It was also a revitalized Guam that I visited. Less than a year before my orientation trip, the 81st Congress had passed the Organic Act of Guam, providing not only United States citizenship for the people but a represen-tative government and a balance of power among its executive, legislative, and judicial branches. President Harry Truman had signed the legislation on August 1, 1950, and Carlton Skinner, the first civilian governor, had sailed for the island in September. When I visited Guam the next June, he had been in office less than a year.

I was excited that June day. I had had a hand in bringing about this monumental transfer of jurisdiction, and now, as an employee of the De-partment of the Interior, I was going to have an opportunity to help imple-ment the new legislation. Within a couple of days the navy would take me with them in a PBY on an inspection trip of the Trust Territory of the Pacific Islands, and after that I would spend three weeks on Guam. As Pacific Island Assistant in the Department of the Interior, I would serve as a liaison between the people of Guam and the federal government for the next four years.

But that is not what this book is about. This book is about the five-year struggle, between 1945 and 1950, leading up to the Organic Act of Guam. It is about the Chamorros and their determination to obtain what Article IX of the Treaty of Paris had promised in 1898: namely, that "the civil rights and political status of the native inhabitants of the territories hereby ceded to the United States shall be determined by the Congress."[13] Without their petitions, without the walkout of their Guam Congress, without their per-sonal appearances before key committees of the U.S. Congress, passage of the Organic Act would never have come about.

It is also about the Institute of Ethnic Affairs and John Collier, its founder, the modest, far-seeing pragmatist whose aspirations for the people of Guam never wavered. Together, the Chamorros and the Institute were able to achieve in a very short time changes that had been sought for centuries. The time was ripe.

And now, let's get on with my story. How did this peaceful revolution start?

Chapter 2

The Institute of Ethnic Affairs

John Collier wrote his letter of resignation from the Department of the Interior on January 19, 1945 (see Appendix 1 for President Roosevelt's response). He had served for twelve years as Commissioner of the Bureau of Indian Affairs — longer than any Indian commissioner before or since. He had been appointed to that post by President Franklin D. Roosevelt in 1933 at the insistence of the new secretary of the interior, Harold L. Ickes. For thirteen years before that, beginning in 1920, Collier had publicly defended the Indians' rights to their own cultural customs. He and Mr. Ickes had become acquainted in the late twenties when Collier escorted a group of Indians across the country to testify on their own behalf in Washington. While in Chicago, to save money Collier and the Indians had been invited to stay overnight in the homes of some Unitarians. It was Collier's good luck to be housed in the Ickes home. That was the start of many long years of working together on the problems facing minorities.[1]

Having decided that he could be more effective outside the government than inside it, Collier resigned from Interior in January of 1945 and began establishing the Institute of Ethnic Affairs. According to its prospectus, the Institute would be a nonprofit organization whose purpose was "to search for solutions to problems within and between white and colored races, cultural minority groups, and dependent peoples at home and abroad." The Ethnic Institute would be interdisciplinary, educational in nature, and would recommend administrative changes requiring governmental action.

Collier was concerned about the "wholeness" of life. He felt the modern-day worker in the industrial age had become "sundered" from every kind of wholeness. Likewise, he sensed that many citizens felt divorced from their respective governments. In the foreword to a pamphlet titled "Operational Research and Action Research," he later wrote:

> Bureaucrats, politicians, and pressure-groups are the predominant operators of the State, or at least of our American State now. None of these classes takes

John Collier was hand-picked by Harold L. Ickes to be Commissioner of Indian Affairs in the Department of the Interior in 1933. He served until 1945, when he resigned to establish the Institute of Ethnic Affairs with his wife, Laura Thompson, and other notable social scientists. Always a modest man, Collier left no photographs for our national archives. He is shown here with his dog, Pixie, in 1947 in the home of the Winquests in Washington, D.C.

overall responsibility; the private citizen feels a power and responsibility less than that of a phantom.

But men cannot live without a feeling — some kind of feeling of belongingness, of power. When belongingness, power, wholeness are unattainable in the work sphere, in the political sphere, in the lapsed local community, on any line truthful and benign, then inevitably the remaining possible ways to attain these essential ingredients are resorted to. Most of these other available ways — drink, obsessive pursuit of sex, spectator-sportsmanship — are of a rather neutral significance, mere dissolutive substitutes for the spiritual nurture that our age denies its men and women. But very wide in the world today is another substitute, not neutral, of groupings of hate, groupings of fear, groupings of scorn: the fascism which threatens all our remaining hopes. In fascism, the withdrawal of significant wholeness from human life has its terminus.

To recapture for human effort — for human life — the master quality, the

Laura Thompson, anthropologist, pictured here with Chamorro assistant Jesse S. Perez, was hired by the Navy in 1938 to do cultural research on Guam. Nine years later she testified before a House committee in support of civilian government under an organic act for the island.

supremely necessary ingredient, of wholeness: this is the overriding task of the epoch of revolution which is upon us. . . .

Operational research and action research use cooperatively and integratively all the branches of knowledge and all the specialized disciplines relative to the particular problem; they use them in active, responsible team-effort, with the administrator, the lay citizen, the membership of the geographical or functional group. Therefore they are one of the master-keys for the opening of the doors which have closed around us all, which shut out the meaningfulness, responsibility and momentousness from our life. . . . They can reach as summons and as nurture and as medicine to the heart of our age's painful, poisoning unorientation and meaning-bereft unrest.[2]

While Collier perhaps coined the term "action research," it was the anthropologist Laura Thompson who had coordinated the program launched by him in the Bureau of Indian Affairs in the early 1940s. As husband and wife, they would again work together applying this concept in the Pacific islands. Both were founders of the new Institute of Ethnic Affairs. Thompson had researched *Guam and Its People* in 1938 at the request of Captain James T. Alexander, then governor of Guam. She served as his Consultant on Native Affairs and after six months was to suggest how the school system and the welfare of the islanders might be improved. It was her book on Guam and other Pacific islands research that had qualified her for work in the Bureau of Indian Affairs.

The Colliers remained in the Washington area after John's resignation from the Department of the Interior in January 1945. Both continued as consultants to the Bureau of Indian Affairs through much of the next year, and John maintained an office there as well as in their country home in Virginia. They gave a lot of thought to the new organization they were creating, and by the time it was incorporated in July 1945 they had attracted as directors some of the most enlightened social scientists, attorneys, and government administrators of postwar America. All are listed in Appendix 2. Some of the best known included Clyde Kluckhohn, Ph.D., a Harvard University anthropologist; Kurt Lewin, Ph.D., director of the Research Center for Group Dynamics at the Massachusetts Institute of Technology; Harold Lasswell, Ph.D., a law professor at Yale University; Philleo Nash, Ph.D., anthropologist on the staff of the White House; and Louis Adamic, Saul Padover, and Carey McWilliams, authors.

Collier spent part of the summer writing a lengthy paper entitled "United States Indian Administration as a Laboratory of Ethnic Relations." It drew on his twelve years as Indian Commissioner and gave specific examples showing how administration of soil conservation in the Acoma pueblo, stock reduction on the Navajo reservation, and economic development through use of a revolving credit fund established by the Jicarilla Apaches had been affected by "action-research." The importance of granting disenfranchised peoples the freedom to grapple with their own problems was a central theme. He wrote:

> It is from the needs of action that knowledge is dynamically empowered. Imperfect action is better for men and societies than perfection in waiting, for the errors wrought by action are cured by new action. And when the

The third edition of Laura Thompson's book, published in 1947, was sharply critical of Guam's naval administration and played an important part in bringing change. Pictured here is the first edition, published in 1941.

people acted upon are themselves made true partners in the actions, and co-discoverers of the corrections of error, then through and through, and in spite of blunders or even by virtue of them, the vital energies are increased, confidence increases, power increases, experience builds toward wisdom and the most potent of all principles and ideals, deep democracy, slowly wins the field.[3]

In a speech before the Women's Alliance of the Unitarian Church at Wilmington, Delaware, on October 29, 1945, Collier further elaborated on the goals of his institute. He asserted that social diversity was the creative force of history, as evidenced by what he called the genius of Christianity, which he pointed out blended Hebraic morality, Greek philosophy, Oriental mysticism, and Roman law. Unfortunately, he maintained, this cross-fertilization of cultures had come under attack with the advent of the machine age, which predisposed mankind to concentrate on selfish material advantages and power struggles. This led to a spiritual bankruptcy permitting the growth of the Nazism and Fascism that had recently brought about such human destruction.

Collier warned that this peril was reemerging after World War II in the form of isolationism, anti-Semitism, and U.S. rivalry with Russia over nuclear weapons. In order to cure this social illness, he said people had to implant in their children the idea that different races need one another. He suggested that his audience take a practical step in this direction by writing their congressmen. Their letters should insist that the United States take the lead on the colonial problem by granting its new Pacific island dependencies self-government under United Nations trusteeship and ending the forty-five-year military rule over Guam and American Samoa.

An unexpected platform for the expression of his hopes came early in 1946 when Interior Secretary Ickes was instrumental in getting Collier and Abe Fortas, then an Assistant Secretary of the Department of the Interior, appointed as advisers to the United States delegation on trusteeship matters at the first session of the United Nations General Assembly, to be held in London. Fortas, an attorney, had worked with Collier on Indian affairs. (Several years later he was appointed to the U.S. Supreme Court.)

Aboard the *Queen Elizabeth* while crossing the Atlantic during the third week in January 1946, Collier and Fortas strategized how to obtain international support for pertinent chapters of the United Nations charter setting forth the responsibilities of national governments toward their colonies and territories. Once in London, they drafted a "Resolution on Non-Self-Governing Peoples." It was endorsed by Secretary of State John Foster Dulles, chairman of the American delegation. Then Collier and Fortas quietly set about getting it approved. After much discussion by all participants in the conference, the measure was finally passed by all fifty-one countries then members of the General Assembly. This was a notable achievement, made possible by the duo's expert knowledge of how to express public policy in legal documents and to their powers of persuasion.

Thus, in London the foundation was laid for a Trusteeship Council under the General Assembly of the United Nations. It would come into existence at the second session of the United Nations Organization scheduled for late spring. A system was established for obtaining annual reports on the millions of people still under the colonial control of the Dutch,

Belgians, French, British, and others in Indonesia, parts of Africa, and southeast Asia. The system also required reports from the United States on its dependencies, including Alaska, Hawai'i, Puerto Rico, the Virgin Islands, Guam, and American Samoa. Year by year governments would be required to file accounts of progress being made to promote the political, economic, social, and educational advancement of the inhabitants of those territories, as well as what was being done to promote their development toward self-government or independence.

The board of the new Institute of Ethnic Affairs had planned to publish its first *News Letter* in January 1946, but because Collier was in London most of that month the first issue was delayed until February. It was put together by John H. Provinse, a director of the Institute who was still in the Bureau of Indian Affairs. The front-page article, entitled "Institute's President Called to London as Special Adviser at UNO Assembly," was written and signed by Provinse as acting president of the Institute. The content was a mixture of pride that Collier was participating in a conference critical to future world policy and regret that he could not be in Washington to further the progress of his new organization.

A short news item in that first *News Letter* enthusiastically reported that the Institute's prospectus had struck a chord with the leaders of far-off Guam, twenty-three of whom had sent in their membership applications and a combined money order of $115. In their joint letter of December 18, 1945, the twenty-three signers expressed the "sincere hope that this new institute will find out sufficient facts which will open the eyes and minds of those big people in the States who are holding the fate of thousands of inhabitants." The *News Letter* article went on to say, "No letter, among the many that came in response to the publication of the prospectus, has been quite so moving as that which came from the leaders of Guam."[4]

The second Ethnic Institute *News Letter,* dated April 1946, is remarkable to this day as a personal account of how the Trusteeship Council of the United Nations was born. It was written by Collier himself and occupied nearly all eight pages. He strongly advocated that the islands of Micronesia once mandated to Japan under the League of Nations should not be annexed by the United States or closed off under a strategic trusteeship agreement approved by the United Nations Security Council, but openly governed under an ordinary trusteeship agreement approved by the United Nations General Assembly. He forcefully argued that United States leadership in this area of world affairs would have a beneficial influence on the fate of hundreds of millions of other people not then in charge of their own political systems.

"Strategic trusteeship" was an idea advanced by the United States at San Francisco when the United Nations Charter was written in the fall of 1945. It stemmed from the military's desire for autonomy over the islands taken from Japan at great human cost. It also stemmed from the "manifest destiny" policy that had been proclaimed by President William McKinley in 1898, under which the United States would become a strong naval power by controlling small islands in the vast Pacific Ocean. Collier strenuously objected to building a virtual iron curtain around Micronesia, and this strategic trusteeship idea soon triggered a tug-of-war among the Departments of State, War, Navy, and Interior.

About eighteen months after the London meeting, the Trusteeship Council was indeed established under the General Assembly. Great Britain, France, Belgium, New Zealand, and Australia all promised to place their mandated areas under it. The United States offered no such prospect for the mandated Pacific islands. Conversely, it was becoming increasingly clear that any "strategic trusteeships" would be established under auspices of the Security Council, where the victors of World War II would have veto power and where the military could maintain absolute control. This spelled trouble.

What the United States would do about the islands formerly mandated to Japan would actively occupy, not only the four departments of the United States government mentioned above and the United States Congress, but Collier, the Institute of Ethnic Affairs, and the news media for the next five years. The battle for control of those islands was a war fought at the very top by men whose names were, and are, well known: Roosevelt, Truman, Forrestal, Ickes, and others. It was a battle that holds lessons for time to come.

Chapter 3

Collier and Ickes Kick Off the Battle

The man who sent Collier to London would sound the battle cry for civilian control of the Pacific islands at the first annual meeting of the Institute of Ethnic Affairs. The meeting was cosponsored by the Institute of Pacific Relations and held in Washington, D.C., on May 29, 1946.

Harold L. Ickes had resigned as Secretary of the Interior on February 15, 1946, and become a syndicated newspaper columnist reaching millions of readers. He was Collier's choice for main speaker, and he delivered what later became known as the opening salvo in the battle to take the governments of Guam and American Samoa away from the Navy and to place the former Japanese islands in the Trusteeship Council under the General Assembly of the United Nations instead of the Security Council.

That speech was extremely frank and hard-hitting. In some ways it deserves an entire chapter of this book. Instead, I have relegated it to Appendix 3 (p. 193), but I urge readers to peruse it — better yet, read it word for word — before going further. It sets the tone for all that follows.

Ickes did his research with the help of Lyle H. Munson, who had been an intelligence officer in World War II. With the Colliers' help and Munson's independent research besides his own vast knowledge, Ickes wrote a speech that cited example after example of how the Navy had been discriminatory and inexcusably inadequate in its administration of Guam and American Samoa for the past forty-seven years. That sad legacy should not be passed along to the islands recently taken from Japan, he asserted. Instead, all of those mandated islands should be placed in the Trusteeship Council and set on the road to self-government. The address was caustic — pure, unadulterated Ickes at his best. No wonder he was known around Washington as "the old curmudgeon." The address was transmitted to Guam almost overnight, and Guamanian members of the Institute of Ethnic Affairs wasted no time in circulating it. They reprinted thousands of copies.

It was less than a month after Ickes delivered his speech that I went to

Harold L. Ickes, Secretary of the Interior from 1933 to 1945, kicked off the battle for organic legislation for Guam in 1946 and stayed with it as a syndicated newspaper columnist until it was enacted in 1950.

work at the Institute of Ethnic Affairs, the third week of June 1946. I had just received my master's degree from the Graduate School of Journalism at Columbia University in New York. While earning that degree, I had simultaneously studied imperialism and world government under Nathaniel Peffer in Columbia's night school. His courses put the cap on what I had learned as a varsity debater on international affairs.

I had been recommended for the position of editor of Institute publications by Betty Winquest, a college classmate and close friend from Nebraska Wesleyan University. She was one of about thirty young college graduates from throughout the country selected in the spring of 1945 for federal government management training by the Institute of Public Affairs. She had gone to Washington, D.C., in the fall, when I went off to New York City, and she had worked in a number of government offices, including the Bureau of Indian Affairs. Collier recognized her many talents and hired her as executive secretary that winter when he began to establish his

Betty Winquest *(left)* and Doloris Coulter *(right)*, classmates from Nebraska Wesleyan University, were hired as Executive Secretary and Editor, respectively, by the Institute of Ethnic Affairs in 1946.

new Institute of Ethnic Affairs. In the spring, when the Ethnic Institute was ready to employ an editor, Betty knew I would be graduating from Columbia and looking for a job. She recommended me, and I went for an interview. It was the only job I applied for, and Betty tells me I was the only interviewee. We were a natural fit.

When I went to Washington for the interview, I knew nothing of the John Collier described in the earlier chapter of this book. Had I known more about his accomplishments, I might have been nervous. But as it was, I found him to be an older gentleman, then sixty-two, scholarly, forthright but quiet-spoken. He didn't have to ask what I had done at the Graduate School of Journalism; he knew its reputation. Moreover, unbeknown to me, he had attended Columbia himself when he was in his teens. He told me a little about the new Ethnic Institute, and I asked a few questions. But Betty was the link. If Betty thought I was right for the Institute, that was good enough for him. He had no prejudice against gender or age, and he hired me on the spot for $50 a week. That was the going wage for beginning professionals and the same as Betty was being paid.

The Institute of Ethnic Affairs was first located in two rooms of an old brownstone at 1719 K Street, N.W., in downtown Washington. Betty and I were usually the only occupants of the office as the Colliers generally worked from home. The buildings on that street have since been demolished to make way for lobbyists in sleek new trappings.

Writing and editing the Institute's monthly *News Letter* was my first assignment. A printer had been selected, and three issues had been published before I arrived. I was pleased to see that this journal was a brochure of eight pages printed in two columns on letter-size, rough-stock, ivory-colored paper. It looked very academic, and I liked it that way. In the beginning, most major articles were to be written by authors other than me.

I soon learned that the twenty-three Guamanians who had joined the Institute in January 1946 were well known to Laura Thompson. They knew she was a cofounder of the Institute and that they could trust her. She was one of the main reasons that their memberships had begun coming in.

Soon after the Ickes speech was circulated, forty-one more Guam residents became members. Their names are recorded in note 1 to this chapter and include such familiar surnames as Calvo, Camacho, Flores, Leon Guerrero, Reyes, Sablan, and Sanchez.[1] They sent checks and cash totaling $1,215 to be applied toward the Institute's work. These members were the "American nationals" at the grass roots who gave the Institute's efforts credibility. More than that, they were the Chamorros who for nearly fifty years had been trying to get the U.S. Congress to determine "the civil rights and political status of the native inhabitants of the territories ceded to the United States" as promised by the Treaty of Paris. Now maybe they would be heard!

Betty and I marveled at the additional five- and ten-dollar bills that came by airmail over the summer and fall, especially since we had just learned from the Ickes speech that Guamanian laborers earned only 28 cents an hour and that a pair of shoes on Guam cost $7.10.

In one of the envelopes there was a letter from Simon A. Sanchez, then Superintendent of Schools in Guam, who was designated by other Chamorros to collect and mail in their memberships. He wrote:

> We firmly believe that the Institute is doing its utmost to promote the general welfare of the people, particularly in those places under the United States flag where American ideals and principles are not practiced extensively and where the line of demarcation or discrimination is most noticeable and hurtful to the island inhabitants.

Simon Sanchez was an outstanding civic leader in addition to being Superintendent of Schools in Guam.

We love the American people. We are truly loyal to them. We believe that the principles of democracy as practiced in America and backed by the Constitution of the United States is [sic] the best form of government in the world. We have inexpressible appreciation of the Americans for freeing us from the hands of the Japanese. . . .

We are now living in a new era with many rapid changes but with great hope that the present regime will be forever benevolent, fair, just and without any discrimination as to race, color, nationality or social standing. We earnestly pray that the administrators will encourage maximum individual abilities which will undoubtedly make them more valuable and significant in their island home.[2]

We printed that letter in the Institute's September 1946 *News Letter,* followed by a one-sentence evaluation that Collier wrote: "A clearer expression of our objectives on behalf of dependent peoples would be difficult to phrase."

Guamanians weren't the only ones who read former Secretary Ickes' speech. One can only imagine the ire it raised when studied by naval officers on Guam and high officials in the Pentagon. Information coming back to us from both active and retired naval officers indicated that the Navy didn't know what to do about it. The facts could not be disputed. In June and July the Navy Department appeared to be carrying out a policy of not trying to disprove or defend anything. Instead, it chose to publicize only good deeds claimed or done by the Navy in the islands.

For example, a long dispatch sent by Harrison W. Baldwin to the *New York Times* on August 5, 1946, reported that, due to the "remarkable progress of its [the Navy's] health and sanitation measures, the death rate [on Guam] was halved during the past year while the birth rate was doubled." In a news item for our September *News Letter*, Collier pointed out that cutting the death rate in half in comparison with the time of Japanese occupation when many hundreds of Guamanians were tortured to death and otherwise disposed of could hardly be viewed as an achievement.

To show their support of civil rights for the Pacific peoples, several United States congressmen introduced pertinent legislation. Early in 1946, Representative Andrew J. Biemiller (D., Wisc.) had introduced H.R. 6858 providing civilian rule for the Pacific islands under organic acts administered by the Department of the Interior. On May 29, the very day upon which Ickes delivered his provocative speech, Representative Henry M. Jackson (D., Wash.), introduced H.R. 6605 transferring the Pacific islands to the Department of the Interior. Delegate Joseph R. Farrington (R., Hawai'i), subsequently introduced H.R. 3528 granting Guamanians American citizenship. Representative Robert A. Grant (R., Ind.), introduced a seventy-two-page bill providing both citizenship and an organic act for Guam. It was written by Richard Wels, a young New York City lawyer who had served as a naval officer on Guam and who was to figure prominently later on as an advocate of civilian administration.

Thus, the groundwork for administrative change was laid. Ickes, with his speech to members of the Ethnic Institute, had torched a fire under the United States Navy and the Truman administration. Congress and the people of Guam had picked up the torch.

Chapter 4

To Be or Not to Be a Strategic Trusteeship

Less than a month after I was hired by the Institute, Collier asked me to prepare an article for the *News Letter* explaining the difference between a "strategic" and a "nonstrategic" trusteeship and why the latter was better for the islands formerly mandated to Japan. That writing assignment may have been the hardest I was ever given.

I was told to talk to Emil Sady about trusteeship matters. Formerly a young protégé of Collier's in the Bureau of Indian Affairs, during the war Sady had trained as a military affairs officer in the Navy. In 1946 he was a trusted analyst in the Dependencies Unit of the State Department. He would know what should be written for the *News Letter*.

I read and researched, consulted with Sady, wrote and rewrote most of the summer. The material was new to me and the stakes were so high that I knew I had to get it right. But writing this article gave me the opportunity to apply some of what I had learned in those classes at Columbia on imperialism and world politics. My whole heart was in what I was trying to put across. By the middle of August, I had a seven-page, very readable story that was ready to go to press.[1]

The first section described the islands and their peoples. It contained a brief history and a world map. The second section was a discussion of trusteeship status versus annexation. It quoted President Truman stating in Berlin, on July 20, 1945, shortly before the war in the Pacific ended: "We are not fighting for conquest. There is not one piece of territory or one thing of a monetary nature that we want out of this war." In his Navy Day address in New York on October 27, 1945, Truman had reaffirmed this foreign policy, saying "we do not seek for ourselves one inch of territory any place in the world."[2] At the same time, this section pointed out that the president recognized the need for a single United States policy for administration of the Pacific islands. In October 1945 he had appointed the Secretaries of State, War, Navy, and Interior as a committee to meet and give him a recommendation "satisfactory to all four departments . . . *without delay.*" Still, almost a year later, no action had been taken.

The third section of my article explained that an ordinary trusteeship under the General Assembly would be superior to a strategic trusteeship under the Security Council in that the whole territory would not then be closed off to the world; trusteeship under the Security Council would be tantamount to annexation. By contrast, under the Trusteeship Council, there would be mandatory reporting on the islanders' economic, social, and political progress every year. Full provision could be made for military control of any bases needed, but the islands themselves and their inhabitants would be under civilian administration.

To illustrate the disadvantages of military occupation, my article was full of colorful, current examples of injustice resulting from continued Navy administration of Guam. These examples showed that Navy officers and other personnel were inadequately trained in governing people of other cultures, that their administration was inefficient, and that their methods were authoritarian. There was disregard for human rights, and the military courts were staffed by men who had never studied law. Defendants were considered guilty until proved innocent. Furthermore, naval governors were given new assignments out of the islands every two years or less, providing the government little continuity.

My article was preceded by what might be described as an editorial by Collier explaining the urgency of the issue. He wrote that trusteeship was the "testing ground" for the billion and a quarter politically and industrially dependent people of the world. If it failed, he said, "there is no future except one of tooth and claw."[3] He cited Palestine as "one of the immediate examples."

In a second editorial comment following my article, Collier wrote something called "The Job That Lies Ahead." We had just learned that three of the department heads, instructed by Truman to give him a policy statement, had met in March 1946 without the fourth one. That fourth one was, of course, the Secretary of the Interior. The Navy, War, and State Departments had conveniently waited until Secretary Ickes had resigned in February; then they met without notifying the new Secretary, Julius A. Krug. And what did they do? They voted to formally adjourn until some indefinite future. Collier considered this an outrage and wrote for the September 1946 *News Letter:*

NEWS LETTER
of the INSTITUTE OF ETHNIC AFFAIRS, INC.
1719 K Street, Northwest, Washington 6, D. C.

VOL. I	SEPTEMBER, 1946	No. 4

MICRONESIA AND TRUSTEESHIP: TEST FOR AMERICA AND CRUCIAL NEED FOR THE WORLD

The President
White House   August 30, 1946
Washington, D. C.

We urge that you make clear to the world that the United States intends to place the Japanese mandated islands under United Nations trusteeship and to govern them, as administering authority, through a civilian agency of the government. Indefinite contradictory announcements in press August 29 and 30 by spokesmen in whom final authority does not rest have effect of increasing the confusion in American and world mind.

The General Assembly of the United Nations at its first session adopted resolution inviting States administering territories now held under mandate to undertake practical steps for implementation of trusteeship chapters of Charter in order to submit trusteeship agreements for approval not later than the General Assembly session next September. Australia, Belgium, France, New Zealand and United Kingdom have responded affirmatively to this resolution and to the Charter provisions. The failure of the United States to make clear that it intends to trustee the mandated area which it, as military occupant, administers is injurious to development of United Nations trusteeship system and to traditional position of world leadership by this country in promoting the interests of dependent peoples.

In addition to placing these islands under trusteeship, they should be placed under civilian administration. Government of people by military agencies except in times of national emergency is contrary to American principles of democracy, justice, and freedom and obstructs fulfillment of present and possible future obligations of the United States set forth in Chapters XI, XII, and XIII of Charter. Military requirements can be fully met through trusteeship under Assembly of United Nations, and without subjecting inhabitants of these islands to permanent naval rule.

Therefore, we join our fellow citizens in urging that you declare unequivocally United States intentions, and take the needed steps, to trustee and Japanese mandated islands under the Assembly of the United Nations, with the United States as administering authority, and to place these islands, along with Guam, Samoa and other United States Pacific Island possessions, under the administration of a civilian agency of the government.

> John Collier, President, Institute of Ethnic Affairs
> Richard Wood, President, National Peace Conference
> Justice Owen J. Roberts, President, United Nations Council of Philadelphia
> Norman Thomas, Chairman, Post War World Council
> Mrs. William H. Davis, President, Women's National Democratic Club
> Mrs. Edgerton Parsons, American Section, Pan-Pacific Women's Association
> Dorothy Kenyon
> Harry Laidlar
> Friends Committee on National Legislation
> National Council of Jewish Women
> Union for Democratic Action
> Council Against Intolerance
> Workers Defense League
> Council for Democracy
> Friends General Conference
> United States Student Assembly
> Council for Social Action
> Catholic War Veterans

(Telegram drafted by the Institute for endorsement by citizen groups.)

1

Thirty issues of the monthly *News Letter of the Institute of Ethnic Affairs* were published between February 1946 and May 1950.

Maximum delay, the maximum secrecy, and to give American citizens no handle for coming to grips with the issues of trusteeship and civil liberty for the islands; such is the strategy of the Navy and Army, with the Secretary of State going along. Hush, hush, hush! while a situation disastrous to the trusteeship system, violative of Chapter Eleven of the Charter, weakening the United Nations, and ruinous to the island natives is continued.

Citizens are not helpless. But they must talk to one another, talk to their editors, use the vast organizational and institutional forces which are at their command, and converge their public opinion on the White House.[4]

Fully understanding the power of citizen action, at the end of August Collier prepared a telegram to be signed by interested civil rights organizations and sent to the White House. (In those days, a telegram rather than a letter signified that an issue was of unusual importance.) Philleo Nash, one of Collier's close friends and a member of the board of the Institute of Ethnic Affairs, was then in the White House as the president's adviser on minority affairs. He would see that the telegram reached Truman's busy desk and that its substance was clearly understood.

The message of the telegram to the president was evident in its first line: "We urge that you make clear to the world that the United States intends to place the Japanese mandated islands under the United Nations trusteeship and to govern them, as administering authority, through a civilian agency of the government." It went on to say in the third paragraph, "Military requirements can be fully met through trusteeship under the Assembly of the United Nations, and without subjecting inhabitants of these islands to permanent naval rule." The last line would have the president extend civilian administration to "Guam, American Samoa and other United States Pacific Island possessions" as well as to the islands formerly mandated to Japan. It was signed by sixteen organizations and two individuals. Another important document, it is reprinted in full in Appendix 4.

Contrary to the Institute's hopes, the telegram brought no immediate response from President Harry Truman. It did, however, precipitate some very detrimental action. Soon after the telegram became public, the Internal Revenue Service ruled that donors could not write off contributions to the Institute on their tax returns. That made it difficult, if not impossible, to raise money through foundation grants or individual contributions. It was widely believed that Navy Secretary James V. Forrestal, through a former Navy employee then in the IRS, had had a hand in trying to kill off the young Institute. None of the other organizations that signed the telegram were given such a ruling.

Silence that summer on the part of the Navy in Washington with respect to the Pacific islands was foreboding. But it allowed the Secretary time for strategizing. As we soon learned, Forrestal was lining up news reporters for the Navy to take to the Pacific for the express purpose of disproving

James V. Forrestal became Secretary of the Navy in 1944 and was elevated to Secretary of Defense in 1947. In both positions he fought hard to keep Guam under the autocratic control of the Navy Department.

the allegations in Mr. Ickes' May 29, 1946, speech. Those allegations were given greater currency when Ickes turned his speech into an article for the August 31, 1946, issue of *Collier's* magazine (no relation to John Collier). He gave his article a tantalizing title: "The Navy at Its Worst."

On September 8, Collier wrote a letter to the editor of the *New York Times* disputing a Navy Department report to the United Nations submitted in July justifying military government in Guam. He said the Navy had misled the public, because the so-called experimental farm described in the report provided food only for military personnel and that the native owners who had their farms confiscated for this project never received compensation. He claimed that the Navy's concept of vocational education amounted to nothing more than manual labor. And he charged that military officials had failed to return to Guamanian owners the buses they had expropriated for military use during the war.

Reaction began when Navy Secretary Forrestal sent a letter to the *New York Times* on September 20. In that letter, he made no attempt to refute the criticisms leveled at the Navy. Instead, he reviewed the history of how the Navy had been given authority over Guam and Samoa by President William McKinley and quoted President Herbert Hoover's saying the Navy's "administration has been completely without blemish."[5]

Less than ten days later, Collier responded with another letter to the *Times*, pointing out Forrestal's omission of facts to rebut specific criticisms and noting that it was Mr. Hoover who in 1930 had appointed an American Samoan commission to investigate naval rule. That commission, Collier said, had recommended a bill of rights, an organic act, and citizenship for the Samoans. The Senate had enacted the recommendation, he continued, but the Navy had blocked the bill in the House.

Ickes also replied to Forrestal's letter. In a letter to the *Times* on October 15, he reiterated his former position as a responsible critic of Navy absolutism in the islands and gave new, concrete, documented illustrations of that department's continuing denial of human rights. He mentioned the case of Pedro Martinez and B. J. Bordallo, from whom bus lines were commandeered by the Navy during the war, and to whom no compensation had been paid. He referred to General Order 14-44, dated June 14, 1945, in which absenteeism from work "has been made punishable in Guam by fine and imprisonment." Of freedom of the press, he said, "It would have been more accurate if Secretary Forrestal had said that there would be such freedom if there were a press."[6]

Despite these citations of current cases, Admiral John H. Towers, then Commander in Chief of the Pacific fleet, in a Navy Day address delivered at a luncheon in Honolulu, called Ickes' criticisms "gross misstatements and purported events of several decades past." As military governor of all ex-mandated islands and military commander of the Pacific Ocean areas, Admiral Towers said he resented Ickes' recent attacks.

In his speech, the admiral completely ignored an editorial entitled "Neglect of Pacific Natives" that had appeared just the day before in the *Honolulu Star-Bulletin*. That editorial had summarized a series of reports of conditions in the islands dispatched by the paper's correspondent in Guam and had concluded, "The story reported by creditable eye-witnesses is one of shameful neglect of these Pacific islanders."[7]

The war of words at the highest level of government had begun, and the press was picking up on it. These exchanges were reported in the November 1946 issue of the Institute's *News Letter*, in which we reported, "Now the Navy has invited ten newspaper correspondents to tour the islands.

Whether the Navy will permit reporters to inspect pertinent areas of the islands and talk to the people without benefit of naval presence remains to be seen."[8]

On October 23, 1946, the Second Session of the United Nations General Assembly opened at Lake Success, New York. In his opening address President Truman failed to make any mention of trusteeship matters, even though France, Australia, Britain, New Zealand, and Belgium had submitted trusteeship agreements for approval. In his lead article in the November issue of the Institute *News Letter,* Collier chided the president for this omission, noting that in the Truman administration teamwork was lacking.

In a separate article entitled "How the Military Sways Foreign Policy," Collier maintained that, under a technical arrangement established by President Roosevelt during World War II, the Army and Navy acting together, or even separately, could veto policy proposed by the State Department. That organizational arrangement was known in Washington as SWNCC — the State, War, and Navy Coordinating Committee — and through it foreign policies of even the remotest military interest had to be cleared.

The Institute had been pressing since January 1946 for a decision that would place the formerly mandated Japanese islands under the Trusteeship Council of the General Assembly. This immense region, larger than the United States in area but with a tiny population scattered throughout hundreds of atolls and volcanic islands, would be called the Trust Territory of the Pacific Islands, or TTPI for short. Two weeks after the General Assembly opened, on November 6, 1946, President Truman announced that the United States was prepared to place all of Micronesia except Guam under the Security Council instead. This was to become the only "strategic trusteeship" in the world. The Navy Department under Forrestal obviously had been hard at work behind the scenes.

As soon as he heard the news, Collier was angry, probably as angry as I ever saw him in the five years I worked with him. I'll never forget the expression he repeated around the office and to professional acquaintances to describe what had happened. It had come from a New Zealander who summed up the reaction of foreign governments and many American citizens alike when he said, "We had been expecting something like that to be pulled out of the bag. But it was a bigger and blacker cat than we had imagined."

A big black cat indeed.

Undeterred, Collier immediately went about writing copy for the December 1946 *News Letter:*

> The announcement did not come as a surprise. The silence our government had maintained on this question had been an ominous silence. Scarcely a flicker of hope was given American individuals and organizations who pressed during spring, summer and fall months for trusteeship under the General Assembly. . . . In answering telegrams to the President which requested clarification of policy, the State Department issued only ambiguous words of thanks for your interest in this important subject. . . . Furthermore, it was known that trusteeship was being plotted by SWNCC — State, War and Navy Coordinating Committee . . . [where] the two military bodies on the board could win a strategic trusteeship for the entire area if they so desired. By September it was obvious that Security Council trusteeship was SWNCC's order of the day.[9]

Collier's paramount criticism of the President's announcement was that the entire mandated area would be closed to the rest of the world. That would amount to annexation. The Navy could rule the native inhabitants of the islands in absolute secrecy.

The hub of the area was 6,000 miles from San Francisco; 2,000 miles from Hong Kong, China; 2,000 miles from Darwin, Australia; and 2,200 miles from Vladivostok, Russia. That the United States should need all of the 1,500 islands and coral reefs for military installations to secure the mainland against possible attack by Australia, China, Russia, or Japan was "nothing short of ridiculous," Collier wrote. More from his pen follows:

> We must secure ourselves against eventualities in the Pacific. But just as it is unnecessary to call San Francisco, New York and Honolulu "strategic" and close them off from the rest of the world, so is it unnecessary to call all of Saipan, Rota, Truk and the other islands "strategic" and draw an iron curtain around their shores.[10]

It was this argument, this logic, that would eventually prevail in securing civilian administration for the Trust Territory. But, for the time being, it was lost on the Navy. As early as 1946, the military had plans for using Bikini as a test area for nuclear weapons and probably wished to conduct those tests in secrecy. The forthcoming test was not then known to the Institute of Ethnic Affairs.

"When the military institution makes foreign policy, foreign policy makes toward war."[11] These words opened Collier's article on "How the Military Sways Foreign Policy," in which he discussed SWNCC in the November 1946 *News Letter* (see Appendix 5). They proved prophetic. The military has used the Marshall Islands for scores if not hundreds of nuclear tests since that first test on and around Bikini in 1946. Instead of eliminating nuclear weapons, as has been promised under various international treaties, the United States government has been creating new ones. In this way, the military has been making foreign policy, and the State Department has gone along with it. One can only guess what Collier would have said about how the military influenced our entry into war with Iraq in 2003.

In the 1940s, no organization in Washington other than the Institute of Ethnic Affairs was concentrating on colonial issues. There were all those organizations that signed the telegram sent to President Truman in September, but their agendas were either narrower or broader. No organization other than the Institute of Ethnic Affairs was turning out regular publications on civil rights in the Pacific, except possibly the Institute of Pacific Relations, and it was headquartered in New York City, away from the center of United States government.

No scholars or administrators had the breadth of knowledge about and experience with dependent peoples shared by Collier, Laura Thompson, and Secretary Ickes. In the beginning, they stood alone against the military. No one else had the vision or the profundity of expression that could compare with these three on this subject.

Unable in 1946 to keep President Truman from recommending a strategic trusteeship under the Security Council instead of an ordinary trusteeship under the General Assembly, Collier went about critiquing the proposed agreement. Most of the December 1946 *News Letter* was given over to his comments in an article called "U.S. Trusteeship Draft: Analysis and Recommendation." The draft agreement was so riddled with deficiencies, he wrote, that the most desirable action would be to withdraw it and start over. But that would be difficult to do because Secretary of State John Foster Dulles, who was also the American member of the General Assembly Trusteeship Committee, on November 7 had served notice that it was this agreement or nothing at all. The military had made policy and Dulles had gone along with it.

Article 13, Collier wrote, should be amended so that only the islands or parts of islands used *exclusively* for military purposes would be exempt from the normal functions of the General Assembly and Trusteeship Council. Otherwise the agreement would apply to hundreds of islands, many of which "would not boast the installation of one American gun."[12]

Article 5 was intended to contribute to *international* security. As written, he said, it could lead to a bigger and better armaments race than the world had ever known. He proposed amending it so establishment of bases and maintenance of troops in the Trust Territory would be contingent on agreements made between the United States and the Security Council, as Article 43 of the United Nations Charter provided.

Article 7, as written, would license any Army or Navy administrator to write and change island laws according to his personal whims under the guise of requiring public order *and security*. Collier reminded *News Letter* readers that thousands of acres of land, public buildings, bus lines, and ships were confiscated in Guam and Samoa during the war by our Navy and not returned afterward. In 99 percent of the cases, not one cent of compensation had been paid. In order to protect the islanders' civil rights, the condition of *security* should be struck out, he said.

Collier wanted to amend Article 6 to leave the door open to independence, not just self-government. He thought it was unlikely that the islanders would ever want that status, for economically and otherwise they were confiningly dependent. But he maintained that the people should be given the right to make that choice.

It is certain that drafters in the Departments of War, Navy, State, and Interior as well as advisers in the White House saw all of Collier's suggestions, because by that time our *News Letters* were widely circulated to targeted individuals in key government agencies. We had most of them by name on our mailing list. We also knew copies were passed from hand to hand, or the contents were discussed over interdepartmental lunches.

In a relatively short time, the *News Letter* had become the voice of opposition to continued military rule in the Pacific islands and a small lighthouse of hope for other dependent territories.

Adverse developments in Guam were also reported in the December 1946 *News Letter*. Guamanian leaders well known to Laura Thompson had brought certain situations up to date for us. Devastation of Guam when the Navy retook it in 1944 was mortal. The fighting had gone on for months. Hagatna (or Agana as it was then called by the Navy) was completely destroyed by American bombardment. Guamanians were living in hovels.

Fares on the bus lines taken over by the Navy had been raised from 5 to 25 cents per zone, but neither Bordallo nor Martinez had been compensated for their loss.

A Meritorious Claims Act had been passed by the United States Congress in November of 1945 (Public Law 224, 79th Congress), but most claims remained unpaid. Since so much of the property was destroyed or confiscated for new military installations like the Navy airfield, Guamanians were acutely dependent on prompt and equitable action by the claims commission. Approximately 3,500 claims were pending. Worse, the Navy had pressed Congress to write into the Meritorious Claims Act that it alone should be the court of claims with final authority. In other words, the Navy Department, which had inflicted the damage and confiscated the property, was the court of first and last resort on compensation for the losses.

A similarly negative situation persisted with respect to wage discrimination. The Navy had decreed that Guamanians could be employed only on military unit jobs or by employers hiring fewer than fifty workers, and that their day-labor wages should be 28 cents an hour. The massive employment on Guam after the war was under Army and Navy contractors. These contractors were required to import their labor and were doing so at more than four times the Guamanian pay rates. Contractors were forbidden to employ, after returning to Guam, any native islanders who had been away during World War II, for example. Thus, any citizen, regardless of his race — Chinese, Japanese, Hawaiian, and so on — was receiving a wage four times that of a Chamorro with the same skills on the same type of job. Imported labor received sick leave and overtime pay, but Chamorro workers received neither.

Admiral Charles A. Pownall, governor of Guam, and his superior officer, Admiral John H. Towers, were quoted in the *Washington Post* of November 24, 1946, as endorsing the Chamorros' proposals for citizenship and adjustment of the wage scale. But both changes should be put into effect at the "proper time," they said, meaning nothing should be changed until Guam was rehabilitated. And that could take years.

Two other developments reported in the December 1946 *News Letter* affected me personally. One was an announcement that the *News Letter* would be published on a regular monthly basis and that I would continue to be its editor. The other was that, beginning in January 1947, the Institute would publish "a periodical newspaper" called the *Guam Echo* for its eighty-eight Guamanian members. The second announcement explained why such a publication was needed. It appeared in an article written by Collier and Laura Thompson:

> Few Americans realize that on this island there exists a news vacuum. No newspaper is published for the 23,000 natives; no magazine comes regularly even from the States. There exists no publication in which the people can express themselves.
>
> The *Navy News* is published daily for 30,000 American men and officers stationed on Guam and frequently is read by the natives. But naturally, this paper is geared to the taste of Navy men. World news of interest to islanders frequently is left out. This is no criticism of the Navy's paper, for it is edited for a particular purpose: to build Navy morale, and that purpose usually is excellently fulfilled.
>
> But dissemination of news on Guam leaves much to be desired. One young Guamanian now in the United States confessed that he had not heard of the United Nations organization until he reached this country last summer.[13]

The first *Guam Echo* would be published soon after the first of the year, and primary responsibility for it would be mine.

Chapter 5

The *Guam Echo*

So here we were, moving into January 1947, six months after I had joined the Institute staff. I had proved that I could get my arms around a difficult subject like a strategic versus a nonstrategic trusteeship. I could write in plain English. I could pick up the phone and ask questions of almost anyone in Washington. I could get publications out on time. All this and my general knowledge of imperialism and world government apparently qualified me for my added assignment as writer and editor of the new *Guam Echo*.

The expense of printing a regular newspaper would be prohibitive, so our new Guam periodical would come out in a four-page, letter-size, two-column, mimeographed form. This new publication would cover Washington developments affecting Guam, news from Guam itself, news from the United Nations in New York, editorial comments, and letters to the editor. Islanders themselves had suggested the name.

The paper would be sent to all who paid annual Institute memberships of $5.00 (or more). It would also be sent by request to Institute board members, selected members of Congress, one or two advisers in the White House, and friends with whom we worked in the State and Interior Departments. It was not sent to the Navy Department, but we were told the Navy was able to scrounge copies from various sources in both Washington and Guam.

The first issue was delayed while we moved to 810 18th Street, a square modern structure of steel and glass known as the Otis Building, not far from the Department of the Interior. We were on the third floor, which we reached by elevator, and we now had two fairly large rooms, one for Collier alone and one for Betty and me.

That first issue, published in early February 1947, was full of good news. Several new bills affecting the political future of Guam had been introduced in January, and that became our lead story. Each bill was briefly described (see Appendix 6).

GUAM ECHO

Vol. 1, No. 1   February 1947

Temporarily published by the Institute of Ethnic Affairs
at the request of members in Guam

BILLS FOR GUAM

The political future of Guam will be determined by passage or rejection of certain measures introduced in the United States 80th Congress.

H. J. Res. 80, introduced by Henry Jackson of Washington, provides for civilian administration under the Secretary of the Interior over the Caroline, Marshall, and Marianas Islands and Guam and American Samoa. Any unexpended balance of funds allocated for expenditure by the Navy Department in the administration of native affairs is made transferable to the Department of Interior.

S. J. Res. 51, introduced by Hugh Butler of Nebraska, is identical to the Jackson Resolution.

H. R. 874, introduced by Willis W. Bradley of California, would confer U. S. citizenship upon inhabitants of Guam, as would H. R. 1417, introduced by Delegate Joseph Farrington of Hawaii.

H. R. 64, introduced by Robert A. Grant of Indiana, is a 72-page document providing citizenship and an Organic Act for Guam. It allows that the Governor, appointed by the President, may remain on active duty in the naval or military service during his term and provides a salary scale for administrators that Guamanians probably could not afford. The bill is minutely detailed, providing for everything from a Marianas Commission to regulations for commitment of the insane. Some say the bill contains too much detail for an Organic Act, that some of its subject matter would belong to the Guam Congress for enactment in ordinances from time to time.

Other bills providing for citizenship and an Organic Act are anticipated. Observers in Washington expect that

STATEHOOD FOR HAWAII

Guam isn't the only American possession seeking more liberty. At the opening session of Congress, ten bills providing statehood for Hawaii were introduced.

Delegate Joseph R. Farrington led the campaign by introducing H. R. 49.

"I'm not a numerologist," he said. "But I have confidence that H. R. 49 will enable Hawaii to become the 49th state this year."

Guamanians will support the principle of all bills but no one bill in particular until more bills have been introduced and committee hearings scheduled.

It has been suggested that Guamanians may request that any bill granting them self-government be referred to the Guam Congress for approval of detail before ratification by the U.S. Congress.

* * * * *

RESOLUTION FROM GUAM

Copies of the Joint Resolution, No. 1, of the 8th Guam Congress, to the effect that Guamanians be granted citizenship and an Organic Act, were enthusiastically received by the Institute of Ethnic Affairs and interested individuals in Washington and New York.

Cabinet members, presiding officers of the House of Representatives and the Senate, and special committees seemingly have not yet received official copies of the resolution although it was designated in the bill that copies would be sent to them.

Thirty-seven issues of the monthly *Guam Echo* were published between February 1947 and May 1950.

A yellowed clipping from the December 20, 1946, *New York Times,* tucked into my file of Ethnic Institute press releases, quotes Representative Henry Jackson saying as he reintroduced his bill of the year before:

> The native peoples of the former Japanese-mandated islands in the Pacific were not belligerent enemies of the United States in the late war. They are a liberated people, friends of the United States and not conquered enemies to be ruled with bayonets under military administration. . . .
>
> The people of Guam have been loyal Americans since 1898, when their island was acquired by cession from Spain. To this date the United States has failed to fulfill its pledge contained in the Treaty of Paris, pursuant to which we agreed to define by act of Congress the civil rights and political status of the native inhabitants of Guam.

We made a point of listing the names of all members of the House and Senate subcommittees dealing with island affairs (see Appendix 7). We also explained how to address them properly. In a paragraph under all those names we wrote: "Congressmen urge that you write them how you feel about civilian administration for Guam. What you — the people — say has far more influence on Congressmen's votes than what people thousands of miles from the scene tell Congressmen about the situation."[1]

A second story on the front page of that first *Guam Echo* reported that on January 4, 1947, the 8th Guam Congress had passed Joint Resolution No. 1, requesting that Guamanians be granted citizenship and an organic act. This was considered a very significant development. The news had been enthusiastically received by the Institute board and other interested individuals in both Washington and New York.

The article stated that cabinet members, presiding officers of the House and the Senate, and pertinent committees of the Congress had not yet received official copies of the resolution, although it was stated in the bill that copies would be sent to them. Apparently the Navy was having trouble digesting the implications of that resolution; it was slow about notifying Congress.

We reported, on page three, that a request for civilian administration and home rule had also come from American Samoa. When Martin Brunor, a New York anthropologist, had returned to the States in October after four frustrating months of trying to help the Samoans establish a wood handicraft business, he brought with him a proposed bill for self-government signed by four hundred native chiefs. Brunor had turned that document over to the Institute of Ethnic Affairs, and Collier had sent photostatic copies of it to the Territorial and Insular Affairs Subcommittees in the House and Senate.

In Guam and Washington the question had been raised whether an organic act and civilian rule would cut Guam off from federal funds. A three-paragraph article, written by Collier, explained that Puerto Rico had once been governed by the U.S. Navy but that an organic act and help from the Interior Department meant that the U.S. government in 1947 was allotting to Puerto Rico about $50,000,000 a year, or about $25 per person. If Guam were given the same amount per capita, Collier asserted, it would receive about $575,000 a year. As another example, Collier stated that American Indians were once governed by the U.S. Army. In 1934 Congress enacted and President Roosevelt signed the Indian Reorganization Act, under which tribes could adopt their own constitutions and ordinances. In 1947 the federal government through the Interior Department was receiving more than $30,000,000 a year, or about $75 per each of the 400,000 Indians. For Guam, with its much smaller population, a similar percentage of federal allotment for schools, medical service, and all social services would mean about $1,725,000 a year.

To put Guam in perspective compared to other dependent areas of the world, we reported on page four that after 250 years of colonial rule by England, India would soon be given its independence; Burma had just been granted the right to elect a Constituent Assembly in preparation for independence from England; the French were fighting desperately to hold on to Indochina (which became Vietnam), but on July 4, 1946, the United States had granted the Philippines independence and signed a treaty for the strategic defense of that new country in return for the lease of military bases at Subic Bay, Clark Field, and elsewhere.

We also reprinted a column by Drew Pearson describing, tongue in cheek, how Ickes had finally gotten General MacArthur and Admiral Nimitz to speak to each other. Ickes had asked the Navy if he could send one of his staff with the newsmen invited by Forrestal to tour Guam and the Trust Territory. The Navy had hemmed and hawed, then bucked the question up to MacArthur, who kindly obliged Nimitz by saying no.[2]

In what was labeled an editorial on the fourth page, I wrote something about "The Right to Know":

This first issue of *Guam Echo* is our answer to Guamanians' call for news. It is an expression of freedom of the press as Americans know that freedom. It is partial fulfillment of every individual's right to know. . . . It should reach every family and be read by all. For only then will Guamanians keep abreast of what is happening in the world and understand the part they have to play in history.

This is YOUR paper. It was named by you. Someday it will be edited and printed by you. Do your part now to let it echo your hopes, your grievances, your news, and your views. Help it speak for Guamanians.[3]

That little paper was on its way to making a difference in the lives of thousands of islanders. Nothing I have written since has been as gratifying as the *Guam Echo,* and I've had fifty years of writing and editing for Fortune 500 corporations and nonprofit organizations. Eventually, the *Guam Echo* fulfilled its mission.

Over the summer and fall of 1946, we had received many reports from Guamanians verifying what Ickes had said about naval government at the Institute's meeting in May, so I was able to start "Guam Looks to the 80th Congress," the lead article I wrote for the January 1947 *News Letter,* with the following claim: "The people of Guam are sick and tired of being wards under the thumb of the United States Navy. . . . The 80th Congress will meet this month to find the 23,000 "nationals" of this island in the Pacific ready to fight for citizenship and an organic act."[4] At a special session of the Guam Congress on December 14, 1946, a committee had been appointed to draft a resolution recommending enactment of just that.

Guamanians had come to realize that an organic act was a form of local constitution that would give them a government with checks and balances — an elected legislature that would enact local laws, an executive branch that would administer those laws, and a judicial body that would interpret the laws. For Guam, an organic act could mean real lawmaking by the Guam Congress that then sat only as an advisory body, a civilian governor who might actually be one of their own Chamorros, and a court system with the right of appeal.

Guamanians knew that their petitioning could lead to a showdown struggle that would result either in opening a new chapter of self-government for them or the shutting of that door forever. They were determined to succeed. In 1946, Guam was still front-page news in many continental U.S.

newspapers. The memories of the many thousands of Americans who had served on Guam during the war were still fresh. In time to come, military secrecy could shut Guam out of world affairs. If anything were to happen, it had to happen soon. That's why the Guam Congress had appointed a committee to prepare a resolution requesting U.S. citizenship and an organic act for introduction right after the first of the year.

Through Emil Sady, we at the Ethnic Institute knew that the State Department believed civilian government for Guam to be consistent with American traditions and with the objectives of the United Nations Charter. Through Roy James we knew that the Department of the Interior was prepared to become the administering civilian agency. Only the Navy Department was raising objections. Part of the Navy's strategy for maintaining control had involved taking ten hand-picked newspaper reporters on a tour of the islands in November, all expenses paid, and wining and dining them in such a fashion that they would write only reports favorable to continued naval administration. Unfortunately for the Navy, the plan boomeranged. The reporters found ways to elude military surveillance and talk to the islanders alone. Excerpts from printed accounts in their newspapers throughout the country became part of my article in the January *News Letter*. Lloyd Norman, of the Chicago Tribune Press Service, wrote:

Opposition grievances against the navy follow:

1. The navy is throttling free enterprise. Sales taxes and price fixing do not permit a fair profit.
2. The navy government is essentially military in nature and its high handedness is not suitable for civilians who have been American subjects for 47 years.
3. The navy takes a patronizing and condescending attitude toward the Guamanians, treating them as inferiors.
4. Medical care is on a charity ward basis with little sympathy or interest shown except in grave emergencies.
5. The navy has taken the best land and the most attractive parts of the island for its installations.
6. The navy is building homes for the families of its officers and men but has done nothing to rebuild the old city of Agana to provide homes for the 20,000 persons whose homes were devastated by American guns and shell fire during the war.
7. The navy has played favorites, especially with the Guam Commercial

Company. The company's cargo is unloaded rapidly while other business men on the island have to wait weeks for their cargoes to be delivered.[5]

John G. Norris, writing in the *Washington Post,* stressed Guamanians' wage discrimination grievances.

Any "citizen," regardless of his race — Chinese, Japanese, Hawaiian, etc. — receives a wage four times that of a Chamorro with the same skill on the same type of job.

A Chamorro electrician, for example, makes 43 cents an hour. An imported Civil Service electrician working on the same United States Government project, doing similar work, gets $1.80 an hour. An imported electrician working for a private contractor doing naval work on the island is paid $1.95 an hour.

Chamorros generally are not allowed to work for private contractors.[6]

Roland Sawyer, writing in *The Christian Science Monitor* on December 5, stated: "It is not overstating the case to report that the form of government which exists here is autocratic and undemocratic."[7] On December 17, in the same paper, Sawyer observed that the Navy had missed or chosen to ignore the real issue: "That issue is whether or not a military group should govern civilians; whether or not a military caste by its nature can govern civilians adequately in time of peace."[8]

Eugene Rachlis, who was in the Washington Bureau of the *Chicago Sun* when he made the trip, closed an article he wrote for the December 9, 1946, *New Republic* magazine with these words: "Naval rule results, at best, in humanitarian paternalism towards the members of communities which happen to be near military bases. The principal goal of military government of the Pacific islands is not democratic political development and economic advancement for the Pacific peoples. It is a military rule for one purpose: military defense."[9]

My article in the January *News Letter* went on to corroborate what the reporters had written about wage discrimination. We had learned, for example, that imported continental American automotive mechanics were paid $66.40 for a forty-hour week, while the Navy was paying Guamanian automotive mechanics of the same grade for the same amount of work only $15.60 per week. The Navy was paying Guamanian launderers 28 cents an hour, compared to $1.27 for Hawaiian and American launderers brought into Guam by contractors.

Civil rights were being denied. Executive Order Number 20-46, issued by Admiral Charles A. Pownall, then governor, prohibited Guamanians from riding in any government-owned vehicle without a proper pass from the military authority charged with custody of such a government-owned vehicle. Executive Order Number 21-46 restrained all civilians who were not permanent residents of Guam from entering any Guamanian home, village, or community without a written invitation from an adult member of the family visited and a written pass from the commanding officer or camp commander of that civilian.

Shortly after Ickes' indictment of Navy rule in May, the Navy had made a pretense of improving its government by a change of name. It had replaced "Naval Military Government" with "Naval Civil Government." Guamanians found any improvement indiscernible. Letters to the Institute revealed as much desperation as Guamanians ever allowed themselves to feel. One half-seriously asked the Institute, "Must we give up the fight and all try to move to the United States?"[10]

By January of 1947, the Navy was agreeing that citizenship and an organic act for Guam were good ideas, *but not for now.* My article reported that the strategy of the Navy was to get by the 80th Congress without an organic act for Guam and Samoa. For success it was relying on time and inertia, on the waning of public interest and Guamanian hope. As reported in the *Washington Post,* on December 9, 1946, Secretary Forrestal was proposing another investigation, this one conducted by a committee of notable hand-picked civilians. Such a study would discourage Congress from acting while awaiting the committee's report. Echoing comments by Collier made earlier, my article concluded:

> The thorough, impartial investigation that should be made could be effectively conducted only by Congress. The obvious faults of Naval administration can be corrected only by passing an organic act. The people of the island are prepared for a fight to the finish. Individual Americans, organizations, newspapermen and Congressmen, too, must work to secure for Guamanians cherished human rights they have earned by their loyalty and paid for in suffering and in blood.[11]

A big box in the body of my article listed twenty-one bulleted points explaining what an organic act could mean to Guam. Nearly all of them eventually were covered in the final legislation.

That January *News Letter* also informed readers that on December 13,

1946, eight trusteeship agreements submitted by five former mandators were approved by the United Nations General Assembly, making possible establishment of the last remaining major organ of the United Nations — the Trusteeship Council. The United States was not one of the five; the agreements had been submitted by Australia, Belgium, France, New Zealand, and the United Kingdom. No less than 228 suggested modifications to the draft trusteeship agreements had been considered in nearly six weeks of deliberation. United States consultants, including John Collier, had been active in obtaining many of the modifications. UN Secretary General Trygvie Lie was directed to convoke the first session of the Trusteeship Council no later than March 15, 1947.

Our very first *Guam Echo* had been published in early February of 1947. So much was happening so fast that we decided to publish a second issue before the end of February. For one thing, Roy James and others had talked Julius A. Krug, the new Truman appointee who succeeded Ickes as Secretary of the Interior, into seeing the Pacific islands for himself. Roy had worked as an officer in the Naval Military Government in Guam until the spring of 1946 when he joined the Interior Department. Now Roy and several other Interior Department officials were accompanying the Secretary on a swing through Shanghai, American Samoa, Guam, Okinawa, Tokyo, and Hawai'i. With them were several Army and Navy officers.

Although the Interior Department under Secretary Ickes had been strongly opposed to continued naval rule of Guam and Samoa, the new secretary, a former naval officer himself and a close personal friend of Secretary Forrestal, was thought to be lukewarm toward civilian administration. The Institute board and staff didn't know what to think about him. His trip had come about rather suddenly. However, when the group reached Tokyo near the end of their trip, we were reassured. On February 25, Secretary Krug told the Associated Press that he approved of American citizenship for Guamanians and Samoans. He said he was not prepared at that time to state how much local rule the natives should be given, but that they should receive "a measure of the freedom we have at home." He said the United States had learned from experience that native leaders govern well when left alone.[12] This was the first public statement made by the new Secretary relative to the future of the Pacific islands. It certainly merited a special issue of our new Guam "newspaper."

"Krug Favors Citizenship for Guam" was the headline on the lead story of the *Guam Echo,* dated February 27, 1947. The article explained that

Secretary Krug would present to President Truman his proposals for the islands soon after his return on March 4 and that hearings on bills in the Congress would then be held.

Another front-page story notified Guamanian readers that they would be visited by a second high-level group of civilians being sent there by Navy Secretary James V. Forrestal. That group would become known as The Hopkins Committee and included Ernest Martin Hopkins, retired president of Dartmouth College; Maurice Joseph Tobin, former governor of Massachusetts; and Knowles A. Ryerson, dean of California University's College of Agriculture. They were to (1) study the conduct of naval government of Guam and American Samoa; (2) recommend legislation including an organic act for island government and U.S. citizenship for the natives; (3) recommend measures for improvement of native health and educational programs; and (4) recommend measures for rehabilitation and stabilization of the island economy, including the establishment of civilian wage scales.

In still other ways, the Navy was firming up its control over the Pacific islands. Readers of the *Echo* were told that Admiral John H. Towers would step down as Commander in Chief of the Pacific (CINCPAC) on February 28, 1947, turning over his command to Admiral Louis E. Denfield. Towers would go to Washington to head the Navy's powerful general board there. He had made it known that he wanted Denfield to be named "Governor General" of all the former mandated islands, with both military and civil authority delegated to Denfield. Under the current setup, the naval governors of Guam and Samoa reported directly to Washington on government matters and to CINCPAC on matters strictly military. Admiral Towers felt that CINCPAC, being charged with defense of the Pacific, should not be bypassed on government reports.

Further complicating matters was a speech made to Congress by Representative Mike Mansfield, a Democrat from Montana, also reported in the February 27 *Guam Echo*. Mansfield had recently visited the Far East. When he came back he said he believed the Navy would be the best administrator of the mandated islands for the time being. Concerning citizenship, Mansfield correctly pointed out that the Guamanians had petitioned for it on a number of occasions but the U.S. Congress had not yet acted. As far as health conditions were concerned, he said that Guam had become one of the cleanest and most wholesome islands in the tropics.

Senator Hugh A. Butler (R., Nebr.) on April 9, 1947, introduced in the Senate a bill, S. 1078, identical to Poulson's bill in the House.

To this health-care claim Laura Thompson asserted in the same *Guam Echo* that the Navy often was given more credit for its health program on Guam than it deserved. She pointed out that Guamanians had petitioned for water purification for forty years before the Navy consented to chlorinate the public water supply, a process that cost only $5,000. And she noted that in the large hospital on Guam, to which the Navy pointed with pride, before Pearl Harbor there was not even a ward for the isolation of communicable diseases such as tuberculosis and pneumonia.

As a counterpoint to Senator Mansfield's remarks favoring continuing naval government, we printed parts of a statement by Senator Hugh A. Butler, a Republican from Nebraska. It had accompanied his introduction of S.J. Res. 51, which, if enacted, would provide for civilian administration of Guam, Samoa, and the mandate islands:

> The native populations of those islands have no civil or political rights. There are no independent courts. The Naval governors are, in effect, executive, legislative, and judicial branches of the government, all rolled into one. . . .

Government of this type would be burdensome even if conducted by a civilian. Certainly it is doubly so when the rule is that of a man trained in military methods — with all that that implies. The Congress of the United States has a final responsibility for the welfare of these people. We cannot dodge that responsibility. We ought to give them a truly American form of government.[13]

Chapter 6

The Fight for Civilian Government

Stopping in Hawai'i on his way home from Shanghai, American Samoa, Kwajalein, Guam, Wake, and Japan, Interior Secretary Krug left no doubt about his personal conviction that increased self-government and civilian administration were best for the Pacific islands. In an address before the Hawaiian Legislature on February 28, 1947, he strongly supported statehood for Hawai'i, then added: "the native populations of Guam and American Samoa have made great progress under naval administration. But now they are ready for the next step in the American tradition, which is civil political administration, responsible to the people who are governed."[1]

Back in Washington, on March 7, he testified before the House Public Lands Committee, saying that he was "very certain" that a greater degree of self-rule for the Pacific islands was desirable. Asked about General Douglas MacArthur's position, he said, "In Tokyo the general told me that he was in accord with the policy of extending civilian administration and more self-rule to the islands."[2] It is interesting to note that this testimonial came on the very day that the proposed trusteeship agreement covering most of the islands of Micronesia was put before the Security Council, where the United States could exercise a veto, instead of the General Assembly, where issues would be decided by majority vote.

Opponents of the draft agreement had hoped Russia would raise its powerful voice, because through this document key islands scattered across 3,000,000 square miles of the Pacific Ocean could be closed off to the world. In other words, an iron curtain could be drawn around them, enabling the United States to construct military installations there in secrecy anytime, anywhere, it pleased. That was certainly contrary to the spirit of the United Nations Charter. Russia's surprise approval of the proposed agreement late in February left both proponents and opponents scrambling for words. Neither side had much to say publicly. Even editorial comment was conspicuous by its absence.

Julius A. Krug suc-
ceeded Harold L.
Ickes as Secretary of
the Interior in 1946.
A friend of the Navy
and noncommittal
at first, he became a
strong supporter of
civilian government
for Guam and all
Pacific islands.

On March 3, 1947, four days before the Security Council was scheduled to vote on the proposal, Collier sent a letter to the *New York Times*. It was the first comment, either pro or con, to appear on the *Times* editorial page since the Russian position became known. In that letter Collier adamantly claimed that the proposed strategic trusteeship agreement, "faithless to the spirit of the Charter of United Nations, now has served an added sinister purpose, curiously unforeseen by ourselves." Just as certain congressmen and Navy spokesmen had justified the draft agreement by reiterating that we had paid for those mandate islands "with our blood," Collier continued, so Russia could argue that it had the right to unilaterally take under its wing other disputed regions of the world "paid for with Russian blood."[3]

The letter began to wake policy makers up, but not soon enough. On March 7, when the Security Council met, it approved the proposed agreement with three minor amendments. Collier wrote in the March *News Letter,* "Russia's surprise move [approval of the agreement] crystallized for the world what formerly had been clear to only a few specialized groups, that by proposing a virtual land-grabbing trusteeship agreement, America inadvertently had shut her lips on her own voice."[4] No words could better express what we at the Institute felt.

Unknown by Collier or other Institute members at the time was a tacit understanding between Russia and the United States that the United States would acquiesce to Soviet retention of four Japanese islands in the southern Kuriles north of Japan in return for American control of Micronesia.[5] This became clear to me only in 2005, when Robert F. Rogers, in a phone conversation, called my attention to page 206 of his book, *Destiny's Landing,* where the secret accord was described. Also, not generally known at that time was the fact that the U.S. military wanted to use the isolated atolls of the Marshall Islands to test nuclear weapons. The first test, in fact, had been conducted on July 1, 1946, with an explosion on Bikini Island.

Truman's placing of the Micronesian trusteeship under the Security Council instead of the General Assembly was a real blow to those of us who favored civilian administration of the islands. But the battle wasn't over yet. In fact, it was far from over. President Truman had not yet announced which agency should administer those mandated, now trusteed, islands. He wouldn't announce it for another two years. The outcome explains why I was able to call this book *We Fought the Navy and Won.* A victory with respect to civilian government was in the making, but there were many more ups and downs to come.

In the next *Guam Echo,* dated March 20, 1947, we were able to report that Interior Secretary Krug was now ready to give wholehearted support to civilian administration of Guam, Samoa, and the Japanese mandate islands. Testifying before the House Public Lands Committee on March 7, he had said:

> I feel that the islands in the Pacific that are American-owned now and those that will be held under trusteeship arrangement should be accorded a form of civil government giving them national autonomy if possible. . . . It would be wise if we give them at least a separation between the courts and the law making and the law enforcement . . . [instead of] a single individual who, under a charter, makes the law, enforces the law, and decides whether he is doing it right. I think that is an intolerable situation.[6]

If the Guamanians were "fighting" for civil rights, and they were, some were doing it in a most genteel manner. While in Guam, Krug had been invited to the home of Agueda Johnston, a most knowledgeable and gracious host. We didn't mention her by name in the March 20 *Guam Echo,* but we

Agueda I. Johnston
was the first Chamorro
woman to work for civil
rights for the islanders.

did write, "The Secretary of the Interior, who now has the distinction of being the only cabinet officer ever to have enjoyed the hospitality of a Guamanian home, has indeed become a 'friend of Guam.'"[7] Mrs. Johnston had helped win him over. I can't help observing here, based on my future visits in the homes of people all over the world, how much more could be gained through this kind of diplomacy in contrast to what our political leaders often try to achieve through violent, military force.

Representative Norris Poulson (R., Calif.), Representative Clair Engle (D., Calif.), Delegate Joseph R. Farrington (R., Hawai'i), several Army and Navy officers, and several Interior Department staff members, including Roy James and Carlton Skinner, who later became the first civilian governor of Guam, were members of the Krug delegation on that trip throughout the Pacific.

Upon their return to Washington, Representative Poulson told me for publication in the March 20, 1947, *Guam Echo:* "I propose to introduce an Organic Act for Guam which will give the people of Guam a measure of local self-government, American citizenship, a decent system of courts, and a Resident Commissioner in Washington to look after their interests in the future. These long-suffering and loyal people deserve all we can do for them — and deserve it now!"[8] Representative Engle said, for publication in the same *Echo:* "I found Guamanians to be intelligent, splendid people, capable of handling a wide degree of self-rule. They should have their own courts, their own legislature. This, I believe, is not inconsistent with United States defense purposes."[9]

Most of a news article by Buck Buchwach that had appeared in *The Honolulu Advertiser* on February 27 was also reprinted in the March *Guam Echo:*

> The towering head of the Interior Department strongly endorsed the substitution of civilian administration for military government of these islands and said he advocated such a change "soon." He said such a change could be accomplished even in areas which the military has labeled strategic.
>
> "There is no more strategic area in the Pacific than Hawaii, and you have civilian rule here," he pointed out. . . . "There is no reason why many of the things now done by the navy [referring to transportation, communication, and medical facilities on Guam] can't be continued. . . . The navy is doing an excellent job. That isn't the question. . . . The question is whether those people are entitled to the same type of government that we are. I feel strongly that the basic principle of our government is civilian government for civilian people. That is why I am for statehood for Hawaii and civilian administration of Pacific islands."[10]

In that *Echo,* we published the names of eight members added to the House Subcommittee on Territories and Insular Possessions (see Appendix 7). We also printed our first letter-to-the-editor. Signed simply "A Guamanian" to protect the writer from possible recriminations, it said in part: "The short visit made by the Secretary of Interior Krug and his party was most gratifying. It showed that at last an effort has been made to see the fire behind the smoke . . . While we are waiting for the result of these investigations, our feeling is like that of a person standing on one leg. When is the other one to be let down? We hope Congress will decide before we get too exhausted."[11]

By this time, 143 Guamanians had joined the Institute, 54 of them in the previous two months. Encouraged by Collier and by all they were reading in the Institute publications, more and more Guamanians were beginning to speak out.

Warned by us about the possible bias of the Hopkins Committee, the islanders were prepared when that high-powered trio appeared early in March. Shortly after their visit, a leading Guamanian wrote to the Institute, "The Dr. Ernest M. Hopkins Commission will be a success . . . if the Commission will recommend what they heard from the crowd that met them at the Guam Congress Hall. . . ." He went on to recount what the Guamanians had said. His rather long letter may be read in Appendix 8. We printed it in the March *News Letter* because it was important that readers know what Guamanians had told the Hopkins Commission. Collier wrote in response for publication in that *News Letter:* "If these views of the people are conscientiously reported and if recommendations as to legislation are based thereon, Secretary Forrestal will have what amounts to a mandate for civilian administration. The time to relieve Naval Civil Government officers of duty in Guam and Samoa then will have come."[12]

Nearly three more years would pass, however, before Guam actually got its organic act. There would be many more political skirmishes before the die was cast. Sparks flew next on the Hill when Representative Poulson, in a speech before the House on March 31, 1947, charged Navy Secretary Forrestal with "deliberately withholding" from Congress all knowledge of the resolution passed by the Guam Congress three months before. Poulson also accused the Secretary of withholding from Congress the bill enacted in 1945 by the *General Fono* of American Samoa proposing an organic act for that island.[13]

This speech brought a sharp retort from Secretary Forrestal the very next day in the form of a letter addressed to Congressman Richard Welch, chairman of the House Committee on Public Lands, on which Poulson also served. It was actually carried to Welch's office by then Undersecretary of the Navy, John L. Sullivan, and various naval officers for introduction into the *Congressional Record.* No copy was furnished to Poulson.

In essence, the letter said that Secretary Forrestal understood such a bill had been passed by the Guam Congress on January 4, but no copy had been forwarded either to the governor of Guam or to Washington. Late in February, the Guam governor had directed his attorney general to prepare copies of the resolution, signed by the presiding officers of the Congress. The copies were not delivered to the governor until March 15, and still had not reached the Secretary of the Navy as of the date of the letter, April 1, 1947. In regard to the Samoan resolution, the Secretary said he understood it was embodied in the report of the Hopkins Committee, which would

Representative Norris Poulson (R., Calif.) introduced H.R. 2753 granting Guam an organic act soon after accompanying Secretary Krug on a tour of the Pacific islands in the winter of 1947.

reach his desk sometime that week. The Secretary ended his letter, "Be assured that I have not deliberately withheld either of these matters from the Congress of the United States and immediately upon their receipt I shall transmit them expeditiously."[14]

Congressman Poulson absolved the Secretary of any personal knowledge of the petitions in a speech to Congress on April 3, but made plain that

> I am not withdrawing from the position I have taken in calling for an end to naval autocracy in Guam and American Samoa. . . . What is it that has aroused the Gold Braid Department of our Government and has prompted the Secretary of the Navy to have his letter placed in the Record of Congress? . . . The thing that brought out the hatchet men is the Poulson Bill, H.R. 2753. . . . The rub is, gentlemen, that by providing for a new form of government my bill in reality points out the evils of the existing form of government in Guam.[15]

This exchange showed the congressman's true mettle, as did the comments made by Harold L. Ickes in his syndicated newspaper column a few days later:

> There can be no doubt that the Navy had knowledge of the action on January 4 of the Guamanian Congress. . . . The conclusion cannot be escaped that the Navy knew of these petitions and was desperately anxious to keep them from reaching the Congress, at least until the latest, hand-picked group, headed by Dr. Ernest M. Hopkins, sent out by the Navy with whitewash buckets, could file its report defending the dictatorial naval rule of these two American possessions.[16]

I could only smile as I read again in 2005 Ickes' words about the Navy's "whitewash buckets." How wonderfully forthright he could be! And how unabashed regarding stature or rank, even when dealing with the Secretary of the Navy and the retired president of Dartmouth University.

As part of the seesaw going on between proponents of civilian government and advocates of continued naval administration, Representative Poulson had introduced H.R. 2753 on March 24, 1947, scarcely three weeks after his trip through the Pacific with Interior Secretary Krug. It proposed U.S. citizenship and an organic act for the people of Guam. On April 9, an identical bill, S. 1078, was introduced by Hugh A. Butler (R., Nebr.) in the Senate.

News of these bills was conveyed to the Guam people in the sixth issue of the *Guam Echo,* dated April 14, 1947. Poulson told us that his office had forwarded copies of his bill to leading members of the Guam Congress. But knowing that not many Guamanians would be able to lay their hands on it that way, we spelled out for our readers the main provisions, as listed below. Incidentally, nearly all provisions were included in the final bill that the White House instructed the Interior Department to write two years later. If enacted, the Poulson and Butler bills would:

1. Transfer administration of Guam from the Navy Department to the Interior Department;
2. Place the reins of administration in the hands of a civilian governor appointed by the president with the advice and consent of the U.S. Senate;
3. Set up a two-house legislature to enact laws, modeled upon the Guam Congress, members to be paid $15 each day Congress was in session plus travel expenses for one round-trip each session;

4. Provide for a Resident Commissioner in the U.S. House of Representatives, elected by the people of Guam;
5. Establish a District Court of Guam with the right of appeal to the U.S. Supreme Court;
6. Extend the power of local taxation to the Guam Congress;
7. Establish private commercial banking facilities in place of the naval-owned and -operated Bank of Guam;
8. Enforce equal pay for equal work in Guam;
9. Extend to Guam U.S. Public Health Service, the National School Lunch Act, vocational education aids, soil conservation, and other social and economic services.

Washington observers familiar with all bills on this subject agreed that the Butler and Poulson bills seemed to meet most adequately the needs expressed by Guamanians. Both bills provided a framework for good government and left the details to be worked out by the Guam Congress and other officials. The "miscellaneous provisions" extending social and economic services to the islanders were not carried in any other bill.[17]

As it happened, the Hopkins Committee report, an eighty-page document, was filed with Secretary Forrestal on March 25, the day after the Poulson and Butler bills were introduced. The report was not released to the press until May 11, 1947.

Basic recommendations of the committee were threefold: (1) that the people of Guam and American Samoa be made United States citizens as soon as possible, (2) that the future government of both American possessions be under an organic act, and (3) that general control over the islands be retained in the Navy Department for the immediate, though undefined, future. Writing for the May 1947 issue of the Institute *News Letter,* Collier stated: "In making public the report, Secretary Forrestal announced his concurrence in the recommendations for citizenship and an organic act. If enacted by Congress these represent the longest strides toward democracy taken in the history of American control of the islands."[18]

Paradoxically, Collier continued, the major factual part of the report substantiated the points used by critics of naval administration as arguments for an immediate change to civilian government. Yet the Hopkins Committee had not been able to go that far in their recommendations. In fact, what they wrote flew in the face of what the Guamanians had told them. The report stated: "Nowhere did your committee find any expression

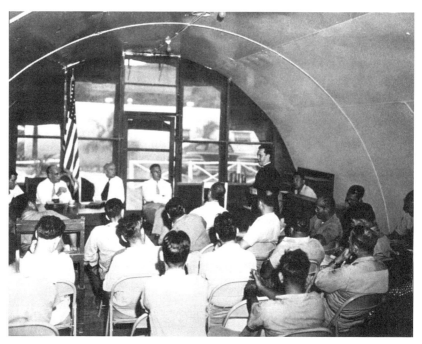

The Hopkins Committee held hearings on Guam and recommended civilian government—"but not now." It misrepresented how the Guamanians felt about naval
government.

of desire to be removed from under the auspices of the Navy, but on the
contrary, whenever discussion of the matter came up, apprehension was
expressed as to whether from any other department than the Navy, service
so vital to them as these in their possession could be afforded."[19]

This ran counter to the anonymous letter from a leading Guamanian
printed in our March 1947 *News Letter* (see Appendix 8), and everybody
concerned knew it. The Hopkins Committee had chosen to ignore the fact
that the Interior Department for many years had administered far-flung
Hawai'i, Alaska, the Philippines, Puerto Rico, and the Virgin Islands. It
also chose to ignore Interior Secretary Krug's statements, given nationwide publicity at the end of his inspection trip, urging that the islands be
placed under civilian rule immediately. A solemn mood had settled over
all of us at the Institute, which contributed to the title on Collier's analyti-
cal article in the May 1947 *News Letter,* "Time Only Can Tell. . . ." It ended
with the following conclusion, "The Hopkins Committee has thrown its
weight, if not its facts or argument, behind continuation of naval rule,

while suggesting that at some indefinite future date, under an organic act, some new, presumptively civilian, agency should replace the Navy."[20]

It was always amazing to me that Collier could lay his hands on government reports so quickly and analyze them so promptly. He had the mind of a prosecuting attorney, though he had never studied law. Because we thought our readers would be interested in many aspects of the Hopkins Report, we devoted the entire May issue of the *Guam Echo* to direct quotations that provided a summary of each section. With Collier's help, we were able to publish that *Echo* only four days after the eighty-page report became available. We noted that a fuller analysis was in the May issue of the Institute *News Letter* and that copies of the full report were available in the office of Guam governor Pownall.[21]

Congressional committees in charge of island affairs spent most of the month of May digesting the Krug and Hopkins reports. But by May 27, 1947, the House Subcommittee on Territorial and Insular Affairs was ready to hold the first of several hearings on pending bills. A blue-ribbon panel had been invited to appear. The first day would feature Representative Robert A. Grant, sponsor of H.R. 3044; Senator Hugh A. Butler, sponsor of S. 1078; and John Wiig, Honolulu attorney who was chief of police in military government on Guam during the war — all friendly witnesses. On the second day, Interior Secretary Julius A. Krug would lead off, followed by Navy Under Secretary John L. Sullivan; Assistant Secretary of State John H. Hilldring; Representative Willis W. Bradley, Jr., former naval governor of Guam; Maurice J. Tobin, member of the Hopkins Committee; Richard H. Wels, a New York attorney who had served with the Navy on Guam during the war; and our own Dr. Laura Thompson, author of *Guam and Its People*. Finally, on June 2, Former Interior Secretary Harold L. Ickes would appear with Secretary Hilldring, taking the stand again (see Appendix 9).

Before the morning of the first day had passed, it was clear that citizenship and organic law were no longer at issue. Everyone agreed that these rights had been too long denied and that any bill for the islands should embody these principles. In a surprise move on the second day of the hearings, the Navy, Interior, State and War Departments made a joint statement favoring government by civilians "at the earliest practicable moment."[22] The four departments must finally have met and come to an agreement! But what kind of agreement? Civilian government? Yes. They said it out loud, before a congressional committee. Fantastic! But, "at the earliest practicable moment." What did that mean? Therein lay the problem. In their joint statement and the bill accompanying it, the four departments had recommended that "the timing of the transfer and the designation of the agency to which the transfer is made be delegated *to the President* . . ." (italics mine).[23] So the four department secretaries had passed the buck to the president. And what did they think he would do about the timing? When questioned by the subcommittee, Navy Under Secretary Sullivan estimated that this changeover could come within five or ten years. Interior Secretary Krug said he thought it could be accomplished sooner, but he refused to mention a specific time.

Krug repeatedly was called inconsistent for the stand he was taking on delayed civilian administration. Newspaper clippings dated late in February, when Krug was returning from his swing through the Pacific, were called to his attention by the congressmen. In these clippings, he was quoted as favoring a change to civilian administration "soon."

Republican Congressman Poulson accused Krug of "compromising his principles" by going along with the Navy Department in order to make a show of unity within the Democratic administration. He said, "The Navy Department is the winner and Interior Department the loser in this compromise. For by your joint bill, the Navy is left in control, and nothing in it compels the President or Congress to place jurisdiction in any other Department ever."[24]

Poulson continued by chiding all the department heads, stating that although their joint statement stated that they favored civilian rule, the bill they submitted failed ever to use the term "civilian." At the end of a year, or five or ten years, he said, the president could name the Navy as the designated administrator. Assistant Secretary of State Hilldring said the State Department "likes this bill because it envisages early turnover to a civilian agency." To this, Poulson sharply replied, "We go by what is in the law, not by what departments say they mean."[25]

Tobin of the Hopkins Committee and Congressman Willis Bradley urged that the transfer of jurisdiction be postponed for months or even years. They argued that the effectiveness of reconstructing war-torn Guam would be impaired if the changeover were made "now." When pressed to explain in just what way reconstruction would be impaired, Under Secretary Sullivan said, "The Navy is making an effort to adjudicate those [war] claims as quickly as possible. We have a team of experts out there now. To transfer the job to Interior Department would delay payment of claims."[26]

Ickes challenged the efficiency of the Navy. He promptly observed that at the rate the Navy Claims Commission was going, according to figures in the Hopkins Report, settlement would not be completed for twenty years. The report said about 420 cases had been settled or processed to Washington by March 1947, fifteen months after the Navy Claims Commission was authorized, leaving more than 6,300 claims to go. He pointed to the Federal Security Agency and the Interior Department as two civilian agencies fully experienced in the problems of reconstruction that could efficiently take up wherever the Navy left off.

Laura Thompson called the Navy's refusal to lend money on the basis of claims indicative of a "lack of confidence which the naval government itself has in its own ability or intention to settle such claims in the near future." She pointed to the impracticability of the naval government's elaborate plan for the rebuilding of Agana, "which to this day remains a grass patch." She also noted that the cost of Guam's naval government — $88 per capita — was higher than the cost of any state in the union.[27]

The third edition of *Guam and Its People* by Thompson was just off the press in Hawai'i and was made available to members of the subcommittee. In the May issue of the Institute *News Letter,* it was described by a reviewer as "the authoritative book on the Chamorros, their extraordinary history, their almost unexampled capacity for adjustment and survival, assimilation and adjustment; with a factual, dispassionate examination of naval rule from 1899 to the present."[28]

Immediate transferal of jurisdiction was urged by Representative Grant, Senator Butler, Richard Wels of New York, and John Wiig of Honolulu.

In the final questioning of Secretary Hilldring on the third day of the hearings, shortly before the subcommittee adjourned, it seemed clear that members of the House were trying to pin the departments down on a reasonable date for the transfer and write it into the bill, along with a stipulation that the Department of the Interior should be the civilian agency to which authority would be transferred. Representative William Lemke, Republican subcommittee member from North Dakota, told Hilldring, "the more you testify, the more I am convinced that Guam and Samoa should be given civilian administration immediately."[29] Representative Fred Crawford seemed to sum up the sentiment of all members of the subcommittee when he said to spokesmen of the four departments, "You have a long way to go to convince me that civilian administration should not be instituted now."[30]

If legislation could go forward, we editorialized two days later in the June 4, 1947, *Guam Echo,* the ultimate decisions would no longer rest with the president. Interior would be written into the bill as the administering agency and a date for the transfer of jurisdiction would be named by Congress. We speculated that a new bill could be written before Congress adjourned at the end of July and that it could be enacted early in the next session of Congress.

An editorial from the *Honolulu Star Bulletin,* dated May 13, 1947, and reprinted in the June 4 *Guam Echo* proved prophetic. It noted that the Hopkins Committee report was not conclusive, and that Congress itself should visit the Pacific islands. On the first day of the House hearings, May 27, Richard Wels had strongly suggested that a party of Guamanians selected by the Guam Congress be transported by the Navy to Washington to testify. Under Secretary Sullivan had responded that the Navy had no objection, provided an exact time could be set and expenses could be met. The subcommittee voted to go into executive session on the subject.[31]

The very next day, I phoned Representative Crawford, chairman of the subcommittee, to see what he thought about the proposal so I could write it into the June 4 *Echo.* He said plans for bringing Guamanians to Washington could not be completed before a couple of weeks, implying that a second hearing on the bills would have to be scheduled. Passage of legislation would then be delayed. On the third day of the hearings, June 2, he had commented publicly that, as far as he was concerned, it was not necessary to bring Guamanians in to testify. He said he was convinced that they wanted citizenship, an organic act, and civilian rule. Over the phone, he repeated that they should get them "now."

Guam was at that point within a whisker of getting the changes its people wanted. But on June 18, 1947, at an executive session of the subcommittee, instead of reporting out an existing bill, members voted to go to the islands and see for themselves what the Navy, War, State, and Interior Departments had been unable to agree on. A vote on any bill would be postponed until after that. Tentative plans were made for the delegation to leave soon after Congress recessed in July. A new bill would be prepared for presentation the following January.

How could the Institute object to that? Collier had always been supportive of a congressional investigation, so the proposed trip could only be considered a bump in the road to civilian government. There was no way around it. What might have been a quick fix for the islands through almost perfect legislation then pending became a postponed dream for Congressman Crawford and the Guamanians. To my mind, the subcommittee's decision reflected the prospect of a pleasant summer junket to the tropics for certain congressmen — but of course I knew better than to say so. We would just have to wait out another investigation. In some ways, the Navy had won another round. It had achieved the inaction of the 80th Congress that it had hoped for.

Chapter 7

The Press Weighs In

Perhaps pressured by the House hearings, the Secretaries of State, War, Navy, and the Interior, on June 18, 1947, finally sent to President Truman their recommendation on how the Pacific islands should be administered. This was the answer he had requested more than twenty months before (see Appendix 10). It came the very day the House subcommittee had passed up the opportunity to report out a bill and voted instead to make a trip to the islands.

The communication from the Secretaries recommended that legislation for Guam "be enacted at this session" of Congress, that legislation for American Samoa be presented to the next session, and that organic legislation for the Trust Territory be prepared sometime after the Security Council acted favorably on the agreement to be presented for approval shortly.[1] Alas, it was too late for anything to be done by the 80th Congress. As a result of their hemming and hawing at the House hearings, the four Secretaries had failed to present a united front, and, in effect, the administration had dropped the ball.

The announced agreement was full of ambiguities. It was made to look as if all four departments favored civilian government for the Pacific islands, but there was a conditional provision in Section 4 postponing the transfer of administration to an unnamed civilian agency to "the earliest practicable date, such date to be determined by the President." Meanwhile, the Navy should continue to have administrative responsibility on an interim basis pending the transfer. (See Appendix 10.)

Ickes declared for publication in the Institute's June–July 1947 *News Letter:* "The Congress will not be taken in by this tricky language. This is one of the Navy's famous delaying actions, a strategy that may be appropriate in battle, but not when human liberties are at stake."[2] He called the argument that problems of reconstruction must be resolved before the Navy could hand the government over to a civilian authority "purest hokum."[3] Despite its shortcomings, those of us at the Institute of Ethnic Affairs thought the letter of agreement represented a real breakthrough. For the Navy and War Departments, advocacy of civilian administration, even "at the earliest practicable date," represented a major change in the policy that had stood since 1898 when President McKinley by executive order had placed the government of Guam in the hands of admirals.

By Interior, State, and President Truman, this June 18 communiqué was interpreted as an unequivocal, irreversible statement of support for civilian government, not only for Guam and American Samoa, but for the new Trust Territory of the Pacific Islands as well. To the Institute and other advocates of human rights, the letter brought hope for justice not only in the Pacific islands but for dependencies worldwide. In transmitting the recommendation to Senator Arthur H. Vandenberg (R., Mich.), then president of the Senate, which he did the very next day, President Truman wrote:

> It has long been my view that the inhabitants of Guam and Samoa should enjoy those fundamental human rights and that democratic form of government which is the rich heritage of the people of the United States. . . .
>
> I hope that the Congress will approve legislation for the purposes indicated in the enclosed report and that such legislation will provide for the full enjoyment of civil rights and for the greatest practicable measure of self-government.[4]

I was charged with preparing the lead article for the June–July 1947 *News Letter*. It was to be a running narrative of what I had already written for the June 4 *Guam Echo* plus this new development. In "Congress Looks to Guam," I explained that the administration's recommendation that legislation for Guam be enacted at this session came the day after plans were made for a congressional inspection of the Pacific islands, and that Representative Crawford had told the *News Letter* that this recommendation would not change the House subcommittee's plans for visiting the islands. The soonest legislation for Guam might be expected would be early in 1948. "Though congressional action thus has been delayed," I wrote, "the U.S. Government has taken its longest strides in fifty years toward democratic liberties for these islanders."[5]

Crawford actually introduced H.R. 4340 on July 23, 1947. Drafted after the subcommittee hearings in June, this bill set forth what the Departments of the Navy and Interior had seemed loath to do. It placed Guam under the Secretary of the Interior instead of the Secretary of the Navy and

Representative Fred L. Crawford (R., Mich.), a thirteen-year veteran of the House Public Lands Committee, was one of the strongest supporters of an organic act for Guam.

provided that a governor of Guam would be appointed by the president of the United States. That governor would then appoint heads of executive departments with the advice and consent of the upper house of a two-house legislature. Judicial power would be vested in a District Court of Guam that would be part of the United States court system. A Resident Commissioner in the U.S. House of Representatives would represent Guamanian interests in Washington. This bill would be among others discussed when the congressional committee went to Guam.

The whole front page of the August 12, 1947, *Guam Echo* was used to describe the Crawford bill, and Guamanians were given a measure of the man when we wrote that Crawford had chosen to stay on the House committee dealing with U.S. territories and islands even though his seniority in Congress qualified him for placement on other committees with greater political advantage. He had served thirteen years on the House Public Lands Committee and would personally conduct the hearings that would be held on Guam.

While Crawford's bill was being printed, Congressmen Norris Poulson and Willis Bradley sent letters to the *New York Times* defending their own bills for Guam and attacking certain provisions of others. Poulson called Bradley's bill the "Navy-Interior bill" coming out of recommendations of the Hopkins Committee. He criticized it for omitting two basic liberties — trial by jury and equal protection of the laws. Representative Bradley, who had served as naval governor of Guam twenty-three years before, countered by writing, "The simple truth is that trial by jury would be one of those Anglo-Saxon things forced upon Guam." He claimed that it was foreign to Guam's more than three hundred years under the flags of Spain and America and said as far as he knew Guamanians did not want it.

Bradley's assertion brought an immediate rejoinder from Guam. One of the islanders wrote the following in a letter to the editor of the *New York Times*, signed simply "A Guamanian" to protect the identity of the writer.

> Mr. Bradley is essentially a Navy officer, and his letter obviously attempts to support the Navy in its current fight to retain its supervision over Guam. . . .
>
> Mr. Bradley's statement that we do not understand such an arrangement [trial by jury] is erroneous and is based on a gratuitous assumption. That it is foreign to us because we have never had it under a naval government which has been consistently undemocratic and totally un-American is a foregone conclusion.
>
> Recall that the Japanese never had a democratic form of government in 2,000 years, yet General MacArthur reports periodically that they have learned the meaning of democracy and are practicing it with commendable results. . . .
>
> Fundamentally, the Naval Government of Guam is a continuation of Spain's despotic regime. We want neither of these two alabaster models. We want the American democratic form of government, which has been too long denied us.
>
> Mr. Bradley also forgets that the present generation of Guamanians is a product of American education, culture, and tradition. . . .
>
> Our struggle is against the half-century-old naval dictatorship, and our only desire — it should be clear by now — is to share fully in the constitutional and natural prerogatives of free men. Among these prerogatives are the right of trial by jury and equal protection under the law, which the Bradley Bill, H.R. 3564, would deny us.[6]

This was one of the strongest statements ever to come from Guam. It clearly showed the writer's understanding of the separation of powers, which is so fundamental to democracy. Collier and others of us in the

Institute were jubilant upon its publication. Even though legislation would be delayed, Guamanians were clearly on record as to what they wanted.

An equally heartwarming message had come from American Samoa shortly before. It was a report of what High Chief Mariota T. Tuiasosopo of American Samoa had told the Hopkins Committee in April. Written by Jules France for the *New Republic,* it was a strong condemnation of what the chief called "an eighteen months government." Tuiasosopo explained that naval governors were rotated every eighteen months and that "there has never been an instance where the policy inaugurated by a former Governor was continued by the one succeeding. . . . The present form of government is too complicated," he said. "By this, I mean that its operational mechanism is beyond the reach and understanding of the average Samoan."[7]

Much of the article was reprinted in the August–September 1947 *News Letter* and may be summarized by the author's opening paragraphs:

> The Honorable Mariota T. Tuiasosopo is an earnest, self-educated admirer of American democracy. He likes the whole idea so much that he's been trying to get more of it for his people in American Samoa.
>
> An official orator for the Samoan Assembly, and a "high talking chief" of the Eastern District, Tuiasosopo has refused to be discouraged by the peculiar fact that you can apparently live under the American flag without enjoying the heritage of self-government. . . .[8]

Here we were at the end of the Institute's second summer with clear statements favoring civilian administration from leading spokesmen in both Guam and American Samoa when fate took another discouraging twist. A resolution passed by the Guam Congress on September 6, 1947, read that naval administration should be retained in Guam "on an interim basis, pending the transfer to a civilian agency at the earliest possible date . . . when the Island has been completely rehabilitated and economy of the island fully restored." It threw us into momentary despair.[9]

Fred Crawford, chairman of the House Subcommittee on Territories and Insular Possessions, told me for publication in the *Guam Echo,* "It cuts the ground out from under those of us who have advocated civilian government for Guam in the near future and may endanger passage of an organic act of any kind."[10] Crawford was definitely irritated by this turn of events. So irritated, perhaps, that he may have postponed the congressional trip to the islands. Two days after the Guam resolution was received, his office called the *Guam Echo* to inform us that during most of October,

Congressman Fred Crawford would be in Alaska, where his committee would be conducting hearings on statehood. His spokesman said it looked like a special session of the U.S. Congress would be called after that, so a trip to Guam by his subcommittee might have to be postponed for many months. We put that shocker in a box on page one.

Why would Guamanians seek to retain naval control?

A member of the Guam Congress then visiting Washington said, "I am embarrassed by such action." He speculated that some of his fellow legislators wished to act "diplomatically" with the Navy. Another Guamanian also temporarily in the United States suggested that some Guamanians feared they would lose Navy business if they supported civilian government. In a letter to the Institute he wrote, "I feel that what Guamanians really want can best be expressed by a general plebiscite since our [Guam] Congress has chosen to misrepresent our desires."[11]

All three of these comments were printed in the September 26, 1947, *Guam Echo.* We also wrote that the Guam Congress resolution of September 6 had reached the Navy Department in Washington on September 25 and was immediately forwarded to other federal government offices. This stood in great contrast with how slowly the Navy had acted on Guam resolutions recommending a change to civilian government. Not only that, it had been released to the press September 26, the very day after it had been received.

Rumors that such a resolution might be passed had been circulating in Washington all summer. The Navy, obviously, was getting to the leaders in Guam. We were told the September 6 resolution was considered superior to the one presented at July and August meetings of the Guam Congress in that it did speak of naval administration "on an interim basis." But the underlying premise of the resolution was wrong. It was wrong to give the Navy more time to improve its administration, and it was wrong to think the Navy could rehabilitate the island in a few months or years.

Collier had had plenty of time to think about what the Navy was strategizing. So he wrote what follows for that September 26, 1947, *Guam Echo:*

John Collier Comments

The text of the resolution follows the Navy's line in Washington: Civilian rule but only after the Guamanian economy has been fully restored and rehabilitation fully finished. That can mean a lifetime hence. It can mean never. And it can mean that no sound economy for Guam will ever be achieved.

Short of a plebiscite of all the people of Guam, held after debates wherein all the issues and alternatives were made plain, the Guamanians' friends will continue to believe that Guam wants what it so long and vocally has wanted, that is, American rights. Among the oldest and most precious of these rights is the right not to be ruled by the military in times of peace — or even in war, except during extreme brief emergencies.

At the present time, when rumors of a new world war [over Korea] fill the air at home and abroad, the Army and Navy get money from Congress with less difficulty than do the civilian agencies. That circumstance is no argument for surrendering the rule over our lives to the Army or Navy. Congressional resolution or no resolution, I simply do not believe that the Guamanians want thus to surrender their own American cause and birthright.

And I predict that those mainland Americans who see wellbeing for the Islanders will go right on in their effort for civilian rule — and will win it for Guam as for the other Islands.[12]

This statement certainly served notice to the Navy and anyone else who was listening that the Institute of Ethnic Affairs and its friends were not giving up. Collier wasn't the least fearful of the Navy or any other part of the United States military. They had their place and he was completely respectful of it. After all, they had just won, in effect, two wars — one in the European theater and another in the Pacific. Both wars had been fought against totalitarian, autocratic rule and in the interest of human rights. The people of the United States were united in their fight for freedom and democratic government — more united than they had ever been before or have been since. Millions of young men and women my age had enlisted in the armed services. They had seen duty and felt obligations that broadened their vision. Some, like Roy James, Emil Sady, and Richard Wels, had come home imbued with the ambition to carry on the good fight. What Collier's Institute of Ethnic Affairs proposed and stood for was an extension of civil and human rights to all non-self-governing, dependent people everywhere, respect for the dignity of every individual. It drew together like-minded people. The governments of Guam, American Samoa, and the Trust Territory of the Pacific Islands provided the Institute's first theater for direct action — and it would be nonviolent action, a battle won through logic and legislation representing the wishes of the indigenous inhabitants involved. A handful of other sociologists and seasoned civil servants like Harold Ickes participated in the fight for civilian government for the Pacific islands, but it was John Collier who led the way.

The intensity of that fight and the public attention it was receiving was revealed in a column written by Mary Van Rensselaer Thayer in the August 14, 1947, *Washington Post,* which we reprinted by permission in the September 26, 1947, *Guam Echo.* Note in her article, again reprinted there, all the prominent magazines of the time that found this struggle to be newsworthy.

Battle over the Islands

In the current *Harper's Magazine,* John Marquand fires the latest broadside in a stimulating tug-of-war between the Navy and the Interior Department. The to-do is whether Navy or civilian administration will get final control in the Pacific islands newly under our flag. The battle, which is being fought in magazines and newspapers with no clinches barred, may well blossom into a major campaign issue. Heretofore, our territories, such as the Virgin Islands and Puerto Rico, have been administered by the Interior, but after the war, on-the-spot Navy stayed put in the Pacific with Admiral Charles A. Pownall made Governor of Guam.

The opposition's opening shot was published just a year ago in a *Collier's* [magazine] article authored by Harold Ickes and politely titled, "The Navy at Its Worst!" Navy public relations, stung by the Ickes tough-talk, sprang into action. They sent Rear Admiral Carleton H. Wright to a coupla-islands, then back for a peek at every rock and coral reef in the area. Admiral Wright immediately became an island expert and was made right bower to Admiral Pownall as high-sounding Deputy High Commissioner of the Trust Territories of the Pacific.

The DHC of the TT of the Pacific turned author and on May 3 the *Saturday Evening Post* tossed in its hat by publishing his, "Let's Not Civilize These Happy People." Then Interior countered, murmuring that Admiral Wright got into trouble VJ-Day when the sailors under his command at San Francisco went on a terrific victory binge. The Navy, a bit too high pressured, complacently invited a group of newsmen to look over the islands. As usual, the press bit the hand that feeds it, dug up informed natives, and reported all was not over-rosy. The Interior won the next round with a *Life* editorial appearing last week and authored by the astute Gilbert Cant. The Marquand opus, called "Why the Navy Needs Aspirin," then made its debut in *Harper's.* The Interior meanly rates it as one of the better bits of Marquand fiction. To those who know the drawly New England author, it's obvious the Navy joy ride was pleasing, the happy islanders to be envied by anyone living at Newburyport on the chill Atlantic coast. So far the score stands a bit in favor of the Interior, as President Truman has advised Congress that the islands should be placed under a civilian agency.

There's no doubt, though, that the Navy is doing a superb public relations job and they may get to the top of the heap. To devotees of the Brewster investigation, here's a nice little squabble to fill in the void until our Senators, refreshed by vacation breezes, return to Washington and a second round of Sherlock Holmesing.[13]

Civilization has always looked to educated young people to provide leadership for the future. So it was with considerable pleasure that we were able to report in that same September *Guam Echo* that seven Guamanians had received college scholarships and on August 31 had arrived in San Francisco, where they separated to travel on to their respective schools. Their names appear in my end notes.[14] The four-year scholarships were arranged by the bishop of Guam, the Most Reverend Apollinaris William Baumgartner, O.F.M. Transportation was provided by funds from island taxes and contributions from interested Guamanian organizations.

Still another item with academic overtones was printed in that issue of the *Guam Echo*. We announced that every week for the next two months and possibly longer, John Collier would teach a course in sociology at City College in New York. As I look back, this was probably the first acknowledgment by Collier that he and Laura Thompson could not live comfortably without supplementing his retirement funds.

The Institute budget had remained minuscule. The IRS ruling had precluded application for tax-free grants. There was a little income carried over from work the Institute was doing on inter-American projects formerly handled by Nelson Rockefeller, and there were a few thousand-dollar grants that got the Institute started. But there was rent to pay, printing expenses, and mailing. The Institute's whole endeavor probably cost less than $10,000 a year. Betty and I continued to draw our checks, which had gone up from $200 to $230 a month, about $2,760 a year. Collier still drew no salary or expenses. I don't remember that we ever discussed compensation. There just wasn't much to talk about. But Betty and I never feared losing our jobs or having to look for other work. We were too busy to think about things like that. Betty kept the books, and they were always in the black.

Even at our modest salaries we knew we were much better off than the Pacific Islanders about whom we were writing. We were able to report in that September 26, 1947, *Guam Echo* that the settlement of property dam-age claims was picking up. Claims were then being settled at the rate of three to four hundred a month. In the summer of 1947, six property dam-age claims over $5,000, totaling $166,500, were being processed in Wash-ington. Settlement of land-damage claims was going much slower. Accord-ing to Navy spokesmen in Washington, the Guamanian judges presiding in Island Court had been indisposed toward handling those cases because many of them involved Guamanian relatives or close friends. But John C. Fischer had just been appointed Presiding Justice of the Court of Appeals in Guam, and the rate was expected to increase noticeably.

Fischer's appointment was intended, in part, to bring balance to that ju-dicial body, then composed of two Guamanians, an Army officer, and a Ma-rine Corps officer, with a naval officer as presiding justice. Upon Fischer's arrival in Guam, the naval officer was to be released to other duty.

Judge Fischer was a civilian appointed by the Navy. The decision to ap-point a civilian grew out of a Hopkins Committee recommendation. Col-lier thought Fischer's legal experience well qualified him for the job. For three years he had been attorney for the Seattle Real Estate Board, and before that he was general counsel of the Bonneville Power Administration and had developed a new method of land condemnation. He was living in Washington and for four years had been serving as a judge of the U.S. Board of Veterans Appeals.[15]

Other *Guam Echo* news of the month included the fact that headquar-ters of the High Command of the Pacific islands trusteed to the United States would be moved from Hawai'i to Saipan sometime soon. Admiral Louis E. Denfield was then High Commissioner of the Trust Territory of the Pacific Islands. We added a fifth page to that September 26, 1947, *Guam Echo* in order to reprint most of a syndicated newspaper column by Harold Ickes that had been published in newspapers across the country that very day. It was the first public disclosure of what had happened to the Bikini islanders when the United States conducted its first postwar test of nuclear weapons on their island more than a year earlier.

Ickes' column explained that on July 1, 1946, a Nagasaki-type atomic bomb had been dropped at Bikini Island from the Superfortress *Dave's Dream*. Of seventy-three vessels anchored off Bikini, five were sunk and nine heavily damaged, including the battleship USS *Arkansas* and a Japa-nese cruiser. The column continued:

Bikini Natives

To set the stage for the bomb test, the benevolent U.S. Navy persuaded the 160 natives of Bikini to move to neighboring Rongerik Island "as their contribution to the advancement of science." The Navy generously provided free transportation, and news-reel cameramen were on hand for moving day. . . .

Now comes word that the natives are actually and literally dying of starvation. As late as a month ago, the Rongerik Islanders, late of Bikini, were in the last stages of dire want. Neither chickens nor pigs exist on Rongerik. Those who know report that domesticated animal life on the island is restricted to one old dog so under-nourished that it has developed rickets. The desperate people have been reduced to cutting down their few coconut trees in order to eat their hearts.

The Deputy High Commissioner of the Trust Territories, who has responsibility for the government and welfare of these people (under a mandate of the United Nations to the United States) is Rear Admiral Carleton H. Wright. He is the humane brass hat who wrote the recent article in *The Saturday Evening Post* entitled "Let's Not Civilize These Happy People." I suspect that even a little food would persuade these unhappy people to adopt unanimously a resolution declaring that, not for the world, would they substitute civilian for Navy rule. This is the way it has worked in Guam. . . .[16] (See Appendix 11.)

This last sentence referred, of course, to the resolution passed by the Guam Congress on September 6, 1947, favoring continued rule by the Navy until rehabilitation of the island could be complete.

Ickes' column caused another ruckus with the Navy. Captain Walter Karig, U.S.N.R., in Washington was the first to respond. In a letter to the *Washington Evening Star* on October 1, he said Mr. Ickes didn't know what he was talking about as he had never been to the islands. By contrast, Captain Karig asserted that he recently had been to Rongerik and he knew for a fact that Ickes' charges were untrue. On the same day, the report upon which Ickes had based his story was released by the Navy. It was written by Dr. Howard G. MacMillan, an agricultural specialist working for the U.S. Commercial Company responsible for delivering food to the outlying islands, and it corroborated all of Ickes' statements.

The very next day, October 2, the *Honolulu Star-Bulletin* ran an article stating, "The report now made public by the Navy bears out the assertions of Harold L. Ickes." It went on to quote Admiral Louis E. Denfield, High Commissioner of the Trust Territory, as having admitted that he had

After viewing the atom bomb test at Bikini, July 1, 1946, James V. Forrestal went to Guam, where he made an inspection and gave a Fourth of July address at Agana. Here he is leaving The Bank of Guam followed by Rear Admiral Charles A. Pownall *(in doorway),* Governor of Guam.

known of the Bikini islanders' plight the previous February whereupon he ordered that something be done to aid them. And now — seven months later — the Navy was prepared to move them to Ujelang, a larger and far more lush island about five hundred miles to the southwest, provided the people wanted to go. A few days later, the Navy took King Judah and other native representatives to Ujelang. The Bikinians subsequently announced their desire to move there.

Commander E. B. Miller, naval administrator, was sent to Rongerik on about October 15 to deliver evacuation orders. With him went photographer Robert Ebert of the *Honolulu Star-Bulletin* to see what relief the Navy had provided in the two months since the MacMillan report had gone in, and in the two weeks since publicity had been given the unfortunate situation.

On the island Ebert found and photographed Bikinians eating the heart of a palm and green coconuts because they still had not been given sufficient ordinary food. In the native store he found two boxes of thread, a few pencils, one hunting knife, and several bars of GI soap — but no food.

About the middle of November *The Honolulu Advertiser* reported that evacuation preparations had been started and, according to the naval officer in charge, the migration would be accomplished in December. These plans were abruptly changed, however. On December 2, with the announcement of plans for an atomic bomb test on Eniwetok, the Navy disclosed that the Eniwetokians would be moved to Ujelang instead and that the Bikinians would have to pick a new site. They were then offered Kili, Ujae, and Lae, which they rejected in favor of Ujelang.

All of this was reported in the December 26, 1947, issue of the *Guam Echo*.[17] I remember being shocked that tests of the terrible bombs like those that had been dropped on Hiroshima and Nagasaki were still going on. But the full impact of nuclear weaponry was not well understood by most of us in those days. How the islanders were being treated simply reinforced what we at the Institute of Ethnic Affairs already knew — that the Navy's main interest was military preparedness, not caring for people who might be in their way. Also, it became crystal clear that the United States could do anything it wanted with islands in a "strategic trusteeship." As was becoming evident, the Navy's interest in retaining administration of the Trust Territory as well as Guam was boundless.

Chapter 8

The Navy versus the Guamanians

As we have seen, the Navy was relentless in its public relations attempts to maintain control of the government of the Pacific islands. In the fall of 1946, it had transported news reporters throughout the islands, expecting them to report favorably on naval administration. In the late winter of 1947 it had dispatched the Hopkins Committee to the Pacific to do what Ickes called a whitewash of conditions. Both efforts boomeranged. In May, Admiral Wright wrote "Let's Not Civilize These Happy People" for publication in the *Saturday Evening Post*. During the summer, he was promoted to Deputy High Commissioner of the Trust Territory of the Pacific Islands. The Navy's next step, early in September 1947, was to persuade the Guam Congress to tack onto a resolution requesting United States citizenship and an organic act a provision that would continue naval government until rehabilitation of the island was complete.

In October 1947, the Navy decided to bring Admiral Charles A. Pownall, then governor of Guam, to Washington to confer with Island Government officers in the Navy Department. At a press conference on October 31, just before returning to Guam, Admiral Pownall stated that he definitely favored citizenship for Guamanians. Asked when the Navy intended to "get out of Guam," he replied that that was "a matter of law."[1]

To achieve an organic act and a change of federal jurisdiction at the same time would be "quite a chore," the admiral commented. He cited the Guam Congress resolution for retention of naval administration to show that Guamanians were hesitant about going from "known to unknown conditions." Unless naval civil government became unbearable, he said, the people probably would not want a change.[2] Asked to comment on pending legislation, he said he had little to add to Under Secretary John L. Sullivan's statement of the previous spring, maintaining that the Navy should govern Guam until rehabilitation could been effected. Admiral Pownall, like Sullivan, estimated that rehabilitation would take from five to ten years.

What to do about the status of Guam and other Pacific islands became a subject of concern for the military in Washington, D.C. Shown here at a staff meeting in 1948 are *(left to right)*: Major General Hoyt S. Vandenberg, Chief of Staff, U.S. Air Force; Admiral Louis E. Denfield, Chief of Naval Operations, U.S. Navy; General Omar N. Bradley, Chief of Staff, U.S. Army; Secretary of Defense James V. Forrestal; Lieutenant General Albert C. Wedemeyer, Director of Plans and Operations, U.S. Army; Vice Admiral Arthur W. Radford, Vice Chief of Naval Operations, U.S. Navy; and Lieutenant General Lauris Norstad, Deputy Chief of Operations, U.S. Air Forces.

Asked how the Navy was progressing with its rebuilding program, Admiral Pownall said the cornerstone of the Guam Congress building had been set in place on October 4 and that streets and drainage facilities for Agana were being laid out. He said the Navy still controlled 50 percent of the land on Guam and that it had not yet determined how much would be required for military purposes. "Housing is our greatest problem," the governor said. He acknowledged that many employees of contractors had left Guam because they were dissatisfied with housing and recreation facilities.[3]

Speaking of the economic policy of the Navy in Guam, Admiral Pownall said it was founded on two precepts: (1) to make the people self-supporting, and (2) to avoid outside exploitation. He added that it was the Navy's purpose to avoid monopoly groups. That is why the Guam Commercial Company was encouraged by the Navy, he said. Asked if membership in the Guam Commercial Company was limited to Guamanians, the governor said no. He did not state who else held stock, but emphatically declared that federal employees (Navy personnel) did not. The success of the Navy's economic policy seemed illustrated by the amount of revenue resulting, the governor said. When the Navy took over the government in May 1946, tax revenue totaled $4,500 a month. Now it totaled $145,000 a month. This would help make island government self-supporting. For the fiscal year 1949, the Navy expected to get as much as $1,500,000 from island revenue taxes to run the government, he stated. This was half the total appropriation requested for fiscal year 1948 for the administration of Guam, American Samoa, and the Trust Territory of the Pacific Islands.[4]

Asked to explain why the Navy should pay less than contractors for the same kind and amount of work, the governor explained that Guamanians' cost of living was less than that of other employees on Guam. Guamanians paid no rent, enjoyed free hospitalization, and got their transportation to and from work free. However, he frankly admitted that hospitalization facilities for Guamanians were inadequate. He commented that money from the Susanna Hospital fund was being transferred to the Guam Memorial Hospital and that the Navy was in the process of setting up a board of trustees. The new hospital, estimated to cost about $1,000,000, would be financed largely by individual subscriptions. Recently, $10,000 had been raised in one day, he remarked, noting that this was far short of the goal.

Asked why he found it necessary to constitute a new Superior Court of Guam to settle land cases when the Island Court was set up for that purpose, Admiral Pownall replied that in many cases the judges of the Island Court owned the land in question and therefore were ineligible to sit in judgment. He said the Superior Court definitely was not a device to take land adjudication out of the hands of the natives. Asked if there was appeal from the Superior Court, the governor said yes — to the Secretary of the Navy. With this press conference, the Navy had seemed to score another point. The governor portrayed the islanders as being content with the government they had.

Almost as if to offset Admiral Pownall's endorsement of continued naval government, on October 29 the President's Committee on Civil Rights recommended: "the enactment by Congress of legislation granting citizenship to the people of Guam and American Samoa. This legislation should also provide those islands with organic acts containing guarantees of civil rights, and transfer them from naval administration to civilian control. Such legislation has been introduced in the present Congress."[5] This was one of thirty-five specific recommendations for wiping out segregation and discrimination from the American way of life. It was embodied in a

176-page report submitted to the president by a fourteen-member committee headed by Charles E. Wilson, president of General Electric, after nearly
a year's study.

This good news was carried in a box on page 1 of the October 31, 1947,
issue of the *Guam Echo,* alongside the report on Admiral Pownall's press
conference.

Some bad news was carried in a box on page 2. A special session of the U.S.
Congress called for November 17, 1947, had made it necessary for Congressman Crawford to postpone the congressional trip to Guam indefinitely.

A second piece of bad news informed readers that on October 29, the
Navy Department in Washington had issued the following press release:
"Chiefs of the Island of Tuituila meeting in general assembly last week
adopted a resolution that American Samoa continue under the Naval Civil
Administration. The assembly by acclaim gave the civil government a vote
of confidence and pledged full support and cooperation."[6] Of course, this
was completely contrary to what Mariota T. Tuiasosopo, the High Talking
Chief of American Samoa, had told the Hopkins Committee. Here was
more proof that naval officers in the field were bringing pressure to bear
on the islanders. It was another good try at reversing public opinion in
Washington.

On the other side, evidence that Guamanians were standing up for their
convictions came in the form of an October 19 letter to the editor of the
Navy News on Guam from Mrs. C. A. Siguenza, protesting the discriminatory attitude of some American servicemen toward the native islanders. The
fact that another Guamanian asked that the letter be reprinted in the *Guam
Echo* underscored the widespread feeling Guamanians had that the Institute
of Ethnic Affairs would try to set things right. We published the letter in the
October 31, 1947, *Guam Echo.* In it Mrs. Siguenza was suggesting that Guam
become more like Hawai'i, where she had lived for thirty years, and where
all races worked well together.

The Navy got still another shot in the arm in November when a subcommittee of the House Committee on Armed Forces, headed by W. Sterling
Cole (R., N.Y.), returned from a two-month inspection tour of all major
military outposts in the Pacific as well as Turkey, Greece, Italy, Austria, and
Germany. About the administration in Guam the subcommittee reported:

> We were happy as well as gratified to find that the relationship between the
> Guamanians and the Naval Government at Guam was completely whole-

some and satisfactory; in fact there appeared to be some apprehension on the part of the Guamanian officials that this relationship might be disrupted by Congressional or Executive action resulting in the Insular Affairs being placed with some other agency of Government. It is hoped for the sake of the people of Guam this will not take place, at least until there is greater evidence of a desire on the part of the Guamanians than now exists that it be done or some more compelling reason advanced than presently appears that it should be done.[7]

Expressing great concern over this recommendation, Congressman Crawford, chairman of the House Subcommittee on Territories and Island Possessions, told the *Guam Echo* on November 25, 1947, that he intended to press the Armed Forces subcommittee for the particulars upon which they based their recommendation. He said the subcommittee may have been influenced by the large military contingent on the trip. Whatever the case, he said, "these reports come back with great official sanction," adding that "they should serve as a warning to dependent peoples to work harder if they hope to achieve civil rights at this time."[8]

Of course, we duly reported all this in the November 28, 1947, *Guam Echo*, underlining Crawford's following words:

So far as I can see, if the dependents of the U.S. proper, and by that I mean the citizens and subjects of the United States residing in offshore areas detached from the mainland of the United States, are to receive the kind of treatment from their Government which we are advocating that the people of other countries are to receive in the way of self-government, it is now very clear that they are going to have to fight for it with all their might in the way of protests, resolutions, personal messages to departments of government which now supervise them, and to constantly keep before the House and Senate a bill of particulars as to how they are being taxed without representation.[9]

This was a real wake-up call to the leaders in Guam. If they were to achieve self-government, they were going to have to be more vocal, more activist than ever before. This was asking a lot of people unaccustomed to confrontation and the democratic process, people who lived thousands of miles away from the center of their government. But the Guamanians were learning. And they had already demonstrated that they were willing to fight for the ideals they believed in.

Fortunately, in those years immediately following the war in the Pacific, democratic change was uppermost in the minds of opinion leaders throughout the world, and the power of the press was on the Guamanians' side. Newspapers from Baltimore to Honolulu were printing editorials about Guam, and we were reprinting them in the *Guam Echo,* whether pro or con. Our little "newspaper" was giving the islanders direction and confidence. They knew they could trust us. The November 28, 1947, *Guam Echo* carried excerpts from five newspapers. One, from the *Honolulu Star-Bulletin* of November 12, expressed the following lament: "It seems doubtful now if Congressman Crawford can get to Guam this year, and possibly not even in 1948. For 1948 is 'election year' and congressmen up for re-election are unlikely to have many weeks to spare in a Pacific tour and checkup. This is unfortunate, for the future administration of Guam is no academic issue—it is immediate, urgent and of international importance."[10] The editorial went on to explain that only a congressional investigation seemed likely to settle the debate on Navy versus civilian administration.

The *Omaha World Herald* weighed in on November 13, backing the bill introduced by Nebraska Senator Hugh Butler:

> Said the Nebraska Senator: Military dictatorship . . . absolutism beyond compare . . . undemocratic and un-American. . . . How can we preach democracy in the Near East when we practice autocracy in the Far East? . . .
>
> The fuss Mr. Butler and others are raising is fully justified, and the time to do something about it is not five or 10 years hence, but now. It is to be hoped that Congress will pass Mr. Butler's bill and that the President will sign it.[11]

The *Baltimore Sun* likewise noted the five- or ten-year wait proposed by the Navy and wrote on November 8, 1947: "Civil administration, however, is bound to be a continuing headache for the Navy, because navy men, as a class, lack the temperament for, and interest in, such work. This was recently demonstrated in the Navy's handling of the 160 ex-natives of Bikini. . . ."[12]

A second reference to Guam appeared in the *Honolulu Star-Bulletin* on November 14, only two days after the one quoted above:

> It is of special note that President Truman's Committee on Civil Rights has found reason to recommend establishment of local self-government for the people of American Samoa and Guam. . . .
>
> The findings on Guam and American Samoa constitute only a small part of the Truman committee report. . . .

. . . But the recommendations of the President's committee on Guam and Samoa will not be lost. They will add to the accumulating evidence in favor of civil administration for those two areas under the U.S. flag.[13]

Earlier, on October 28, *The Honolulu Advertiser* had come out in favor of continued naval administration. Influenced, perhaps, by admirals assigned to the Pacific Command headquartered in Hawai'i, or maybe to differentiate its point of view from that of the *Honolulu Star-Bulletin,* its editorial writer wrote:

> There has been talk of turning Guam and Samoa and all of the Trust Islands over to the Interior Department. That should not be. . . .
>
> This would result in duplication. The Navy would have to furnish ships, bases, communications and personnel anyway at what would have to be considerable extra cost to taxpayers.
>
> America owes Guamanians a debt of gratitude which would not be repaid by further confusing their status now. When reconstruction is complete let us give them territorial status or some form of independent civilian government.[14]

Also reported in the November *Guam Echo* was a resolution passed by the 48th National Encampment of Veterans of Foreign Wars, held in Cleveland, Ohio, in September, calling for "establishing a civilian administration for Guam with American citizenship for citizens of Guam."[15]

Obviously, a great many veterans knew and cared about Guam. Not only that, there were enough veterans living in Guam that the Veterans Administration announced in November that it would open a VA office on the island after the first of the year. It would serve under the Honolulu office.

The newspaper editorials became what we now call "third-party endorsements" of a certain point of view. We at the Institute were gratified that so many highly respected publications agreed that civilian administration was what Guam and Samoa should have. When congressmen read those editorials, they knew it wasn't just the Institute talking.

At the bottom of page 5 in the November issue of the *Guam Echo* was another appeal for Institute memberships at $5.00 a year, more or less, as a contribution to the work of the Institute. Even a smaller contribution would entitle the sender to receive the *Guam Echo* regularly. Air mail was still only 6 cents a copy and labor at the Institute was cheap — just Betty and me as paid staff. The July issue had carried a little letter from John Collier referring to those Guam contributions:

Dear Friends:

By way of the *Guam Echo,* I direct my very sincere and deep appreciation to the fifty-two Guamanians whose contributions made up $1,000 sent to the Ethnic Institute on July 9. To each of you, the Board, the staff, and I say "thank you."

And to all who are members, I send greetings of friendship. Your helpfulness and indomitable spirit have served well in making Guam's needs and hopes the concern of many people in the States. . . .

John Collier[16]

The November appeal brought in another $776, which we reported in January 1948. At that time, Guam membership stood at 226, including eight students in the United States. It was these small sums that kept us going. Betty and I never missed a pay check, and we never asked for a raise.

Chapter 9

Rehabilitation of Guam Begins

The first issue of the *Guam Echo* in 1948 spread the good news that on January 12 the U.S. Senate had approved a bill, S. 1675, authorizing $106,714,500 for Navy construction on Guam. That was in addition to the $92,000,000 already authorized for shore construction. When passed by the House and signed by the president, the new legislation would authorize:

- $24,000,000 for the naval base at Apra Harbor
- $30,000,000 for the naval air station
- $14,000,000 for the naval ammunition depot
- $6,750,000 for supplemental radio activity
- $4,750,000 for a permanent radio station
- $14,675,000 for a naval supply center
- $9,800,000 for a fleet marine base
- $1,780,000 for a submarine base[1]

This was good news because it would mean greater employment in Guam. Not counted in the $106,714,500 figure was an additional $18,000,000 for Army construction in the Marianas, much of which would probably wind up on Guam. Now, if only the wages paid Guamanians could be higher.

The original total estimate for projected Navy construction in Guam was about $2,000,000,000, with an approximately equal amount for the Army and Air Force, according to the Cole Report delivered November 19, 1947.[2]

The January *Guam Echo* also reprinted excerpts from a story in the *Honolulu Star-Bulletin* recounting the success of a new small business — the Guam Commercial Company:

> Before the war, five families were credited with control of Guam's economic life. There was little thought of competition. Enterprising young men went into these firms and relatives of the controlling families generally held the inside track.

But the war changed all. It wiped out everything except the Guamanian people. Agana, the capital city, was destroyed and Guamanians became wards of the United States, dependent upon the military for food and shelter. Century-old business vanished. . . .

An infant corporation born in Guam's postwar turmoil with the Navy as midwife is challenging the island's prewar business hierarchy. . . .

The article described how during its first fourteen months the company cleared $204,424, but that its cash registers "now ring merrily to the tune of $200,000 gross monthly."[3]

Even though business was picking up, salaries for public-service jobs were still down. Another article excerpted from the January *Hawaii Educational Review* reported that the average teacher on Guam received only about $1,500 a year, whereas before the war, teachers were among the best paid of Guam's civil servants. "Now policemen, postmasters, and even clerks are paid higher salaries," the article stated.[4] As a result, the article continued, Guamanian pupils evaluated by American-made standardized tests fell considerably below United States norms. This problem was being addressed by teachers' institutes, scholarship programs, and increased professional training including summer sessions for teachers at the University of Hawai'i. The article also noted that only 40 percent of needed classroom space was available.

Nearly two pages of the January *Guam Echo* were devoted to "The 1948 Outlook on Guam Legislation." We reported that Representative Fred Crawford believed that identical Crawford and Cordon Concurrent Resolutions, introduced in the House and Senate on December 19, had the best chance of passing. Those resolutions would establish a joint congressional committee to make an on-the-spot study of the Trust Territory and all other Pacific islands subject to U.S. authority.

With 1948 being an election year, the congressmen would be forced to give primary attention to matters directly related to their home districts. If an organic act for Guam were not passed at this Second Session of the 80th Congress, the legislative process would have to start all over again. The next session, in 1949, would be the First Session of the 81st Congress in which no bills from the 80th Congress would be carried over. Furthermore, new representatives, who would know very little about Guam, might be elected. If the administration were to change from Democratic to Republican, new friendships within the executive departments would have to

Senator Guy Cordon (R., Ore.) was chairman of the Senate Subcommittee on Territorial and Insular Affairs in 1947–1948 and very supportive of organic legislation.

be formed by the Guamanians and new support sought for Pacific islands legislation. It was, therefore, very important that an organic act be enacted before the end of 1948.

The American legislative system is such, we continued in the *Echo,* that letters from persons for whom the legislation is intended are always given major consideration by senators and representatives. As Guamanians had no elected representatives of their own in Washington, we urged them to write to Representative Fred L. Crawford, House Office Building, Washington 25, D.C., or Senator Guy Cordon, Senate Office Building, Washington 25, D.C., both of whom were chairmen of the subcommittees that would hear the Guam bills. All pending bills on Guam government had been set out by number and briefly described in the December *Guam Echo* so Guamanians could readily identify them in writing letters.[5]

A full page of the January 30 *Echo* was devoted to the new "Code of Guam," published by the U.S. Government Printing Office. Study of it by Collier had produced some interesting contrasts with laws and practices of the States. For example, it was unlawful to own a radio on Guam unless special authority was granted by the governor and a license fee of $1.00 paid. All cameras had to be registered with the government and a fee of

50 cents paid. Delinquency in the payment of poll taxes was considered a misdemeanor punishable by jail.

More good news regarding rehabilitation of the island was reported in the February 28, 1948, *Guam Echo.* The lead story revealed that the House Committee on Appropriations had received from the Bureau of the Budget a recommendation that $1,600,000 be allowed for land on Guam to be acquired by the Navy for military purposes. If this worked out as planned, we wrote, the Navy would be able to make land settlements in the spring. Meanwhile, property damage claims on Guam were being processed. We listed eighteen of the claimants, the damages claimed, and the amounts allowed. They ranged in size from $6,000 claimed by Jesus T. Gutierrez and $5,375.50 allowed, to $195,945.91 claimed by Jose M. Torres and $168,454.54 allowed. Total amount claimed was $491,859.97 and total amount allowed, $402,985.46. Eleven personal injury and death claimants were also named.[6]

Always trying to give our readers in Guam an international context for their thinking and positive models of self-government, we frequently wrote about other dependent territories. The February *Guam Echo* contained a column about President Harry Truman's first visit to Puerto Rico and the Virgin Islands on February 20–22, 1948. While there, he signed the Elective Governor bill, which, beginning the next November, would permit the people to decide by ballot who should govern them. In a formal speech at the capital, San Juan, the president told the Puerto Ricans that they should have the right to determine their own political destiny. Some wanted independence from the United States; others wanted statehood; still others preferred a Commonwealth status (which they eventually achieved in 1952).

In the Virgin Islands, the president and his party were met by Governor William H. Hastie, the first African American to govern that possession. Residents there had no desire for independence but requested increased federal aid to help them get on their feet economically. The president promised to do what he could for them.

In commenting on the president's trip on February 24, 1948, the *New York Times* wrote, and the *Echo* reprinted: "President Truman's Caribbean vacation tour . . . should have the effect of focusing more public and Congressional attention on those outlying possessions of the United States. Perhaps the President can also make a trip sometime soon to the Pacific, where we have equally pressing 'colonial' problems."[7]

Before vacationing in the Caribbean, President Truman had, in fact, spoken about other outlying territories. In a special message to Congress on civil rights on February 2, he said: "The present political status of our territories and possessions impairs the enjoyment of civil rights by their residents. I have in the past recommended legislation granting statehood to Alaska and Hawai'i, and organic acts for Guam and American Samoa, including a grant of citizenship to the people of these Pacific islands. I repeat these recommendations."[8]

Response to this recommendation came three days later when Senator Guy Cordon introduced S.J. Res. 196, authorizing an investigation of the Trust Territory, Guam, and Samoa by a Senate Commission. This resolution differed from his earlier resolution, S.J. Res. 37, in that the investigating commission would be composed solely of Senate members instead of House and Senate members. Senator Cordon thought it might have a greater chance of enactment. On February 23 it went to the Senate Committee on Rules. But that committee had not been disposed to act rapidly on any Pacific islands legislation. So we warned our readers that S. Res. 196 would be apt to lie in state there for weeks unless public pressure was applied. We wrote: "At this point, there is little doubt that the most that will come from Congress this year is a decision to send a committee out to inspect the various islands. If more is wanted by the Guamanian people, more time, money and effort will have to be spent arousing the American public and Congressmen to Guam's needs."[9]

About this time Roy E. James, chief of the Pacific branch of the Division of Territories in the Department of the Interior, announced that he would resign to run for Congress on the Republican ticket in Pennsylvania. This was great for him, but it left something of a void for the people of Guam and for me. I was accustomed to talking with Roy by phone nearly every day and learning what was happening in Congress or elsewhere that I should report in the *Guam Echo*.

Roy James was well known to the Guamanians. A navy commander during the war, he served in the Military Government on Guam in 1945, and in the spring of 1946, after mustering out of the service, he joined the Department of the Interior to further the welfare of the islanders. In 1947 he visited Guam as a member of Interior Secretary Krug's party. In a short article about him in the February *Guam Echo* I wrote: "In Washington James is recognized as the champion of Guam rights. He has consistently fought for citizenship, organic legislation, and civilian administration. Toward these ends he has written articles, written speeches, advised Congressmen writing bills and participated in interdepartmental conferences. He has probably done more than any other one man in behalf of the people of Guam."[10]

James' opponent in the November election was Francis E. Walter, a Pennsylvania Democrat who had been in Congress since 1933. Roy and his family moved to Pennsylvania, and he undoubtedly threw himself into the campaign with the same vigor he had brought to Pacific island affairs. But he was unable to defeat the incumbent.

Highlighted in a box on page 1 of the February *Guam Echo* was the fact that Francisco (Frank) B. Leon Guerrero, a leader in the Guam Congress, was on his way to Washington. He was going to meet with members of the U.S. Congress. It would be May before he actually got there because he was visiting several Guam students in college on his way across the country.

Faith in the Institute of Ethnic Affairs and the *Guam Echo* kept growing. In response to our December appeal for contributions, we heard from several prominent people and reported their written remarks in subsequent issues of our little paper. Harold L. Ickes wrote, "I have been very much interested indeed in the *Guam Echo,* and I hope that you will be able to continue with it. I am glad to enclose a check for $25.00."[11]

Congressman Willis W. Bradley, Jr., former governor of Guam, wrote: "A publication such as the *Guam Echo* serves a very useful purpose in bringing together comments (both critical and commendatory) about matters pertaining to Guam and the Pacific Islands. I believe the *Guam Echo* is presenting the case of Guam fairly and I have confidence that it will be of assistance to those of us who are endeavoring to obtain citizenship and an organic act for the people of the Island."[12]

Jerry Tallmer, assistant editor of *The Nation,* wrote, "important news not covered elsewhere. Has given us an idea for at least one article and several editorial bits and for reference. . . ."[13]

Henry A. Murray, an Institute board member and director of the psychological clinic at Harvard University, wrote, "I have found the *Guam Echo* concisely informative and interesting and shocking! More power to you! The trend of U.S. policy seems to be going toward a more humane and just treatment of the population of the Trust Territory. The Institute is no doubt largely responsible for this improvement."[14]

Cordial written support came also from California Congressman Norris Poulson, Hawai'i Delegate Joseph R. Farrington, and Illinois Congressman Edward H. Jenison. In February, Jenison wrote:

I had the opportunity to visit the island very early after the return of our forces during the war and, as a naval officer, know many of the fine people in the island community. For these reasons I am much concerned with the legislation now before our Public Lands Committee on the government of Guam.

As you may know, I am not one of those who felt that the Navy had failed altogether either before or after the war. But, on the other hand, I am very much convinced that we can improve conditions and hasten the movement toward a model democratic community.[15]

To say the least, these expressions of faith and goodwill helped shape the attitude of those in a position to bring about change. And attitudes were changing — slowly, but changing — at least in Washington. Attitudes of many naval officers in the field, however, remained entrenched in the status quo. Some did their best to delay or extinguish any hope for a transfer of jurisdiction.

The next surprise for the Institute of Ethnic Affairs came in March 1948. A resolution unanimously approved by ninety-three Samoan chiefs, meeting in General Assembly on Tuituilla on February 17, asked that any and all bills pertaining to Samoan affairs "be not considered for ten years or more by Congress." It went on to state the assembly's "unanimous wish that Naval Civil Government be continued in American Samoa."[16]

This was another big blow! Or so it seemed.

The first we heard of it was when the resolution was transmitted to Congress by the Navy Department on March 18 and released to the press. Its immediate effect was to cause congressmen and department officials to question the advisability of enacting *any* pending bills extending self-government and other liberties to *any* Pacific islanders.

This measure was contrary to everything we had been told. It seemed obvious that naval officers in Samoa had been hard at work lobbying the local legislature, as they had the Guam legislature. The fact that the resolution was couched in perfect legal phraseology when the Samoans were known to conduct business in their native language clinched our assumptions.

Faithfully adhering to the Institute's policy of transmitting both good and bad news to the islands as soon as possible, we made this the lead story of our March 31, 1948, *Guam Echo:*

This Samoan resolution, which comes on the heels of the Guam resolution passed last September favoring retention of Navy rule until rehabilitation is effected, puts the President and his Cabinet in the embarrassing position of seeming to favor a change the people do not want.

That the inhabitants of Samoa do not want government by law instead of government by men seems highly unlikely in view of the fact that they have been petitioning the U.S. Congress at intervals since 1900 for organic legislation (a form of Constitution) and a Bill of Rights. . . .[17]

We went on to support the congressional investigation proposed by the House subcommittee and to urge that the Cordon and Crawford resolutions be brought out of the Committees on Rules, where they had been resting for several weeks. Collier sent a letter to the *New York Times* recommending the same:

> Repeatedly, the Navy has stated or implied, through its local officers, that the issue was one of continuing to receive medical aid, schooling and other public services, or of doing without them; one of maintaining Samoan culture or of having it destroyed. No such issue exists in reality. Having an organic act involves no loss of any public service; having a democratic civilian rule in place of an absolutist Navy rule involves if anything increased dignity for the Individual Samoan and respect for Samoan culture. The Navy, in face-to-face and all-penetrating contact with the Samoans, as with the Guamanians, presents them with fictitious alternatives. . . . What is called for is an investigation of the facts by a commission. . . . Resolutions setting up Congressional commissions for this purpose have been introduced. If nothing more, the Samoan measure should serve to bring these resolutions out of the Committees on Rules.[18]

This letter did, in fact, cause the House Rules Committee to report out H. Con. Res. 129 the very next day, April 20. It was passed by the full House a month later, on May 20, amended in the Senate on June 12, and cleared by the House with amendments on June 18. It authorized a committee of twelve to make a survey of all the Pacific islands under United States administration. Three committee members would be from the Senate Interior and Insular Affairs Committee, three from the House Public Lands Committee, and three from each of the Senate and House Foreign Affairs Committees (see Appendix 12).

At an organizational meeting on June 29, 1948, Senator Cordon was named chairman; Representative Crawford, vice chairman; and Representative James G. Fulton (R., Pa.) of the House Foreign Affairs Committee, secretary. The only problem remaining was finding time to go. Because 1948 was an election year, some congressmen would be campaigning for the rest of the summer and into the fall. So the committee tentatively planned to leave San Francisco on November 9 and return to the States on December 20. Senator Wiley, however, planned to make the trip by ship during the summer, stopping at Guam en route to Japan.

I interviewed Congressman Crawford by phone about his expectations, and he told me for publication in the June *Guam Echo* that he for one would not be "sucked into any boot-licking trip to the Pacific islands. Too many people connected with the Joint Committee are too much satisfied with letting the Navy recommend what should be done. . . . It is my aim," Crawford said, "in the first instance, to make Guamanians and Samoans citizens of the United States, and in the second instance, to give them a bill of rights and every constitutional protection."

Referring to United States participation in the United Nations Trusteeship Council, Crawford noted that "this country likes to set itself up as an example when it sits around a table in the family of nations." Declaring that legislation for inhabitants of the Trust Territory should not be given precedence over legislation for U.S. nationals in Guam and Samoa, he said he definitely would not be content with protecting the constitutional rights of the Trust Islanders while leaving Guam and Samoa "under the heel of the Navy."[19]

In April 1948, the State Department finally fulfilled President Truman's directive of the previous June that it prepare and present to Congress organic legislation providing for civilian government for the Trust Territory. A bill had been drafted. Navy and Interior were still working on organic legislation for American Samoa. Crawford's bill, H.R. 4340, transferring the government of Guam from the Navy to the Interior Department would be central among those discussed by the Joint Committee when members departed for the Pacific.

In preparation for the trip scheduled for November 1948, the Joint Committee held an open hearing on July 7 at which spokesmen for the State and Interior Departments argued strongly for civilian administration of all the islands in question. A statement prepared by Oscar Chapman, Under Secretary of the Interior, and carried to The Hill by James P. Davis, Director of the Division of Territories and Island Possessions, asserted that administration by a military agency would reverse the precedents of American history. Secretary Chapman pointed out that the Philippines, Puerto Rico,

Oscar L. Chapman, as Under Secretary of the Department of the Interior succeeding Julius A. Krug, helped convince the U.S. Congress that national security did not require military government where there were military bases. Chapman was elevated to Secretary in 1948.

and the Virgin Islands had all at one time been under military or naval administration; but they had been transferred to the jurisdiction of a civilian agency, and all had since progressed to independence, election of their own governor, and other aspects of self-government. He went on to say:

> I do not intend to minimize the importance of any of the Pacific islands to our national security. It is our view, rather, that the safeguarding of that security does not require the jurisdiction of the Army or Navy to be extended to the civilian populations. There are military installations in Alaska, in Hawai'i, in Puerto Rico and the Virgin Islands and, for that matter, in California and other states, but it has not been necessary to broaden the military or naval jurisdiction beyond the confines of the bases. . . .
>
> . . . [T]he total cost of administration by the Interior Department would

be no more and would probably be less than administration by the Navy Department.[20]

After the filing of Chapman's statement, Davis repeatedly emphasized that his department was not advocating administration under Interior Department over administration by any other civilian agency. Instead, he said Interior was leaving final disposition up to the president.

Benjamin Gerig, chief of the State Department's Division of Dependent Area Affairs, referred to the principle of civilian administration agreed to by the four executive departments — State, Navy, War, and Interior. He stressed the obligations of the United States toward non-self-governing territories under the United Nations, stating: "America's traditional role as protagonist of the interests of non-self-governing peoples . . . will be put to the test as America's own administration of dependent areas is critically examined in the forum of the United Nations."[21]

Spokesmen for the Navy Department appeared before the committee in closed sessions on the afternoon of July 7 to discuss control of Pacific outposts from a strategic viewpoint. Their statements were not made a matter of public record. Soon after, however, on July 13 Admiral DeWitt C. Ramsey, the new High Commissioner of the Pacific Islands, who had just made a three-week inspection tour of fourteen islands, spoke to the press in Honolulu, reintroducing the military once again into this jurisdictional seesaw by stating that only the Navy had the logistic support — transportation, supply facilities, and so on — necessary for island administration. His statement was interpreted by the stateside press as an indirect reply to recommendations for civilian government made by the State and Interior Departments at the July 7 hearing. A report of Admiral Ramsey's statement was carried in a box on page 1 of the July 31, 1948, *Guam Echo,* alongside the lead article describing the congressional hearing. It was important for readers in Guam and elsewhere to know that the fight was still on. Top brass in the Pacific was coming on strong. Nothing would be resolved before the Congressional Joint Committee could go and see for itself what seemed to be right. But elections in November loomed ahead, and everyone involved knew that the proposed organic acts would be put on hold.

Guamanians were used to waiting. It had been four years since the United States Navy retook Guam from the Japanese, and the Guamanians were still waiting for compensation for war damages. The Land Acquisition Act of 1946 had authorized the Navy to acquire land on Guam needed

Land available on Guam for rebuilding by the islanders was limited after World War II because about half the island was then held for military use by all branches of the armed services.

for present and future military installations, but funding was two years in coming. Finally, the necessary appropriations bill went through the Congress, and on May 10, 1948, President Truman signed H.R. 6055, which became Public Law 519, and the first $1,600,000 was appropriated for land acquisition.

This good news was sent to Guam via the May 29, 1948, *Guam Echo,* in which we reported that the compensation for land acquisition would be figured according to present land values, while war damage claims were being figured on prewar appraisals. The $1,600,000 was expected to take care of only part of the necessary purchases, because land value had gone up since 1946 when acquisition was authorized. More money would be sought from Congress the next year. The Navy Department in Washington stated that the actual amount of land required for military purposes had not been determined. About half of Guam's 209 square miles were then held for military use by all branches of the armed services. Some of it was being leased to Guamanians at 6 percent per annum of the appraised value. Now it could be gradually acquired by outright purchase.

Meanwhile, something of a brouhaha was developing over Tumon Beach. Early in April Guamanian civilians got the impression that the Army wished to acquire the entire Tumon Bay area for recreational purposes. In an article that appeared in the *Guam News,* formerly the *Navy News,* on April 24, Vincent R. Palomo, chairman of the Guam Chamber of Commerce protested. The beach was then open to civilians and service personnel alike, and the chamber wanted it kept that way. In fact, the chamber sent a cablegram to Defense Secretary James V. Forrestal, formerly Secretary of the Navy, on April 25, reminding him that it was the only beach open to Guamanians and that it had on it burial grounds of Guamanian ancestors. On April 29, 1948, the Army Department in Washington referred the matter to General Douglas MacArthur, commander-in-chief of the Far East Command in Tokyo. MacArthur inquired of Major General Francis H. Griswold, commanding general of the Marianas-Bonin area, and on May 11 replied to Washington that combined Army–Air Force requirements would involve only half of the beach and that the governor of Guam would be arranging a conference of all interested parties soon.

Governor Pownall had, in fact, on April 26 sent a message to each member of the Guam Congress advising that there was adequate land in the Tumon area to meet all needs. Nevertheless, the Guam Congress on May 1 approved a resolution that was to be forwarded by the Navy to the U.S. Congress requesting that all beaches be declared public property and that no further monies be approved for the purpose of purchasing or leasing additional Guamanian lands for military organizations other than what was now occupied for national defense. As usual, the Navy in Guam delayed transmittal of the resolution — this time waiting more than thirty days. On June 30, the Navy Department in Washington reported that the resolution had been received by them "two or three weeks ago," or about a week before Congress adjourned on June 20. They said that time did not permit them to forward it to Congress before adjournment. Furthermore, officers in Washington maintained that further acquisition of any portion of Tumon Beach was never contemplated. All of this was pieced together and published in the June 30 *Guam Echo.* In an Editor's Note, we observed: "If there is any significance in the Tumon Beach story, it lies in the fact that this is one of

By protesting against the Army's attempt to reserve all of Tumon Beach for recreation by the military, the Guamanians were exercising the power of dissent.

the few times when Guamanians have strongly protested an act either accomplished or contemplated by their Government. . . . Generally, it is safe to assume that where there's smoke there's a fire. But that is something, perhaps for the Congressional committee to investigate. The whole land problem is one of the most ticklish on Guam."[22] It was heartening to us that the Guamanians were learning to speak up. As many authorities on government have observed, democracy depends on dissent. It is better to protest and try to resolve differences than let trouble brew.

Public Law 519 for land acquisition on Guam also appropriated nearly

$500,000 for property damage and personal injury and death claims. Over $400,000 was allowed for twenty-nine large claimants named in the February 28 *Guam Echo.* The General Baptist Mission Church and eleven more individual claimants were listed in the May 29, 1948, *Guam Echo* as beneficiaries of this appropriation.

While Congress in Washington was approving bills for the rehabilitation of Guam and listening to arguments from State and Interior favoring civilian administration, the Navy was doing its best in the field to undermine change. George Weller, a reporter for the *Washington Evening Star,* came back from a trip to American Samoa in July and reported that High Talking Chief Tuiasosopo had changed his tune and was now opposing citizenship for his people and more self-government. Having been brainwashed to believe that "equality" would cause the islanders to lose their customs and culture, Tuiasosopo had told Weller that the Samoans were happy with the legislative assembly the Navy had given them, and in ten more years they might be well enough educated to "look toward citizenship."[23]

Weller's story in the Washington newspaper reinforced what we had learned and reported about the Samoan resolution passed by the *fono* in February. We advised in the July 31, 1948, *Guam Echo,* "the right of legislative assembly guaranteed in Samoa is no greater than the right allowed in Guam and it, like the Guamanian privilege, may be taken away at will of the Governor since there is no Organic Act or other force cementing it into law."[24] To counteract what the Samoans and Guamanians were being told, we printed in that same issue an editorial that had appeared in the *Honolulu Star-Bulletin* on May 25:

The Navy and "Trust Territory"

Naval administration of the "trust territory" in the Pacific inevitably means fairly frequent changes.

Rear Admiral Carleton H. Wright, USN, who is first deputy high commissioner of the trust territory, is to be relieved of that duty in July. He has served in the post for less than a year. He will be succeeded by Rear Admiral Leon S. Fiske, USN.

Only a few weeks ago there was a change in the high commissionership. Admiral Louis Denfield went to Washington several months ago as chief of naval operations. As the top admiral in the Pacific, he was also high commissioner for the Trust territory. A considerable time elapsed before his successor as ranking admiral was named to the high commissionership.

Shifts in naval command were made about every two years. Here are Admiral DeWitt C. Ramsey *(right),* who had just been promoted to Commander in Chief of the Pacific and U.S. Pacific Fleet, with Under Secretary of the Navy W. John Kenney and Vice Admiral Arthur W. Radford, Vice Chief of Naval Operations. Both Radford and Ramsey tried very hard to keep Guam under auspices of the Navy.

The successor is Admiral DeWitt C. Ramsey, USN. He, too, will in the course of time, be transferred, in accordance with the custom of the navy.

These shifts are likely to be made about every two years. And in many cases, the newly appointed commissioners and deputy commissioners are likely to have little close acquaintance with the human problems involved in the administration of this trust territory. . . . There are, in these far-scattered little atolls, islands and islets, not many more than 50,000 people — mostly Polynesians and Micronesians.

But each is a human being. Each is a ward of the United States. Each is a life entrusted to our care.

And the trust territory as a whole presents a combined problem of human relations and economic liability that is urgent, exacting, complex.

The frequent shifts in naval command, illustrated by the transfers men-

Emil J. Sady, first a military officer in the Navy, joined the State Department (later Department of the Interior) after World War II and constantly supported civilian government by the people of Guam.

tioned earlier, call for the development of a resident staff that shall not be subject to these recurrent changes.

Otherwise the 50,000 wards of the United States can not possibly be given the informed, sympathetic attention which their utterly dependent condition requires.

This staff should be made up of men and women who look on their duty with the zeal of the missionary.

Their work requires technical competence and real devotion.

Amateurs, time-servers and men named merely because they are due for a navy transfer will not fit the requirements.

It is a lonely duty, at best. It is often duty in unpleasant climatic conditions. But it is a duty which the United States has assumed.

And until civil administration succeeds that of the navy, it is a conspicuous responsibility of the navy and whose performance is being narrowly watched.[25]

This editorial said very well what John Collier, Laura Thompson, and others had been trying to communicate for a long time. Who but an editor living in Hawai'i could have said it so well?

Perhaps Emil J. Sady, who had just been appointed chief of the Pacific Branch in the Territories and Island Possessions Division of the Interior Department, succeeding Roy E. James. As a young military government officer in the Navy during the war, Sady had begun work in the Division of Dependent Area Affairs in the State Department soon after his discharge. He was an excellent replacement at Interior of the highly regarded Roy James. Sady had been my mentor two years before when I struggled with the *News Letter* article describing a strategic versus a nonstrategic trusteeship. After that, I talked with him by phone almost daily, just as I did with Roy. Emil was intimately familiar with the workings of the United Nations trusteeship system. His assignment in the State Department involved not only the Trust Territory of the Pacific Islands but the future of Guam and Samoa as well. All of that had required frequent negotiations with the Navy, War, and Interior Departments. Politically, Emil was a friendly negotiator and very astute. In the summer of 1948, the future for the Pacific Islands looked pretty bleak to both of us. Naval officers in the field had made serious inroads against the civil rights for which we were working. They had turned the islanders themselves against civilian government, or so it seemed.

Then one of Guam's budding statesmen came to Washington, and prospects began to change.

Chapter 10

F. B. Leon Guerrero Goes to Washington

It was toward the end of August 1948 when F. B. (Frank) Leon Guerrero, member of the Guam Congress, decided just to walk in on Maurice J. Tobin, U.S. Secretary of Labor. Frank had met with the Hopkins Committee when it came to Guam the year before. Tobin was a member of that committee, and Frank felt he knew him, so without making an appointment, one day in August 1948, Frank just went to his office at 200 Constitution Avenue, Washington, D.C. Tobin was leaving to catch a plane, but he recognized Frank and stayed to talk.

Among other things, Tobin told Frank that he was bound by the Hopkins Committee decisions not to speak out for civilian administration and other rights when he testified before Congress. He personally would have gone further than the Hopkins Committee Report, he said. He wanted Frank to know this, and also, he wanted Frank to talk with Navy Under Secretary W. John Kenney, whom he believed to be of the same opinion. Then and there, Tobin arranged a meeting for the three of them at the Pentagon for August 26.

Returning to the office of the Institute of Ethnic Affairs after his meeting at the Pentagon, Frank was walking on air. According to notes I took at the time and sent to Foster Hailey, an editorial writer at the *New York Times,* Frank said: "I feel like a new man. I went to the Pentagon determined not to give ground if Secretary Kenney began talking about the advantages of continued naval administration. To my surprise, I found Kenney strongly supporting the policy determined by the four Secretaries last year. Kenney and Tobin repeatedly assured me that officials in the top brackets are determined to carry out this policy. Kenney said something about some brass down the line holding different views, but this did not represent policy and would not influence his action."[1] Frank said the three of them went on to talk about the economic instability in Guam, the need for more money for rehabilitation, and wage inequities. Both Kenney and Tobin insisted that Frank write to them upon returning home.

Francisco B. Leon Guerrero became one of Guam's first statesmen. He testified in Washington for U.S. citizenship in 1937 and for an Organic Act of Guam in 1950. His meeting in Washington in August 1948 with Maurice J. Tobin, U.S. Secretary of Labor, and W. John Kenney, Under Secretary of the Navy, helped turn the tide for civilian government.

At this point I suggested to Frank that perhaps the time had come for him to talk to the press and openly state the preference for civilian administration that he had been expressing to us at the Institute since he arrived in Washington in May. Frank said he would have agreed to the press conference proposed by Secretary Tobin that very afternoon but for the fact

Under Secretary of the Navy W. John Kenney being sworn in by Rear Admiral Oswald S. Colclough, Advocate General of the Navy, with John L. Sullivan, the new Secretary of the Navy succeeding Forrestal, looking on

that he (Frank) was leaving Washington for New York City that night and there was not enough time to arrange one.

So we worked out a news release that Frank approved. At first, he did not want to mention Tobin and Kenney by name. But then I told him I would call their offices and get clearance. He was all right with that. Showing the usual Guamanian reticence, he still did not want to state a preference for which civilian agency might govern Guam. I quickly prepared a draft press release and Frank left for the train. Upon leaving, he said he was anxious to get home now that he had something really good to tell his constituents.

To me, this news was almost too good to be true. The next morning I phoned Secretary Kenney and Secretary Tobin to get clearance. My notes say, "They were completely decent about it." After hearing the first paragraph, Kenney said, "That's all right." After a few more paragraphs he said, "I've no objection to that." When I finished, he lectured me a little on how cooperation had been the Navy's aim all along. I told him I thought this commitment on paper would surely make the cooperation more obvious.

Then I called Ickes' office. Lyle Munson, his assistant with whom I always spoke, saw this breakthrough as something pretty big. He urged me to send the news release to as many outlets as possible. So we mimeographed multiple copies of the following release and mailed them not only to newspapers but to congressmen and other interested parties on our list.

FOR RELEASE TO A.M. PAPERS

SUNDAY, AUGUST 29, 1948

Navy Will Support Civilian Administration of Pacific Islands, Guamanian Is Assured

Francisco B. Leon Guerrero, member of the Guam Congress, told the Institute of Ethnic Affairs in Washington after conferring with high officials in Government that he had been assured that the Navy Department "is not going to oppose but will give active support to American citizenship, organic legislation, and civilian administration for Guam."

"I feel like a new man after having talked with Secretary Tobin and Under Secretary Kenney," he said, referring to a conference at the Pentagon on August 26 with Labor Secretary Maurice J. Tobin, who last year served on the Navy's Hopkins Committee which made an on-the-spot study of American Samoa and Guam, and Under Secretary of the Navy, W. John Kenney.

"When I came to Washington in May, I was uncertain about the real intent of officials working in the interests of Guam. But now I am sure that persons in the top brackets are really in favor of granting us American citizenship and civil rights under a civilian administration.

"It is my information that this is the objective of men all down the line," he added. "There may be some who on a personal basis oppose civilian administration. But many, both in and out of the service, have expressed willingness to help us achieve a true form of American government."

The Guam Congressman declined to state a preference as to the civilian agency to which jurisdiction over Guam might be transferred.

"That's up to the United States Congress or the President to decide," he said. "With the Joint Committee coming out in November, we should have results. I have utmost confidence in this particular committee. . . ."

He was referring to the twelve-man committee headed by Senator Guy Cordon (R., Ore.) scheduled to tour Pacific island dependencies from November 9 to December 20 in preparation for writing constructive legislation.

Mr. Leon Guerrero spent three months in Washington as an unofficial representative of the Guamanian people. He left here on August 26 for New York, the first lap on his journey home. He will stop at Grand Rapids, Mich., Chicago, Ill., St. Paul, Minn., and various cities in California before leaving

San Francisco for Guam. While in Washington he was advised that he had been re-elected as Councilman from Agana, the principal city and island capital, in the Guam Congress. He is a practicing lawyer on Guam.[2]

This extremely favorable development as reported in the above press release was soon offset by an announcement on October 27, 1948, from Senator Cordon's office that the Joint Committee investigation of the Pacific islands would be postponed. The entire Senate Foreign Relations contingent found it impossible to make the fall trip and two others had conflicting commitments. This was a serious setback.

The *New York Times* in an editorial on October 31, 1948, only four days after announcement of the postponement, questioned what could be more important than deciding the fate of the people of Guam and Samoa who had been in limbo for fifty years, especially since the United States purported "to speak in world councils on the plight of colonial peoples under other flags. . . . There is no reason why the matter should be allowed to lie dormant through another Congressional session just because Senator Cordon and his colleagues failed to carry out their mission this year."[3]

Foster Hailey, an editorial writer for the *New York Times,* had been my professor of editorial writing at the Columbia University Graduate School of Journalism, and he became a very articulate spokesman on behalf of the Pacific islanders. I was almost surprised to find a file of correspondence with him when I began researching this book, but I obviously had kept him up-to-date on developments in Washington.

In preparation for writing the November *Guam Echo,* I phoned Congressman Crawford (R., Mich.). He expressed keen disappointment over postponement of the trip to the Pacific and said he thought it was the congressmen's "duty to go." He was frank in stating: "I think it is shameful, I think it is disgraceful, I think it is mean and low down on the part of the Administration and Congress in giving all attention and substance to other countries, as we have been doing for several years, and at the same time completely disregarding the interests of our subjects located in off-shore areas. . . ."[4] At that point he forecasted dark days ahead for Pacific islands legislation. The resolution he had helped nurse through the previous Congress was dead. Money appropriated for the Joint Committee's trip would go back to the U.S. Treasury at the end of the year. A new resolution would be required if a future trip were to be planned. Crawford said he doubted there was much enthusiasm for such a resolution. Asked if Congress might act without seeing the islands, he said he could not foresee the disposition of possible new House and Senate Committee chairmen, but, generally speaking, "It looks very discouraging for the Pacific Islands."

The 1948 general elections were soon upon us, and to the surprise of nearly everyone except himself, Harry Truman was reelected president over Thomas Dewey. All of us alive at that time can recall the picture of a Chicago newspaper held high by a grinning Mr. Truman proclaiming that Dewey had won.

Only a few of us remember that Guam's flag was paraded in Washington during the president's inaugural ceremonies. But Betty Winquest and I were there, high in the stands along Pennsylvania Avenue, in the bitter cold. Flags of the forty-eight states, the District of Columbia, and all outlying territories were massed immediately behind President Truman and Vice President Barkley in the march from the Capitol to the White House. It was a thrill to be present.

For the future of the Pacific islands, Truman's reelection was very fortunate. If Dewey had won, advocates of civilian government would have had to start completely over. Truman's election meant that most department heads would retain their positions and most policies would not change.

Many Democratic representatives and senators had been swept in with Truman. Most of the legislators who had introduced bills or otherwise shown interest in Pacific island affairs had been returned to office, with a few notable exceptions. Congressman Willis Bradley (R., Calif.) was not re-elected, nor was Robert Grant (R., Ind.). On the other hand, Andrew J. Biemiller (D., Wisc.) was returned to Congress after a two-year absence. He was one of the first congressmen to introduce a bill on behalf of the islands after the war. All original members of the Joint Committee named to study the islands were returned except Senator Alben W. Barkley (D., Ky.), who was elected vice president.

Chairmanship of House and Senate committees would change in January as a result of the Democratic sweep. Joseph C. O'Mahoney (D., Wyo.) would succeed Hugh A. Butler (R., Nebr.) as chairman of the Senate Interior and Insular Affairs Committee. Andrew L. Somers (D., N.Y.) had been mentioned as possible successor to Richard J. Welch (R., Calif.) as chairman of the House Public Lands Committee.

Bipartisan action was expected on insular affairs. The Democratic majority in Congress would back President Truman's policies. Republicans had introduced many of the Pacific islands bills and could be expected to do so again, or at least to support similar bills introduced by Democrats.

Shortly after the election, on November 11, 1948, Emil J. Sady, chief of the Pacific branch in the Interior Department, left Washington for a six-week trip to the islands. A Thanksgiving Day luncheon in Agana was planned for him by Guamanians. After visiting the Trust Territory and American Samoa, he would return home sometime after Christmas.

Soon we at the Ethnic Institute were involved in preparing the December–January 1949 *Guam Echo.* In it we reviewed a new book called *The Fortunate Islands: A Pacific Interlude,* by Navy Captain Walter Karig. The author claimed to have spent twenty years living among the Micronesians. Although we admitted that it was an exceedingly readable book that could become very popular among stateside readers, we concluded, "In view of the author's reputation as a ghost writer for Navy officials, the possibility that this book is part of Navy Department public relations to encourage continuation of naval government in Micronesia should not be discounted."[5]

A news story on December 8, 1948, in the *New York Star,* said Karig's book "contained the first printed confirmation that the Navy had its own corps of civilian administrators up its sleeve as a strategy to circumvent a take-over by the Interior Department's own staff." The story went on to say that a tour of the Navy Department in Washington "confirmed that the admirals are in favor of the civilian corps of administrators within the Defense Department." Forrestal had become head of the Defense Department.[6] At the same time Navy Under Secretary Kenney told the Washington *Star*:

> I think, at this time, the idea of a civilian corps of administrators under the Defense Secretary must be regarded as just another good notion to be weighed with all the others by the President and Congress. Naturally we will do what they decide.
>
> I wish you would make it very clear that the Navy is anxious to turn over this responsibility as soon as possible to a civilian agency. The Navy does not regard itself as a colonial administrative organization, but a combat organization. But there are many problems involved here which can't be solved overnight.[7]

Secretary Kenney's comments in that last paragraph were the clearest, most unequivocal statement of intent to transfer administration of the islands from the Navy to a civilian agency that we had ever seen. As I was writing up the story, I wanted to believe him. But because of all the other contradictory things going on, I wasn't sure I could.

As the First Session of the 81st Congress opened in Washington on January 3, 1949, Senator Butler (R., Nebr.) reintroduced his bills for civilian government for Guam and American Samoa. They were numbered S. 184 for Samoa and S. 185 for Guam. Hawai'i Delegate Farrington also reintroduced his citizenship bills, H.R. 391 for Guamanians and H.R. 392 for Samoans. Those were the only Pacific island bills introduced at the beginning of the year.

On January 12, 1949, Senator Joseph C. O'Mahoney (D., Wyo.) reorganized the Senate Committee on Interior and Insular Affairs. The group decided not to establish standing subcommittees, as had been the custom in the past, but to act as a unit. Special subcommittees would be appointed by the chairman as required (see Appendix 13).

On January 24, Andrew L. Somers (D., N.Y.) reorganized the House Public Lands Committee, as it was still called. He named Monroe M. Redden (D., N.C.) chairman of the Subcommittee on Territories, to succeed Fred L. Crawford (R., Mich.).

Open hearings on Pacific island bills were scheduled by the Senate Committee for four days, beginning January 31, at which time Interior Secretary Krug and his staff would be asked to explain the functions of that department. We noted in the *Echo* that this background session was unprecedented and had the advantage of giving committee members a general view of problems with which they could expect to deal before specific measures came up.

Perhaps responding to Representative Crawford's admonitions to make their wishes clearly known to the U.S. Congress, or maybe urged by F. B. Leon Guerrero who had recently returned to Guam from Washington on December 10, 1948, the Guam Congress passed another resolution calling for citizenship and an organic act "providing a satisfactory determination of our civil rights and political status." Unlike the September petition of the year before, it contained no mention of continued naval administration. A draft of the resolution reached our office early in January. When I called Captain Peter G. Hale, Navy chief of the Office of Island Governments, about it, he expressed doubt that it ever got as far as the governor of Guam. He had never seen it, he said. We printed the draft we had in the

December–January 1949 issue of the *Guam Echo* so decision makers in Washington would know the Guamanians' intent.[8]

At the same time, various offices of the U.S. government were being deluged with petitions and counterpetitions from Samoan chiefs. The chiefs were clearly at odds with each other. In an interview with the *Honolulu Star-Bulletin* on January 6, after his trip to American Samoa, Emil Sady said:

> The whole basis for Samoan opposition to American citizenship, an organic act, and transfer to civilian administration is misinformation, misunderstanding, and a certain amount of misrepresentation of facts.
>
> There was a feeling that the American Bill of Rights applied to Samoa would destroy their long-established native rights and result in a breakdown of their system of chiefs. Many thought that American citizenship would require them automatically to pay federal income tax. In all these things they were misinformed.[9]

Sady also said he asked around to learn how thoroughly the Interior-Navy bill for organic legislation had been circulated and found very few people who had even seen it.

In an interview with me for the December–January 1949 *Guam Echo,* Sady expressed confidence that the president's policy of civilian administration of the islands under organic acts could be carried out in an orderly fashion without waiting much longer. He promised to supply a longer statement for our February or March *Guam Echo,* which in today's parlance would be a "road map" to the future for all the Pacific islands under American authority.

This was encouraging. But before Sady could get his thoughts down on paper, an unexpected revolt by the Guam Congress pushed the United States Congress along that hypothetical road.

Chapter 11

Guam Assembly Walkout Spurs Congress

It was a short United Press dispatch printed by the *Washington Post* and the *New York Times* on March 5, 1949, that alerted us to what had happened.

Navy Action Protested by Guam Assembly

Guam, March 5 (UP) — The Guam Assembly walked out in protest today against what it said was an attempt by the United States Navy to curtail its legislative authority.

The walkout occurred after the Navy government refused to permit contempt warrants to be served on a civil service employee charged with refusing to answer questions of a congressional committee. Assemblyman Carlos Taitano said the Assembly would remain in adjournment until the United States Congress acts on a bill to give Guam organic and civil government.[1]

This was indeed significant news. For a day or two we tried to get additional facts, but few were forthcoming. There was no possibility of telephoning Guam in those days. So Collier and I worked with what we had and issued a press release on March 8, 1949. Key paragraphs are reprinted here:

Guam Assembly Walkout

"I hope that Congress and the American people will understand the significance of the walkout by the Guam Assembly at their meeting on March 5," John Collier, president of the Institute of Ethnic Affairs, stated today.

"That walkout, staged in protest against naval administration, dramatically indicates their desire for an organic act and civilian government.

"It should prompt the Navy and Interior Departments immediately to forward to Congress the organic acts they have had under consideration for many months. . . .

". . . It is significant that the Guamanians feel they must go on strike to get the U.S. Congress to take an interest in their needs."[2] (See Appendix 14.)

The release, which repeated historical facts and up-to-date legislative developments, was disseminated not only to the newspapers but to members of the concerned congressional committees, the White House, and key officials in the State and Interior Departments. It was also sent to Hawai'i and Guam.

While writing the release, we talked to our contacts at Interior, and three days after the walkout their draft Organic Act for Guam was on its way to the Bureau of the Budget. Navy's draft would not be far behind. From Budget, one or more bills would go to the Congress.

Unknown to me at the time was a fact brought out in *Destiny's Landfall.* Rogers wrote: "[T]he first thing Truman did in March 1949 when he learned of the walkout in Agana was to ask the State Department for an assessment. State replied by the end of March that the Guamanians were loyal and not a security risk to the United States but that, unless a change was made in Guam's government, they could become radicalized. State urged that the Department of the Interior take over in one year."[3]

Also unknown to me was a development that took place two years before, in 1947. According to Rogers: "While the debate over Guam's affairs heated up in Washington, back on Guam Governor Pownall, angry at Guamanian opponents of navy rule who supported the *Guam Echo,* ordered security investigations and special ONI surveillance of F. B. Leon Guerrero and his associates. Pownall released the findings, which alleged that F. B. was a communist subversive. The people of Guam ignored the ridiculous allegations."[4]

In retrospect, these precautions taken by the navy seem akin to Secretary Forrestal's alleged attempt to kill the Ethnic Institute soon after its incorporation through an adverse ruling from the Internal Revenue Service regarding tax-free grants and contributions. Frankly, I'm glad I didn't know about them. In my innocence, I just went on about my work.

On March 10, a copy of the March 5 Guam Assembly motion for adjournment reached our office by airmail. We were preparing the March 15, 1949, issue of the *Guam Echo* and decided to feature the exact wording in a box on page 1. It appears below.

Motion for Adjournment

Inasmuch as this Congress has not been vested with the authority to enforce its legislative powers, I ask the unanimous consent of this body to override the House Rules of the House of Assembly, 9th Guam Congress, in the following manner: I move that the House of Assembly adjourn at this time not to reconvene until such time as this body receives a reply or the action of the Congress of the United States relative to the Organic Act for Guam as passed by both Houses of the Guam Congress.

* * *

Motion made by Assemblyman Antonio C. Cruz, of Barrigada, seconded by Jesus C. Okiyama, of Yona, and carried by unanimous vote.[5]

Alongside the box was my lead story stating that the walkout of the Guam Assembly "has done more than any one thing in recent months to spur action on organic legislation for Guam." We quoted the United Press dispatch and parts of our press release.

On March 9, a letter from attorney Richard H. Wels, a naval reserve officer who had worked in military government on Guam during the war, appeared in the *New York Times,* so we quoted parts of that, too:

> The incident leading to the walkout . . . is of consequence only as an index to the discontent which has arisen from fifty years of neglect on the part of Congress. . . .
>
> Our failure to extend the democratic way of life to our own colonies makes perhaps the most effective argument that the Communists have. They are provided a ready-made challenge to our good faith in our present effort to extend the ways of Western democracy beyond the Iron Curtain. Why, they may well say, do we not practice what we preach?[6]

A few days after the walkout, I called several members of the U.S. Congress to get their reactions. I was sorry to have to write for the March 15, 1949, *Echo* that "the United States lawmakers have so many other important things to consider that the walkout on Guam has excited only a ripple in the stream of affairs."

Representative Crawford told me, "Personally, I feel that it's high time the Guamanians submit unmistakable evidence that they no longer want to live under the domination of the Navy, if that is their desire." He said the walkout made it look like the Guamanians meant business when they asked for organic legislation and civilian administration just before they adjourned. "If that is what they want," Crawford continued, "let them shout it from the housetops." Any action of Guamanians should not be "a half-way measure," he went on, signaling that he had not forgotten that the Guam Congress in September 1947 had asked for continuation of naval administration for an interim period.[7]

H.R. 2987, to provide civil government for Guam, had been introduced by Norris Poulson (R., Calif.) into the House of the 81st Congress on February 24. It was identical to the Crawford Bill, H.R. 4340, of the 80th Congress. And on February 21, Guy Cordon (R., Ore.) had introduced S. Res. 73, reviving a senatorial investigation of Guam and other Pacific islands. But no hearings had been scheduled, due in part to the slowness of the administration in getting to Congress bills President Truman had asked the departments to draft.

On March 13 we learned from a small news item in the *Washington Star* that the Guam legislators' revolt was growing. Governor Pownall had called a joint session of the Guam Congress to explain his attitude and urge resumption of work. Only the fifteen-member upper house (Council) had answered the call, and, after courteously listening to Admiral Pownall speak, it too had voted to adjourn.

There were no further reports about the Guam walkout in the Washington newspapers. For that March 15, 1949, *Guam Echo,* we again had to go with what we had. We knew it would be important for Guamanians to hear what Interior Secretary Krug might think or do about their state of affairs. On the occasion of the Interior Department's hundredth birthday, March 3, 1949, just two days before the Guam Assembly walkout, Mr. Krug had been asked by a member of the Washington press, "What about the Pacific islands?" He replied: "We sent one of our top people out there and he spent three months making a survey. His report makes it clear to me that we are about ready for the President to set a target date toward which we can plan. We might start with Guam, work out the difficulties encountered there, then move on to Samoa and the Trust Territory."[8]

Emil Sady—Krug's "top" person—elaborated for the *Echo.* None of the problems involved in the transfer—personnel, transportation, property titles, utilities—were insurmountable, he said. What was needed was that "target date." Once set in motion, the transfer would not take more than a year.

We filled two pages of the March *Echo* with facts about Guam's housing situation and the need for a new high school building. This information had been sent to us by Simon Sanchez and other Guamanian members of

the Institute. It was important that officials in Washington reading our little publication hear what they had to say. Parts of those articles will appear
in my next chapter. We ended that March *Echo* with the following item:

Guamanians Double Support of *Guam Echo*

For continued publication of *Guam Echo* and other work on behalf of Guamanians, the Institute of Ethnic Affairs in February received over $2,300, an
amount double that received from these people any other time. Money came
from 142 private citizens of Guam in amounts ranging from $5 to $100. Of
this number were 62 Guamanians who had not formerly been affiliated with
the Institute.

The *Echo* is proud to note among its subscribers Guamanian leaders in vir-
tually every walk of life. A high percentage of Congressmen, Commissioners
of all villages, naval government employees, farmers, shopkeepers, tradesmen
—all, by their subscriptions have shown a most gratifying interest in this
office and publication and the democratic principles for which they stand.
The Executive Committee of the Institute on Feb. 7 approved a resolution accepting the money and thanking the contributors. That resolution, signed by
John Collier, Laura Thompson, Felix Cohen, Philleo Nash, D'Arcy McNickle,
Betty Cooper and Doloris Coulter was sent to Simon A. Sanchez, where it will
be made available to all who wish to read it.[9]

No chapter on the Guam Assembly walkout would be complete without
a more detailed description of Carlos Taitano, the young Assemblyman
quoted in the United Press March 5 story that has been compared with the
Emerson's "shot heard round the world." In a poem about the Battle of Lex-
ington and Concord, Ralph Waldo Emerson had written: "Here once the
embattled farmers stood / And fired the shot heard round the world."[10] In
other words, the determination of the American colonists at Concord led
to the establishment of a new nation on earth and encouraged worldwide
movements toward democracy. Without Taitano and his telegrams to the
United Press and Associated Press in Hawai'i, news of the walkout might
never have been known — at least not until much later. Without Collier and
the Institute of Ethnic Affairs in Washington, its shock value and its impact
on moving the Organic Act of Guam through the United States Congress
would not have been nearly as great.

We in Washington did not know Carlos Taitano in 1949. We met him
and his wife, Marian Johnston Taitano, in Washington in 1950 and became
good friends. He was then a law student at George Washington University.

Guam Assemblyman
Carlos P. Taitano pub-
licized the 1949 Guam
Congress walkout
through the UP and
AP in Honolulu and
became known to many
as "Mr. Organic Act."

In the year 2000, I met him again in Guam at the 50th Anniversary of the
Organic Act. Some of what appears here I learned in 2005 from phone
conversations and papers he sent me as I was working on this book.

The decision to stage a walkout, Taitano told me, was not an easy one
for him and other members of the Guam Assembly to make. All activities
in Guam, including communications with the outside world, were under
Navy control. For example, before setting foot on Guam at that time everyone, including returning Chamorros, had to obtain security clearance
from the Navy. Also, there was no such thing as freedom of the press. The
only newspaper published locally was the *Navy News*. From experience,
Guamanians knew that retaliation for anything that displeased the Navy
could be quick and severe. Consequently, the Assemblymen were afraid of
repercussions that might result from walking out of the legislature. Nothing even remotely approaching this revolt had ever occurred during the
previous fifty years of naval government. Carlos was younger than most
Assemblymen. He was convinced that if the political neglect of his people
was brought to the attention of the American public, the U.S. Congress
would act.

One of the relatively few islanders who could trace his ancestry to the original Chamorro settlers of the Mariana Islands, in 1936 Carlos had been sent by his family from Guam to Honolulu at age nineteen to finish his secondary education at McKinley High School and enter the University of Hawai'i, where he became a premed student. He graduated with a Bachelor of Science degree in 1941. He has since written that he was shocked to see "the enormous differences between the U.S. administration of Guam and the U.S. administration of Hawaii, [the differences] between an arbitrary military government at home and a democratic civilian government in Hawaii."[11]

On December 21, 1941, Carlos joined the Honolulu police force as a chemist in the crime laboratory, a position he resigned on April 21, 1943, to join the United States Army. Until the end of the war he served in the southwest Pacific as an infantry officer. While in the service, he learned President Franklin Delano Roosevelt had proclaimed that liberation of people under colonial rule was one of the goals of the war. Carlos believed this to include the Chamorros of Guam and vowed someday to return home and try to convince his fellow islanders to join him in aggressively demanding reforms.

Separated from the U.S. Army in 1948, Carlos did indeed go back to Guam. He was soon elected to the Guam Assembly, the lower house of the Guam Congress. In that capacity, he met two newsmen covering military affairs on Guam, one from the United Press and the other from the Associated Press. He invited them to where he was living and carefully explained what it was like under military rule in Guam by contrast with what he had seen in Hawai'i. He told them that something was sure to happen soon that would bring about change, and he implored them to publicize it. Asked what he had in mind, Carlos said he knew then of nothing specific. The reporters emphatically warned him that any incident had to involve civil and political rights and be newsworthy enough for the wire services to carry it. At the same time, they agreed to help and told Carlos how to reach them in Honolulu.

When the Guam Assembly revolt was building, Carlos saw in the proposed walkout something big enough for the wire services. And when the walkout actually happened, he quietly slipped away without telling the others and telegraphed the two reporters. The result was the United Press report that appeared in the *Washington Post* and the *New York Times*.

After the news reached those two metropolitan newspapers, the Navy

Governor Charles A. Pownall wanted to appoint a new Guam Assembly after the walkout but was dissuaded by Navy Secretary John L. Sullivan.

could not prevent disclosure of future developments. With continuing help from Carlos for the next two weeks, the Honolulu newspapers followed developments closely and carried the most significant happenings under banner headlines across the top of their front pages. When Naval Governor Rear Admiral Pownall called a special session of the Guam Congress, Carlos told the UP, as quoted in the March 11, 1949, *Honolulu Advertiser,* that he did not expect the Assembly to attend. Francisco B. Leon Guerrero, a more senior member of the Guam Congress, was quoted in the same article as saying that operation of the legislature would be a "farce" until the United States passed an organic act.

There were no further reports about Guam in the Washington papers, but an Associated Press dispatch printed in Hawai'i on March 16 verified that members of the Assembly did not return and while the Council members showed up and listened politely to the governor, they, too, voted to adjourn until the U.S. Congress granted Guam an organic act.

An AP dispatch on March 23 related that the governor had "booted out" thirty-four of the thirty-six Assemblymen because they had not answered his call to return to duty. One was excused because he was in the States on business; one other refused to join. Pownall then asked each village commissioner to submit three names from his district. From this list, he proposed to name a new Assembly.

Taitano was quoted in the March 23 dispatch explaining that the revolt had grown out of three major grievances: (1) arbitrary rule by naval government; (2) lack of a constitution or document "anywhere" guaranteeing civil rights, and (3) lack of a court of appeal beyond the Secretary of the Navy. "Guamanians feel this kind of government is fit only for conquered peoples," he said.

As volunteer spokesman for the Guam Assembly in 1949, Carlos Taitano quickly became well known. He was so connected with this catalytic action of the Guam Congress that many on the island began calling him "Mr. Organic Act" — and still do.

By the end of March, we at the Institute had the full story of the Guam Congress revolt. We pieced it together from various contacts and printed it as one long "News Note" in our March–April 1949 Institute of Ethnic Affairs *News Letter,* which was also widely distributed in Washington and Guam. Because it gave the disparate facts coherence and the incident is of such historical interest, I have reprinted it as Appendix 15.

Riley H. Allen of the *Honolulu Star Bulletin,* on March 29, wrote a long editorial calling the walkout "Guam's 'Boston Tea Party.'" While recommending civilian administration and an organic act, he noted that "some high-placed navy officers want the general term 'executive agency' substituted for the more specific term 'civilian agency.' By this they hope to avert or at least delay the transfer from navy to the department of the interior."

Believing the mainland public should have more of the facts, I submitted a 27-inch article to the *Washington Post* that the editors accepted and printed with my by-line in their Sunday paper, April 3, 1949. It started as follows and may be read in its entirety in Appendix 16.

Guam Rebels at New Navy "Rule"

Four years after Agana, the capital of Guam, was reduced to ruins in the Pacific war, the Guam Congress Building emerged from the rubble, built by the Navy with American taxpayers' dollars.

Dedication of this building by Gov. Charles A. Pownall last July marked what Guamanians hoped would be a new epoch in their history. Eleven months before, Admiral Pownall had appeared before the Congress, meeting in a Quonset hut, to proclaim its authority increased from advisory to legislative status, as decreed by Navy Secretary John L. Sullivan.

Now less than a year since that building went into use, the lower house has considered its legislative powers so curtailed by the same Governor who proclaimed them that the members have voted to adjourn until the United States clarifies Guam's political status and protects their rights by act of Congress. . . .

. . . The issue is so explosive that it is regarded in some quarters as likely to bring to a head the transfer of administration of Guam to a civilian agency. . . .

A second editorial entitled, "Guam Needs Congressional Attention" was published in the *Star-Bulletin* on April 23, 1949.

The *New York Times* chimed in with an editorial on May 16, 1948, noting that the organic act adopted by the Guam Congress on March 5 had been forwarded by the Navy to the U.S. Congress "but it is still far from enactment. A matter as important as this should not be buried in channels." This gave me an opportunity to elaborate on what was happening with the Joint Committee supposedly set to go to Guam. In a letter to the *Times* published on May 23, 1949, I wrote:

Forgotten Guam
Investigation by Our Legislators Is Urged or Enactment of Legislation.

If an investigation is all that Congress can promise Guam this year, then that investigation should be set up and secured beyond doubt. If busy legislators are lukewarm to a 9,000-mile trip to spend a few hours on an island, then it might be suggested that organic legislation for Guam, to which there is no known opposition, be enacted without further delay.

Guamanians, tired of waiting for Congress to come to them, now are considering a resolution that would appropriate $10,000 for two delegates to go to Washington. This should indicate how the people feel about their island, which the *New York Times* three years ago called "forgotten Guam." (See Appendix 17.)

The walkout actually ended on April 2, 1949, when Secretary of the Navy John Sullivan advised Governor Pownall that he should invite the elected Assemblymen back, that appointing replacements was not acceptable. The Councilmen (representatives in the upper house) had agreed to stay out beginning March 6, 1949, in support of the Assemblymen. After some maneuvering, members of both houses (known as the Guam Congress) returned a month later and resumed business. But, as reported above, reverberations in the stateside press continued even after they returned. And the Guamanian nationals were more convinced than ever that their civil rights would not be guaranteed until they were given American citizenship and an organic act ordaining civilian government.

Taitano's communication with the UP and the AP on March 5, 1949, the day of the Guam Assembly walkout, was indeed a key element in the success of that event. As Robert F. Rogers wrote in *Destiny's Landfall,* "Members of the U.S. Congress queried the White House for explanations. Pownall had unwittingly done exactly what the reformers had hoped for."[12]

The Guam Congress walkout was certainly a turning point in the Pacific islands' political destiny. It was a catalyst. But another seventeen months would pass before the goals outlined above would be achieved. The two Guam delegates to the U.S. Congress mentioned in my May 1949 letter to the editor of the *New York Times* would be named and funded. They were Francisco B. Leon Guerrero and Antonio B. Won Pat. Guam Assemblywoman Concepcion (Connie) Barrett would come to Washington at her own expense in April 1949 and testify before the Senate Subcommittee on Territorial and Insular Affairs. Mrs. Agueda Johnston, Assistant Superintendent of Schools, would also make a trip to the nation's capital at her own expense and meet with influential officials in September 1949. A six-man House Committee, headed by Representative John E. Miles (D., N.Mex.) would finally leave San Francisco on Nov. 2, 1949, to make a study of the Pacific islands. They returned early in December prepared to recommend organic legislation, at least for Guam, but at the end of the year the First Session of the 81st Congress was about to adjourn, and six more months would pass before the law would be enacted.

Chapter 12

Connie Barrett Goes to Washington

Concepcion (Connie) Barrett was one of the first women to own a business in Guam. She was also one of the first women elected to the Guam Assembly. In the spring of 1949, she combined a buying trip to New York City with a visit to Washington and in her own way made a difference. But before I discuss her activity on Capitol Hill, let me tell a little about what everyday life in Guam was like in those days.

Nothing was depressing Guamanians more than the snail-like pace with which their own rehabilitation was proceeding by contrast with the rapid construction of military housing and other facilities on Guam. Accustomed in prewar days to comfortable and aesthetically pleasing homes, Guamanians for five years since recapture of the island by the Navy in 1944 had been living in shacks made of rough recovered lumber with corrugated iron roofs and no built-in bath or toilet facilities. A few houses had been built, but the shortage of building materials, inadequacies in city planning, injustice, and uncertainties involved in the settlement of land ownership, had delayed new construction. A letter to the editor of the *Guam Echo* from a Guamanian in the fall of 1948 stated:

> Most tragic of all sights are the hundred or so dilapidated, leaky, canvas-topped shanties of Agat, built in 1946 as temporary (six-months) shelters for typhoon victims. Behind the shanty town rises the new city with paved streets, lighting, and sewerage — but few homes. Here is the skeleton of a city, lacking houses to fill out the empty blocks.
>
> The $6,000,000 appropriated by the U.S. Congress for rehabilitation of Guam was spent almost entirely in the capital city, Agana, for the Guam Congress building, a police station, city streets, lights, water, and sewerage. Little evidence of rehabilitation even of public buildings and public facilities exists other than here and New Agat. Generally speaking, paved roads lead only to military installations.

Even in 1949, five years after the end of the war, most of the housing on Guam was built from scavenged materials. Paved roads led mostly to military installations.

By contrast, the temporary quarters for American personnel consist in the main of spacious, well-equipped Quonsets which seem attractive in comparison with Guamanian housing. A large number of permanent single and multiple dwellings have been built for military and mainland civilian personnel. Prefabricated concrete single homes and duplexes are being built with speed. Such units are described in the *Guam News* [formerly the *Navy News*] of Mar. 6 as having a kitchen equipped with electric range and refrigerator, and aluminum cabinets above and below the extended drainboard; a bath with both shower and tub and chromium fittings; a utility room with laundry tub and hot water heater; two bedrooms with Hollywood style beds, and so on.

Guamanians would like to see some of the materials going into Navy quarters made available to them for rebuilding their own homes. Prewar homes in Inarajan and other villages provide irrefutable evidence of the highly developed skill and aesthetic sense of Guamanian masons.

All they need is the building materials. They have the know-how. And many have the money to build.[1]

We published this in the March 15, 1949, *Guam Echo,* along with the following letter about the need for a new high school, written by Simon Sanchez, Guam superintendent of schools.

One of the crying needs on Guam is the construction of a permanent high school building to take care of approximately 1,500 students. It is estimated that the type of building needed will cost between $2,500,000 and $3,000,000. Island revenues are such that the Guam Government could not hope to undertake such a project. Money for such a building could come from the U.S. Congress.

Before the war, Guam boasted a reinforced concrete high school in the heart of Agana. This building, like all other buildings in the city, was destroyed by bombardments of the U.S. armed forces in the retaking of Guam. Students since have been attending schools in Quonset huts.

On Guam there are twenty-one elementary schools and one high school. There are over 9,100 students and 300 teachers. Education is compulsory between the ages of seven and sixteen. Approximately forty-five young men and women are attending colleges in the United States, many on scholarships.

Guamanians strongly believe that education is the fly-wheel of success in the democracy championed by the United States Government. It is our sincere hope that American people throughout the United States will give consideration to the building of a high school to be dedicated to the youths of Guam who suffered through the thirty-two months of enemy occupation during the war.[2]

Earlier, in the December–January 1949 *Guam Echo,* we had written about the disparity in wages paid Guamanians compared with statesiders employed as contract laborers. A letter to the editor from Jose C. Sablan, received in October, had recounted his experience in trying to get a job as an electrician on Guam after he had been living in the United States. He had enclosed a printed form from the U.S. Naval Air Station, Patuxent River, Maryland, stating, "In view of the fact that it is not the policy of the Commander Marianas Area to accept for recruitment applications from Guamanians, Filipinos and American-Japanese, Encl. (A) [your application] is returned herewith."[3] Sablan's letter to me accompanying the form read:

In 1946 the Navy Department reported to the United Nations that the Guamanians were treated in all respects similarly to the Americans except in wages and that was due to the relative difference in their standards of living. The argument does not exist any longer. The standard of living of the Guamanians compares favorably with the average standard in the States. Guamanians use comfortable beds, chairs, and other furniture from the States, wear decent dresses and clothes from the States, and pay higher for foods than the Americans on the island.[4]

I took these documents to Navy Under Secretary Kenney for explanation on October 26, 1948. He expressed surprise at the denial of the application and even with the aid of responsible officers under him was unable to explain it. He consented to have the Navy Office of Island Governments get the facts and advise me whether the policy was still in effect. A long letter to me from that Navy office, dated January 17, 1949, attempted to explain the policy but in reality made no change. We printed the last paragraph in the December–January 1949 *Guam Echo*: "The present situation involving a dual standard of compensation on Guam is not considered satisfactory. However, it appears to be the best available compromise between present necessity and the future welfare of the Guamanian population in a temporary situation that resulted from dislocations of war, the need to build a military base and to rehabilitate civilian facilities of the island."[5]

The policy was patently unfair. Why shouldn't Guamanians be hired to help rehabilitate their own island, we asked. Instead, more than 20,000 foreign laborers were being imported. Why shouldn't Guamanians be paid wages equal to those of the imported workers? Maybe then they could buy and pay for the material needed for their own houses — if the Navy would sell it to them. Maybe more of them could start their own small businesses. Absolutely no allowance was made for the hardships suffered by the Guamanians during two and a half years of occupation by the Japanese. Why didn't the Navy government take this into consideration when it set the postwar wage rates? Instead, the Guamanians were treated like slaves on their own plantation.

Despite the discrimination, a few Guamanians did indeed establish their own businesses. One was a most personable young woman, Concepcion (Connie) Barrett, who, with her husband, started a dress shop and simultaneously was elected to the Guam Congress. She, like F. B. Leon Guerrero, came to the United States in April 1949 and, in her own way, moved legislation for Guam along.

Concepcion Cruz Barrett was one of Guam's first businesswomen and also one of the first women elected to the Guam Assembly. She testified before a U.S. House subcommittee in Washington in 1949, urging passage of an organic act.

Connie went first to New York City to do some buying for her dress shop, and while there was entertained by Laura Thompson and John Collier. The three talked about pending legislation and the importance of Connie speaking to members of the U.S. Congress. Mrs. Barrett came to the States not as a representative of the Guam Congress but as an individual. As she explained, the Guam legislature had no funds for sending an official representative to the nation's capital, so she decided to come on her own, thus making her business trip serve a dual purpose. Upon her arrival in Washington, she went almost directly to the Institute office.

The organic act legislation drafted by Navy and Interior had finally been endorsed by the Budget Bureau, and on May 3 Monroe M. Redden (D., N.C.), then chairman of the House Subcommittee on Territorial and Insular Possessions, introduced it as H.R. 4499. Anxious to hear from Mrs. Barrett while she was still in Washington, Representative Redden hastily set the date for a subcommittee hearing just two days after her arrival. It would be held on May 5, 1949. The bill represented the administration's stand on the legislation, and the number of witnesses was kept to a minimum. Only Interior Secretary J. A. Krug, Navy Captain P. G. Hale, and Mrs. Barrett were called to testify. I accompanied Connie to The Hill, so I could report what transpired in the *Guam Echo*.

Secretary Krug was called to testify first. He read from a prepared statement and said, among other things:

> The 81st Congress has an opportunity to put an end to our neglect of the rights of these people over the last 50 years. I am certain that if the members of the Committee could visit these islands, talk to the people, familiarize themselves with conditions in the islands, no doubt would remain in your minds that organic legislation should promptly be enacted. If such a survey of the islands is possible in the very immediate future, I would strongly recommend it. If not, then I urge that the bills be speedily passed on the basis of the record made at the previous hearings.[6]

At this point Chairman Redden acknowledged that the House of Representatives probably would not have time at this session to consider the Guam legislation due to the number of other important bills pending. He suggested that a trip to the islands might be arranged during the summer after Congress adjourned. Secretary Krug said his trip there in 1947 had been an eye-opener. Much as he would like speedy enactment of the legislation, he wanted the committee satisfied as to the facts.

Speaking for the Navy Department, Captain Hale said he had no prepared statement due to the short notice of the hearing. In general, he said, the Navy was in agreement with Interior Department on the legislative needs of the Guamanians and was anxious for prompt enactment of organic legislation.

Before Mrs. Barrett was called to testify, Chairman Redden announced that the subcommittee just that morning had received a cable from representatives of the Guam Congress. He asked Representative Reva Bosone (D., Utah) to read it:

CABLE FROM GUAM

THIS MESSAGE FOR SUBCOMMITTEE QUOTE GUAM CONGRESS AND PEOPLE ANXIOUS AND EXPECTANT EARLY ACTION BY PRESENT CONGRESS AS PROVIDED BY OVER HALF CENTURY TREATY STOP GUAM CONGRESS UNANIMOUS IN RESOLUTION AND ORGANIC ACT STOP FAVORABLE ACTION BY EARLY ENACTMENT BY UNITED STATES CONGRESS WILL JUSTIFY TRUST

Representative Monroe M. Redden chaired the House Subcommittee on Territorial and Insular Possessions and introduced H.R. 4499.

IN GOD AND AMERICA AND WIDELY RECOGNIZED AMERICAN
PRINCIPLES AND IDEALS.

> Antonio B. Won Pat
> Frank B. Leon Guerrero
> Carlos P. Taitano[7]

The subcommittee pronounced the message very well timed. Then Redden invited Mrs. Barrett to speak. In her prepared statement, she said, among other things:

My plea is not for financial help for the 26,000 Guamanians. It is for something more vital to our community life, and that is for (1) a government under law, (2) American citizenship, and (3) civilian administration. The passage of an organic act, such as the one under discussion today, would accomplish this. . . . We feel that ratification of the Treaty of Paris in 1899 implied a moral and binding obligation on the part of Congress to determine our status. We have been ruled for half a century by the Navy under an Executive Order consisting of two sentences, whereby the Secretary of the Navy and the Naval

Governor of Guam are vested with supreme authority. Even today there is posted in the halls of the Guam Congress building a proclamation signed by the present Governor, which, as I recall, says that "all executive, legislative, and judicial authority in Guam is vested in me as Governor of Guam." We need an organic act so that we may know, among other things, the security of a government by law and not the insecurity of a government by men; so that the Guam Congress may know its responsibilities and powers; and so that we may have courts separated from the executive power.[8]

Connie provided the subcommittee with a copy of the organic act passed by the Guam Assembly on March 5 and by the Guam Council on an earlier date. Both had given it unanimous approval and voted to send it on to the U.S. Congress. In conclusion, she invited the subcommittee to visit Guam and expressed the hope that organic legislation would be enacted without delay. The subcommittee spent more than thirty minutes questioning her about the island economy, rehabilitation, land problems, banking, education, medical services, and shipping. It was an exhilarating day for both of us. We went back to the Institute office to tell Betty about it and to begin writing the *Guam Echo* that we would airmail to more than three hundred leaders on Guam the next day.

In the week that Connie Barrett was in Washington, Betty and I made arrangements for her to talk with key officials everywhere. She was both informative and charming. The names and titles of the persons with whom she spoke constituted a literal Washington "Who's Who" with respect to the organic act. We felt they all deserved credit for moving the necessary legislation along, so we devoted one whole column of the *Guam Echo* to listing them. Because those names need to go down in history, that column is provided in Appendix 18.

On a far less favorable note, we found it necessary to report that a United Press interview with Mrs. Barrett appearing in the April 30 *Guam News,* published by the Navy in Agana, contained misquotes and misinformation. Mrs. Barrett had given that interview to the United Press in Washington. The *Guam News* had taken it off the wire and printed it under the headline, "Mrs. Barrett Asks for Organic Act," which was true. And some of her quotes were accurate. But a carbon copy of the wired dispatch proved that the following paragraph did not go out from Washington.

Mrs. Barrett apparently was unaware that in possessions now operated by the Department of Interior, to which it is proposed to give Guam, the same objections are being raised to the powers of the Secretary of the Interior, who appoints the Governor, and from whose decisions appeals are made to the Secretary of the Interior instead of the Secretary of the Navy. In Puerto Rico recently a violent outburst was voiced against both the Interior chief and the elected governor, whom it was charged was controlled by him.[9]

All this was a fiction of somebody's imagination. Apparently, there were still Navy writers or editors in Guam determined to persuade the islanders that a transfer of their government to the Department of the Interior would be a bad thing.

When James P. Davis, chief of the Division of Territories and Islands in the Department of the Interior, was apprised of this paragraph, he gave a statement to the *Guam Echo* explaining that the governor of Puerto Rico is elected by the people of the island, not appointed by the Secretary of the Interior. The present governor, he said, was elected by 62 percent of the voters and responsible only to them. Mr. Davis continued:

> The Secretary of the Interior has absolutely no power to annul or change any act passed by any territorial legislature — Hawaiian, Alaska, Puerto Rican, or Virgin Islands. The Puerto Rican legislature may enact a bill by a two-thirds vote over the Governor's veto. Should the Governor continue to object to a bill after a two-thirds vote, the measure goes to the President of the United States for decision, not the Interior Secretary. . . .
>
> There has been no protest of any kind against the present Government of Puerto Rico. Of course, political opponents of the Administration frequently oppose and criticize as they do in the United States. But there has been nothing like a "violent outburst" against anybody.[10]

We printed the above statement in the May 6, 1949, *Echo,* setting the record straight and knowing the political leaders in Guam would read it. Mr. Davis remarked to me that this was not the first time erroneous statements about Puerto Rico and other U.S. territories had been circulated on Guam. He also observed that the *Guam News,* the Navy paper, was the only newspaper on Guam, and that in 1947 Guamanians had contributed $50,000 through local taxes to support it.

Ever since the Guam Assembly walkout on March 5, 1949, things had been happening in Washington. Congressional committees were beginning to sit up and take more notice of Guam. Even though we didn't know it, President Truman had asked the State Department for an assessment of the loyalty of the people of Guam, and the report had come back favorable without question. Interior was pressing forward with the organic act it was supposed to write. Even the Navy in Washington was becoming more cooperative. After F. B. Leon Guerrero's visit to the office of Under Secretary Kenney in August 1948, the restraint against civilian administration of the Pacific islands seemed to be softening. But officers in the field were holding back, and President Truman was losing patience. It was time for more definitive action. In May, Truman took the bull by the horns.

Chapter 13

Truman Decides by Decree

In a letter to the Secretary of the Interior dated May 14, 1949, and made public four days later, President Truman directed that Guam be transferred from the Navy to the Interior Department within a year regardless of the status of pending legislation, and that American Samoa and the Trust Territories be transferred within two or three years after that. Truman's letter was the linchpin in all that the Guamanians and the Institute of Ethnic Affairs had been working for since 1945:

> I have today informed the Director of the Bureau of the Budget that the drafts of organic legislation for Guam and American Samoa, prepared by the Department of the Interior, have my approval. The Department of the Interior will have the responsibility of presenting the measures to the Congress. I asked the Secretary of the Navy to assist you. . . .[1]

His letter was printed in full in the May 27, 1949, *Guam Echo* (see Appendix 19). We said it "marked the climax in a four-year postwar effort to achieve civilian government for Guam."

A side bar added that, even though this was "the most significant [Pacific Islands] policy announcement in years," it received only a fifteen-line notice in the *Washington Post* and not even one line in the *New York Times*. Collier editorialized that getting attention drawn to Guam was "like sailing a stick boat upstream." We suggested that the Guamanians double and redouble their efforts to get their organic act passed.[2]

Even without prompting, the Guam Congress had on May 21 passed a resolution thanking President Truman for the transfer, "regardless of what [the U.S.] Congress does about organic legislation for the islands." It was forwarded to the president more than a month later, on June 30, with a letter of transmittal signed by Acting Secretary of the Navy John T. Koehler, strongly recommending that members of the Congress visit the islands before making the transfer.[3]

A companion resolution passed by the Guam Congress asked that a representative group of islanders be allowed to participate in planning the transfer. The Guam Congress was prepared to send two delegates to Washington. Congressman Redden, chairman of the House Subcommittee, notified Guam Congresswoman Barrett that little could be accomplished by Guam delegates coming to Washington that could not be accomplished otherwise, but should they come, "I assure you that my Committee will extend them every courtesy."[4]

The possibility that there would still be foot-dragging by the Navy on the transfer seemed evident when I called Captain Hale's office for the May 27, 1949, *Guam Echo* and found that the organic act approved by the Guam Congress on March 5 had not yet reached members of the U.S. Congress through regular channels. It had been forwarded to the White House on April 6, Captain Hale said, but had not been sent to Congress because the memorial accompanying it called for transmittal "by the President." This seemed to me to be buck-passing of the first order and something of a technicality. Fortunately, Mrs. Barrett had brought a copy with her to Washington and hand-carried it to the House Subcommittee hearing on May 5, so they had it anyway.

By contrast with the Navy, after fifty-one years of indifference the United States Congress now seemed poised to move ahead. Only four days after the president's letter had been sent to the Secretaries of the Interior and Navy, on May 18, 1949, Senator Joseph C. O'Mahoney (D., Wyo.), chairman of the Senate Interior and Insular Affairs Committee, introduced two bills — S. 1892 and S. 1893 — for civilian government of Guam and American Samoa, respectively. They were identical to the Redden bills introduced in the House, May 3, 1949, numbered H.R. 4499 for Guam and H.R. 4500 for Samoa.

More than a month passed before writers at the *Washington Post* took editorial notice of President Truman's May 14 letter. When they did, legislation for the organic acts necessary got another good push. A June 14, 1949, *Post* editorial reprinted in the July 30 *Echo* noted: "A trip to the Pacific islands as the guests of the taxpayers is always attractive, but we doubt that a congressional survey is necessary in this instance. The time has come when civilian rule for these islands ought not to be further postponed for the sake of squeezing in another junket."[5]

Late in July, the proposed organic act for Guam received still another strong endorsement. B. J. Bordallo, president of the Guam Council (the

B. J. Bordallo was an early advocate of civil rights for the people of Guam. In 1937, he and F. B. Leon Guerrero went together to Washington to testify on behalf of U.S. citizenship for the Chamorros. He later worked hard for an organic act providing civilian administration of Guam.

upper house of the Guam Congress), visited Washington, accompanied by his daughter, Barbara, and his sons, Ricardo and Paul, all of whom were attending college in California. They visited Capitol Hill and urged early enactment of the pending legislation.

United Nations Trusteeship Council interest in the rest of Micronesia provided additional momentum. For three days in July, Rear Admiral Leon S. Fiske, Deputy High Commissioner of the Trust Territory, was at Lake Success answering questions about the islands formerly mandated to the Japanese. The U.S. State Department was preparing an organic act for those islands.

The logjam had been broken by President Truman's letter, and developments now began to come hard and fast. The big news for the July 30, 1949, *Guam Echo* was that a civilian governor of Guam, to be appointed by the president at the recommendation of Interior, would take office about

John L. Sullivan was Secretary of the Navy in 1949 when a date for the transfer of administration of Guam was worked out. An orderly transfer to the Department of the Interior followed.

September 1, 1949. Navy and Interior had agreed on a date for the transfer of administration. It would be July 1, 1950. Until then, the new governor would report to the Secretary of the Navy.

James P. Davis, director of Interior's Division of Territories and Island Possessions, told the Associated Press on July 14 that all naval personnel engaged in Guam government would be replaced by July 1, 1950, either with Guamanians or, if qualified Guamanians were not available, with civilians from Hawai'i or the mainland.[6]

This, and more, had been spelled out in a Memorandum of Understanding between the Navy and the Interior Departments, printed in full in the August 31, 1949, *Guam Echo*. It may be read in Appendix 20.

"An orderly transfer." I remember hearing Emil Sady use this phrase over and over. It became a kind of mantra, like a Hindu chant or mystical invocation, which indeed it was. Navy and Interior in Washington were working very hard to make the change go smoothly. Plans were again being made for a joint committee of the House and Senate to visit the islands, departing from San Francisco on November 3, 1949. Representative J. Hardin

J. Hardin Peterson (D., Pa.) became chairman of the House Public Lands Committee in 1949 and had the honor of having his name on the Organic Act of Guam when it was passed in 1950.

Peterson (D., Pa.) had become chairman of the House Public Lands Committee in April when Andrew L. Somers (D., N.Y.) died. Peterson would head the joint committee.

August brought the name of the new civilian governor: Carlton Skinner, then Director of Information at the Department of the Interior. He had accompanied Secretary Krug on his swing through the Pacific islands in 1947. Though formal appointment had not yet been made by President Truman, the *Washington Post* reported that the Navy Department had nominated Skinner on August 31. We carried the news in a box on page 1 of our *Guam Echo* of that same date.

August also brought some very disconcerting news. The House Appropriations Committee was rejecting Interior's request for funds to effect the transfer for lack of congressional authorization for the change. The request amounted to only $600,000 to cover the appointment of the civilian governor of Guam, his staff, and replace military personnel as soon as possible, plus $115,000 for related island activities — $715,000 in all.

At a subcommittee hearing on the bill, Michael J. Kirwan (D., Ohio), chairman, asked, "Is it not quite a while for the Navy to be in charge of an island from 1898 down to 1949; fifty years? And then to want to change it almost overnight?"[7] Interior's James Davis cited the 1947 agreement of the Secretaries of State, War, Navy, and Interior approving civilian administration, and the May 14, 1949, letter of the president directing the transfer regardless of the status of pending legislation. This was anything but an "overnight" change. Nevertheless, when the Appropriations Subcommittee reported the bill out, it wrote:

> The government of the civilian population of Guam has been entrusted to the Navy Department for more than 50 years. There is evidence that the Navy has done an excellent job. The Navy Department budget contains funds for governing Guam during 1950.
>
> Legislation was sought, but not enacted, during the preceding Congress to provide statutory authority for the orderly establishment of civilian self-government on Guam. Legislation for the same purpose is also currently pending before the Public Lands Committee. Without awaiting the enactment of legislation authorizing a change in the government of Guam, the aforementioned budget estimate was submitted in an effort to obtain funds for the Interior Department, the appropriation of which is not authorized by law. Hearings conducted by the committee revealed that this proposal was but the initial step in a matter of great national importance. The hearings also made it apparent that inadequate information has been obtained to warrant even the initiation of so important a move, and the committee is unable to recommend the appropriations requested. When Congress has enacted legislation covering these important considerations and when adequate factual data is available, further consideration might well be given to proposals of this nature.[8]

The strong hold the Navy had on the island — and on some committees of the Congress — was clearly evident once again. Hurdle after hurdle had to be jumped before civilian government could be attained.

When the appropriations bill came to the floor of the House on August 19, 1949, Representative Fred L. Crawford, one of Guam's most consistent supporters of civil rule, said:

> Personally, I think that the Congress has been trifling very seriously with the people of those areas (Guam, Samoa, and the Trust Territory) because upon two or three occasions they have been promised that committees would come

out there and hold hearings on legislation, which is referred to here in this report, but the committees have never gone to hold the hearings. As a result, the legislation is held up here in the legislative committees. Within the last three or four weeks efforts have been made to bring about progress in this matter, and as late as this current week the chairman of the Senate committee, which has jurisdiction over the legislative part of the work in that other body, informed me that he had been unable to get a single member of his committee to agree to go to the islands along with House Members and make the study looking forward to the recommendation of legislation which would authorize appropriations of this nature.[9]

Considering that Representative Crawford was now of the minority party, it is a wonder that he actually went to the floor of the House and spoke out. He could have left everything to the Democrats, as he had suggested he might back in January when I asked him if he was going to reintroduce his bill for an organic act in the new Congress and he said he was going to wait a while and see what the administration was going to do. This support shows the fine character of the man. He cared about the island people, and he believed in democracy. He wasn't going to let politics stand in the way of what was right. Nevertheless, the House passed the supplemental appropriations bill without providing for the transfer of funds.

Knowing this could be really troublesome to the people of Guam, Collier wrote an editorial for the August *Guam Echo* in which he pointed out that Guam was lucky in that it didn't have to be dependent on federal appropriations. Local revenues were constantly increasing, and use of them alone would give Guamanians the power to decide what services they wanted and how these services should be managed. He wrote:

Guam, with a local government of its own, will not have to depend on special largesse of Congress. It can accept only those Federal aids which go as matters of rights to all citizens of the United States — citizenship for Guamanians is taken for granted here. And for the rest, it can, if necessary, meet its own costs of government.

And what an advantage for Guam this will be! It will insure (and perhaps nothing else can insure) real local self-government for Guam. Self-government divorced from control over the social services and over administration and fiscal policies is a shadow of self-government, no more. And self-government dependent on the annual favor or disfavor of appropriation committees of Congress is less than a shadow: it is a misery. . . .[10]

Collier knew whereof he spoke! Year after year as Indian Commissioner he had had to go to the Congress and *beg* for appropriations for the Bureau of Indian Affairs. He could see what a blessing it would be if Guam could pay for local government out of its own resources.

The *Washington Post,* having by this time taken quite an interest in what was happening to Guam and the other Pacific islands, on September 4, 1949, published an editorial noting rejection of the $715,000:

> The denial of this fund does not, as the Appropriations subcommittee apparently thought, prevent the transfer. It does, however, make the changeover infinitely more difficult, inviting the very confusion that ought to be avoided in any such occurrence.
>
> It is to be hoped that the Senate, when the request comes before it, will show a better comprehension of the factors involved and will permit adequate preparations to be made in advance. . . .[11]

All was not lost. The pendulum swung again in the direction of civilian government when on Sept. 7, 1949, President Truman issued Executive Order No. 10,077 transferring Guam from the Navy to Interior. It was printed in the September 15 *Guam Echo* and is reprinted here:

EXECUTIVE ORDER NO. 10,077

TRANSFER OF THE ADMINISTRATION OF THE ISLAND OF
GUAM FROM THE SECRETARY OF THE NAVY TO THE
SECRETARY OF THE INTERIOR

WHEREAS the Island of Guam was placed under control of the Department of the Navy by Executive Order No. 108-A of December 23, 1898; and

WHEREAS a committee composed of the Secretaries of State, War, the Navy, and the Interior recommended on June 18, 1947, that administrative responsibility for the Island of Guam be transferred to a civilian agency of the Government at the earliest practicable date as determined by the President; and

WHEREAS plans for the orderly transfer of administrative responsibility for the Island of Guam from the Secretary of the Navy to the Secretary of the Interior are embodied in a memorandum of understanding between the Department of the Navy and the Department of the Interior, approved by me on August 10, 1949, and it is the view of the two departments, as expressed in that memorandum, that such transfer should take effect on July 1, 1950; and

WHEREAS the transfer of administration of the Island of Guam from the

Secretary of the Navy to the Secretary of the Interior, effective July 1, 1950, appears to be in the public interest:

NOW, THEREFORE, by virtue of the authority vested in me as President of the United States, it is ordered as follows:

1. The administration of the Island of Guam is hereby transferred from the Secretary of the Navy to the Secretary of the Interior, such transfer to become effective on July 1, 1950.
2. The Department of the Navy and the Department of the Interior shall proceed with the plans for the transfer of the administration of the Island of Guam as embodied in the above mentioned memorandum of understanding between the two departments.
3. When the transfer of administration made by this order becomes effective, the Secretary of the Interior shall take such action as may be necessary and appropriate, and in harmony with applicable law, for the administration of civil government on the Island of Guam.
4. The executive department and agencies of the Government are authorized and directed to cooperate with the Department of the Navy and Interior in the effectuation of the provisions of this order.
5. The said Executive Order No. 108-A of December 23, 1898, is revoked, effective July 1, 1950.

> (Sgd.) Harry S. Truman
> The White House
> September 7, 1949[12]

Thus the stage was set for appointment of the first civilian governor of Guam. He had actually been installed four days before this document was signed.

Chapter 14

Skinner Becomes First Civilian Governor

Named Governor of Guam by President Truman on September 3, 1949, Carlton Skinner and his family left Washington on September 14 by ship expecting to arrive in Guam and take the oath of office about September 27.

Skinner was born in California in 1913 and graduated from the University of California, Los Angeles, in 1934. Before entering the federal government in 1938 as Assistant Director of Information, Department of Labor, he had been a staff correspondent for the United Press and *The Wall Street Journal*. On active duty with the U.S. Coast Guard from 1941 to 1945, Skinner received his permanent appointment as Lieutenant Commander USCG Reserve, on August 1, 1943. Upon discharge from military service, he joined the Department of the Interior as special assistant to Secretary Krug and Director of Information. He and Mrs. Skinner had two children, Franz Carlton, age four, and Andrea, age one.

Before the new governor left Washington, I interviewed him for the September 15, 1949, *Guam Echo*. When questioned about his program for Guam, Skinner said:

> My program is to run the government of Guam in the best possible fashion in the interests of the people of Guam. It would be presumptuous of me to announce a detailed program before arriving in Guam. I intend to familiarize myself with local conditions, consult with the Guam Congress, local leaders, and Navy officials so that the policies will be developed cooperatively — they will not be ones which I have brought in from the outside.[1]

Skinner said he felt organic legislation for Guam was most important and that he would do everything possible to bring it about. He was aware, of course, that the Senate Appropriations Committee, on September 12, had held hearings on the $715,000 requested to effect the transfer and, like the House Appropriations Committee before it, had raised questions about turning Guam over to the Interior before Congress passed an organic act.

Carlton S. Skinner became the first civilian governor of Guam in 1949.

He was also aware that he should prepare for a visit from a House committee in the fall.

Through the persistent efforts of Representatives Peterson, Redden, and Crawford during the First Session of the 81st Congress, a bipartisan House committee was named (see Appendix 21). "We want to get out in the villages, talk with the people and find out directly what they want," Crawford told me for the October 31, 1949, *Guam Echo.*[2]

Even before that trip could take place, however, with more unity of purpose than we had previously seen, the House Public Lands Committee on September 30 unanimously voted favorably on H.R. 4499, after deleting Section 22 providing that Guam should be represented in Washington by a Resident Commissioner. The bill was now ready for action on the floor of the House. This favorable action by the committee was probably prompted by President Truman's Executive Order of September 7, which set in motion the wheels of transfer. More than that, it was thought to have resulted from a deep desire to demonstrate that Congress was truly concerned about the needs of faraway voteless Guam. But with the House committee scheduled to visit Guam in November, the bill was set aside until January 1950.

In reporting these developments, we emphasized in the October *Guam Echo* that if Guamanians really wanted a Resident Commissioner, and we assumed they did, they should make this point clear to the visiting congressmen. Section 22 could then be reinserted when the bill came up for a vote.

A visit to Washington that fall by another of Guam's leading Chamorro residents helped prove to members of the Congress that the islanders were ready for a change in government. That person was Agueda I. Johnston, Assistant Superintendent of Schools on Guam. She came to Washington in late September 1949 and arrived in Washington during the week the House Public Lands Committee was considering H.R. 4499. By coincidence she came to the Institute office less than an hour after the bill was favorably reported out, on September 30. Her response to the news was, "I am very honored to be the first Guamanian to know."[3]

Betty and I found Mrs. Johnston likable immediately. She was easy to talk to and well informed. As we had done for Connie Barrett, we arranged for Mrs. Johnston to see several congressmen, including Representatives Crawford, Redden, Jenison, Engle, Kearns, and Delegate Farrington. Mrs. Johnston also spoke with Senator O'Mahoney's administrative assistant and clerks of the House and Senate Insular Affairs Committees.

On October 6, she was invited to pay a return call on Interior Secretary Krug. Two years before, while visiting Guam, he had been a guest in her home. She also met with James Davis, Emil Sady, and others in the Department of the Interior, as well as officials in the Department of State and the Budget Bureau. On October 14, she was a guest of Admiral and Mrs. Thornton C. Miller at a reception at The Navy Club in Washington honoring Admiral C. A. Pownall. All officers who had served on Guam during Pownall's administration as governor had been invited. Mrs. Johnston estimated that two hundred guests attended.

While in Washington, Mrs. Johnston was the house guest of Mr. and Mrs. Al Geiken. Mrs. Geiken was the former Magdalene Portusach, whose father was the naturalized American left in charge when the Navy took Guam during the Spanish-American War. (Nina Geiken, as she was known, subsequently became a good friend of Betty Winquest Cooper and myself through the Guam Territorial Society, which we helped found.)

While in New York, Mrs. Johnston attended at least one day of United

Nations meetings at Lake Success. She had met with Francis R. Sayre, U.S. representative on the Trusteeship Council, while in Washington.

Invited to New York by the Colliers, Mrs. Johnston represented Guam at the annual meeting of the Institute of Ethnic Affairs on October 9, 1949. It was held in offices of the Viking Fund on a Sunday afternoon and evening and attended by a capacity crowd of about sixty members and their guests. Dr. Laura Thompson, author of *Guam and Its People;* Peter Coleman, an American Samoan student in law school at Georgetown University; Emil Sady, chief of the Pacific branch of the Office of Territories in the Department of the Interior; Dr. John Useem, professor of anthropology at Michigan State University, who had done fieldwork in the Trust Territory; and Mrs. Johnston constituted a panel that discussed "Pacific Islands and Trust Territory: A Test of Democracy Abroad."

Dr. Thompson delivered a scholarly paper on "The Ethnic Institute's Effort in the Pacific: Accomplishment and Outlook." She reviewed the struggle for civil rights in Guam, Samoa, and the Trust Territory, stating in part:

> The Institute of Ethnic Affairs, three and a half years ago, chose as a field of primary application the far Pacific islands — Guam, American Samoa, and the American Trust Territory of the Pacific. We believed that the statistical smallness of these Islands and their peoples was no measure of their importance. They existed as America's overseas region for the exercise of trusteeship. They could become a moral asset and a demonstration ground for the democratic and creative application of trusteeship. Such a demonstration would have a worldwide value.
>
> Our effort had a near goal and a far goal. The near goal was civilian in place of naval administration, and organic acts, civil rights and domestic home rule for all the islanders. Opposed to this near goal stood one of the dominant power groups in Washington. With the help of the Chamorros of Guam and much other help, and through President Truman's devotion to civil rights, after three and a half years, the near goal is nearly won. Civil administration is assured. The far goal is yet in the future.
>
> Political rights have been won, or are assured if the effort to win them be continued. Political rights by themselves do not insure human and social well-being. The far result is the conservation of personality and culture by the Islanders, the adjustment by themselves of their societies within a balanced ecological structure. The question is how shall that be assured.

From the beginning, the Institute has brought research to bear on these long-range, continuing problems of the Islands. Trusteeship requires research and the research must attend not only to the islanders but to the web of life they are a part of—the animals, plants, water, soil. Administration must be of the grass-roots type, but it must be experimental and informed with science. It must be democratic in spirit and not only in form. It must believe in the people it is administering and must understand them as components in the ecological life-web. These islanders in proved native capacity are the equals of any people anywhere. If civil rights can be helped to move on into creative administration and self-administration within a conserved environment, these little Islands will become beacons for half the world.[4]

Listening intently to Dr. Thompson's words, Mrs. Johnston grasped the larger context of the Institute's work and thanked those present for their broad vision. She was especially grateful for the progress that had been made toward civilian government for Guam and said: "We want you to know that through the work of the Institute of Ethnic Affairs, a new child was born, called the *Guam Echo*. . . . The progress that has been made is due in large part to the *Echo* and the Institute. . . ."[5]

A congratulatory telegram from the Institute's members on Guam was read at the meeting:

CONGRATULATIONS AND BEST WISHES FOR WORLD-WIDE MEMBERSHIP STOP PEOPLE OF GUAM ANTICIPATE WITH HIGH HOPE FULL CIVIL RIGHTS AND POLITICAL STATUS NEAR FUTURE STOP THE APPOINTMENT OF CIVIL GOVERNOR SKINNER WAS THE FIRST EVIDENCE TOWARD GUAM ASPIRATION STOP WE EARNESTLY COMMEND INSTITUTE OF ETHNIC AFFAIRS FOR CONSISTENT AND WELL DIRECTED EFFORTS ON BEHALF OF GUAM AND PEOPLE.

— GUAM MEMBERS[6]

The stateside members then unanimously voted in favor of electing a Guamanian to the Board of Directors. Selection of the board member was left to the Guam membership, and Simon Sanchez, our usual contact, was notified accordingly. The Guamanian man or woman selected would join what was truly a blue-ribbon board of its time, consisting primarily of prominent anthropologists, sociologists, and government administrators. For the first time, honorary vice presidents representing selected foreign countries were elected, along with Eleanor Roosevelt from the United States. They were Dr. Manuel Gamio of Mexico, Dr. A. Grenfell Price of Australia, and Dr. Richard C. Thurnwald of Germany. Names of the officers and directors are listed in Appendix 22. Betty Winquest Cooper was retained as executive secretary, and I was again named editor.

In January 1950 the Guamanians named Francisco B. Leon Guerrero to be their representative to the board. His selection was very pleasing to the Institute board and staff, as Frank had been one of the very first Guamanians to become a member of the Institute. He obviously was highly regarded by his peers on Guam, having been sent to Washington on their behalf in 1937 and named in 1949 to go again.

All this, and more, was covered in the October 31, 1949, *Guam Echo*. It wasn't often that Chamorros made the long trip to New York and Washington, and it was important to record that Agueda I. Johnston, like F. B. Leon Guerrero, B. J. Bordallo, Simon Sanchez, Connie Barrett, Antonio B. Won Pat, Carlos Taitano, and others, had truly helped to change the course of history.

The Ethnic Institute board agreed at their October meeting that civilian government for the Pacific islands should continue to be the primary short-term goal of the Institute while it branched out to do action research in the Middle East. An office in Israel as well as a continuing presence in New York City was contemplated at the October meeting, but before all that could come about, Congress would finally act on legislation for Guam.

The long-awaited trip to the Pacific by members of Congress finally got off the ground about a month after the Institute board meeting. Leaving San Francisco on November 2, 1949, the Miles Committee visited American Samoa, the Trust Territory, Guam, and the Northern Marianas from November 5 to 26. They then flew to Manila for two days and on to Tokyo to see General MacArthur. Leaving Tokyo December 1, they flew to Wake, Midway, then Honolulu. They remained in Hawai'i for six or seven days to write their report before returning to the States. It was a relatively fast trip, but with enough time in each place to conduct interviews with the islanders and hear their true feelings.

Returning to Washington early in December, the congressmen reported that there was a real contrast to the receptions given them in Samoa, the Trust Territory, and Guam. Samoans called a meeting of the local legislature *(fono)* and met the committee with questions about the virtues of American citizenship and whether that would bring with it certain federal

Representative John E.
Miles (D., N. Mex.) headed
The Miles Committee of
the House that held hear-
ings on Guam in 1949.

taxes. They wanted to know if a bill of rights prohibiting involuntary ser-
vitude might not wreck their *matai* system of land ownership and local
rule.

The people in the Trust Territory were very reluctant to speak. In many
cases they had no opportunity to do so, as the congressmen were whisked
off to meetings with the naval administrators and dinners where not even
the native chiefs were allowed.

Guamanians were reticent at first. Only a handful turned up at the
first day's hearing. Congressman William Lemke (R., N.Dak.) said they
appeared to be afraid of reprisals for something they might say until the
committee assured them that their testimony would be taken in strictest
confidence if desired. By the fourth and fifth days, hundreds of Guamanians appeared to get grievances off their chests. They spoke with confidence
in open session. Hearings went on all day and into the night. Committee
spokesmen reported being gratified that so much cooperation eventually
was shown. Unlike in the Trust Territory, leading islanders were invited to

have dinner with the committee in the home of Governor Skinner. Afterward, some of the Chamorros entertained the congressmen in their own homes.

The "terrible thing" on Guam, Representative Crawford told me for publication in the December 15, 1949, *Echo,* was the land situation. Representative Lemke concurred, saying the situation was "precisely the same as two years ago when Navy Secretary Sullivan promised the House Public Lands Committee that settlement with just compensation would be made promptly. Nothing is being done. And the same lame excuses are being offered, that land settlement is difficult and that there are lots of problems involved."[7] Both Crawford and Lemke agreed that if a similar situation existed in the United States, a situation where the government was taking land without just compensation, it would be cause for revolution. By way of illustration, Mr. Lemke reported that the Guamanian owner of fourteen acres of land where the admiral's house and various other prominent government buildings were located was collecting only $14.10 per year — $1.00 per acre per year. "Only anyone who wishes to insult our intelligence would say that was just compensation," Lemke declared. "Congress can and should do something about organic legislation," Crawford commented to the *Guam Echo.* "But fair settlement of land cases is something that has been authorized and now is long overdue."[8]

Lemke reported that in the Trust Territory the committee found the natives "intelligent, happy, none hungry." High regard was expressed for the caliber of many of the naval reserve officers and their wives serving as teachers, doctors, and administrators there. The committee found many who were genuinely interested in their work and wished to continue to serve, whether under naval or civilian government.

"I definitely look for favorable action on organic legislation for Guam," Crawford concluded for publication in the December *Echo.* He also expected organic legislation for American Samoa and the Trust Territory, although those areas presented more "paradoxes" than Guam, he said.[9] The entire subcommittee was in agreement on principles. Spokesmen said they were fully convinced of the need for civilian administration. They reported confidence in the ability of the people to govern themselves.

Shortly after the congressmen returned to Washington, Governor Skinner flew in for budget conferences. He told me for the *Guam Echo* that the congressional hearings in Guam "were a fine example of democracy." He also commented that congressmen making the trip had done so in the face

of a real hazard. They had arrived in Guam shortly after a typhoon estimated to have done four million dollars'-worth of damage.[10]

The governor was optimistic about passage of an organic act in the Second Session of the 81st Congress. Like Representative Crawford, he expressed the belief that congressmen visiting the island were "completely
sold on the need and justification of organic legislation and civilian administration for Guam."[11] Asked to comment on the progress of the transfer of
government from naval to civilian administration, Governor Skinner said
that "slow progress" had been made. "On the basis of my two months out
there," he said, "I can definitely say that we will not need to make a man-
for-man replacement and that we can make use of many Guamanians and
stateside men already there."[12]

Governor Skinner emphasized that he hoped to recruit from the United
States only a small top-notch staff, thereby effecting substantial savings. He
was glad that Navy Commander Pat Herman was being released to inac-
tive duty upon his return to Guam. Having served on Guam for four years,
Herman was probably the veteran of all statesiders in the Guam government and would continue his duties as executive assistant to the governor.
Isaac F. Warren, who was with Skinner and Herman in Washington, would
also return to Guam to continue working on fiscal matters. After two and a
half weeks filled with conferences in Washington, the three left for Guam
by plane on December 14.

With Christmas and New Year's behind them, on January 16, 1950, the
Miles Committee made public a thirty-two-page "Report on the Pacific Islands to the Public Lands Committee." It contained no real surprises. The
report was divided into four sections: Canton Island, American Samoa,
Trust Territory, and Guam. The committee's twenty-three-point summary
was reprinted in the January 30, 1950, *Guam Echo,* and a front-page story
in that issue quoted the following paragraph about Guam:

> The committee was well pleased with what it found on Guam in the way of
> ability to carry on government, and in the understanding of American tradi-
> tions and practices. For all practical purposes, Guam is an American com-
> munity. English is the language of instruction in the schools and virtually all
> Guamanians speak English. They read mainland newspapers, wear clothes
> made in the States, follow stateside sporting events and are almost undistin-
> guishable, with allowances for climate, flora, and fauna, from a community
> of comparable size in the States. The committee is confident that the people

of Guam will be able to govern themselves under the proposed organic act, and that wise and forward-looking laws will be enacted and enforced. The United States should interfere with local administration no more in Guam than it does in other United States Territories.[13]

The report pointed out that the provisions of H.R. 4499 had been discussed in Guam before the committee's arrival and many persons were eager to testify. All of the hundred who appeared before the committee were enthusiastically in favor of the proposed organic legislation. There was no longer any reason to delay enactment (see Appendix 23).[14]

Betty Winquest, as editor of the January 30, 1950, *Guam Echo,* took pleasure in noting that H.R. 4499 was scheduled to come up for House hearings in February. Getting legislation to this point had been an arduous and drawn-out task. Guamanians were finally going to see some results.

Looking back, I know that extraneous events almost capsized the Institute during those strenuous months and years. But at this juncture, it was still afloat. One of the most detrimental influences of the time was the House Un-American Activities Committee and Senator Joseph McCarthy (R., Wisc.), who, incidentally, was not on that committee. The Ethnic Institute was never attacked by the HUAAC or McCarthy, but their poisoned air was all around us. Contributions to most nonprofit organizations dried up, as donors were unwilling to risk winding up on their blacklists.

More than that, as mentioned in Chapter 2, an adverse ruling from the Bureau of Internal Revenue in 1946 prohibited Collier from applying for grants from individuals or foundations accustomed to tax write-offs. Over the years, a few thousand taxable dollars were sent to the Institute by Collier's friends, such as Henrietta Durham and Millicent Rogers, who had previously worked with him on human and civil rights for American Indians; but they were not enough to support an Ethnic Institute director. In the fall of 1947, Collier began teaching sociology part-time at New York University. After commuting to New York City for most of a year, he and his wife gave up their house in Vienna, Virginia, and moved to Manhattan. We talked frequently by phone, and Collier returned to Washington for days at a time as he continued to direct the Institute. Betty and I were still able to occupy the Institute office on 18th Street and publish the *News Letter* and *Guam Echo.* But funding was truly running out in the spring of 1949.

Fortunately, in June 1949, when Mr. Collier was unable to attend the

Second Inter-American Indian Conference, held in Cuzco, Peru, on June 24 to July 4, 1949, I was sent in his place as an adviser to the fourteen-member United States delegation and paid a per diem of $30 a day by the Interior Department. Prior to the conference, I worked with Collier and Simon Wilson of the State Department in soliciting academic papers to be written and presented by U.S. delegates to the conference.

In 1940, Collier, as head of the U.S. Bureau of Indian Affairs, had been instrumental in establishing the Inter-American Indian Institute headquartered in Mexico City. Each of the fourteen affiliated countries of North and South America had a National Indian Institute (NII). When Collier left Interior, he in effect took the U.S. NII with him because it was not then being funded by the U.S. Congress. Shortly after I joined the Institute of Ethnic Affairs, he named me executive secretary as well as editor of Institute publications and we worked together writing articles for the *News Letter* about Latin American Indian projects with which the U.S. NII was associated. Shortly after my return from Peru, I wrote for the June–July 1949 *News Letter* a long article on the Cuzco Conference. I also wrote and supervised publication for the United States government the official fifty-four-page final report of that conference.

Subsequently, William Warne, Assistant Secretary of the Department of the Interior, who had headed the U.S. delegation to Cuzco, asked if I would be willing to join Interior to continue the Inter-American Indian work I had been doing. Because the future of the Ethnic Institute was so uncertain, Collier approved the idea, and I said yes. At Collier's recommendation, I was employed at the GS-11 level, and my salary was doubled to something over $5,000 a year. I didn't actually move to Interior until January of 1950. Until then, I continued to work at the Ethnic Institute office, where I still wrote the *Guam Echo* and edited the *News Letter,* in addition to writing and publishing the *Report of the U.S. Delegation to the Second Inter-American Indian Conference and the Final Act.*

Over the years, Guam members had become increasingly supportive of the Institute, and it was largely their memberships that had kept us going. In February 1949, $2,300 had come from 142 members — an amount double that received from Guam at any other time. Of those 142 members, 62 had not previously been affiliated with the Institute. They included leaders in virtually every walk of life — Guam congressmen, commissioners of all villages, bishops and priests, educators, farmers, shopkeepers, tradesmen, and more. In November 1949 another $1,183.30 was received from 118 members, 49 of whom were new. An even greater record was chalked up in January 1950, when subscriptions and contributions from 186 individuals totaling $1,508.00 were transmitted. There were 108 new members among the 186 January subscribers, and this brought Guam memberships in the Institute to more than 500. That was cause for celebration.

Collier had written for the November 1949 *News Letter* that "financial insecurity, which has toppled so many non-profit organizations into oblivion these postwar years, has kept the Ethnic Institute balancing on a razor's edge."[15] Beginning then, the *News Letter* could no longer be printed professionally. Betty began mimeographing it, like the *Guam Echo.* The December issue was skipped altogether. Publication was resumed with Vol. V, No. 1, the January–February 1950 issue. It and the last two issues — March–April 1950 and May–June 1950 — were devoted largely to John Collier's comments on Truman's Point Four Program and new adverse developments regarding property and cultural rights of the American Indians.

Among other things, the very last issue of the *News Letter,* dated May–June 1950, named two winners of Opportunity Scholarships being granted by the John Hay Whitney Foundation. Betty and I, with Collier's support, had worked hard to get Pacific Islanders included among applicants for those scholarships. So it was with pride that we announced the names of those first winners. They were Peter Tali Coleman of Pago Pago, the capital of American Samoa, who would "continue his law studies to become the first lawyer from Samoa," and Pedro Cruz Sanchez of Tamuning Village, Dededo, Guam, "who will pursue graduate work in education." Peter Coleman later became a popular governor of American Samoa, and Pedro Sanchez, son of Simon Sanchez the respected Chamorro educator, became the first president of the University of Guam.[16]

In January 1950 when I began working full-time in the Interior Department, there was so much to do on Inter-American Indian affairs that I could not simultaneously keep up with all that was happening in the Pacific islands. The rest of the Guam effort to obtain citizenship and self-government was played out without my direct involvement. The Organic Act of Guam was actually passed without anyone telling me when it took place. How could that have happened? I know I was engrossed in preparing a budget for the National Indian Institute. But the islands were never far from my mind.

Fortunately, I have been able to obtain copies of the last three *Guam Echos* — written, edited, and saved by Betty Winquest Cooper. They tell the end of the story. Betty's writing was so much like my own that when I read those issues for the first time in 2004, I felt I must have written them myself. Betty, like me, wrote of new hope and continued delays. This mode went on for another six months.

Chapter 15

The Organic Act Becomes Law

Early in 1950, the Crawford bill, H.R. 4499, was transformed into the Peterson bill, H.R. 7273, incorporating some of the twenty-three changes suggested by the Miles Committee. The change of sponsorship reflected the change of political party leadership brought about by the 1948 elections. Peterson (D., Fla.) introduced H.R. 7273 on February 13, 1950, and less than ten days later, on February 22, the House Public Lands Committee issued a favorable report with the recommendation that the full House pass the bill. In the interest of historical reference, here is what the committee said in its report on the bill:

Report No. 1677:

The purpose of H.R. 7273 is to confer U.S. citizenship on the people of Guam, to grant them a bill of rights, to establish a representative form of government in accordance with our democratic tradition, to provide effective protection of the rights of individuals under law through an independent judiciary, to define the scope of executive authority of government, to accord the greatest practicable measure of local self-government, and to fulfill the international obligations of the U.S. Government with respect to Guam.

The Eighty-first Congress has an opportunity and the responsibility, by enacting H.R. 7273, to put an end to our neglect of the rights of the Guamanian people over the last 50 years and to fulfill our international obligations under Article IX of the Treaty of Paris of 1898 and under Article 73 of the United Nations Charter. Enactment of H.R. 7273 will provide additional evidence to the peoples and nations of the world of this Government's traditional policy of promoting the political, economic, social, and educational advancement of dependent peoples. Failure to do so would be a severe blow to the aspirations of millions of dependent peoples all over the world. To permit the executive branch of government to exercise complete legislative, judicial, and executive authority over Americans is contrary to every basic principle of democratic government. Ours is a Government of laws and not of men, and only the Congress, by law, can define the civil rights and political status of the people, insure democratic lawmaking processes, establish an independent judiciary, and define executive authority. Until Congress does act, Guam will be subject to the good will or arbitrariness, as the case may be, of Federal officials having responsibility for the government of Guam. To remedy this situation, the Congress, in this committee's opinion, should act now. There are no more patriotic, loyal people under the American flag than the Guamanians. Guam was the only important area under U.S. jurisdiction which was occupied by the Japanese during World War II. Throughout the Japanese occupation Guamanians demonstrated their great loyalty and devotion to this country. Many of them endured cruel torture and performed unsurpassed acts of heroism [up] to the [time of the] victorious return of the American forces. They are Americans in every sense except that they lack the fundamental rights under law and the elemental features of democratic government which other Americans enjoy. . . .[1]

It was gratifying to note that much of the philosophy of the Institute of Ethnic Affairs was reflected in the above statement. The writer had picked up on Collier's references to how self-government for Guam would act as a beacon of hope for peoples all over the world. The need of a government of laws, not men, and the importance of an independent judiciary were also among his premises. But this was just the House Public Lands Committee Report. The full House still had to act on the bill.

Pushing H.R. 7273 right along as he had said he would, Congressman Peterson requested a hearing on it before the House Rules Committee and got one for March 7, 1950. On that day, he and Congressmen Crawford, Miles, and Lemke all pressed hard for action. The very next day, the Rules Committee reported out a resolution providing for one hour of general debate on the floor of the House. Granting of the open rule thus cleared the way for House approval — or disapproval. There was really little doubt of approval, if they could get the bill called up.

But that was not to be soon!

The full House scheduled debate for March 15–17, 1950, and the Senate planned to act soon after that. The Navy was notified to bring to Washington the two-man Guam Congress Organic Act Committee. Frank B. Leon Guerrero and Antonio B. Won Pat had been named in January and arrived by Navy plane on March 16.

Antonio B. Won Pat served with F. B. Leon Guerrero on the Organic Act Committee appointed by the Guam Congress to go to Washington in 1950.

Then came the first delay. On March 17, the very first day after the two spokesmen arrived, the House leadership unexpectedly called for adjournment. To allow for future developments, publication of the March *Guam Echo* was delayed until the last day of the month, and at that point the full House voted to take an Easter recess, from April 6 to 18. Consideration of H.R. 7273 would have to come after that. No date was set.

To readers of that March 31, 1950, *Guam Echo,* the continued delays must have seemed interminable and in some ways inexcusable. To Leon Guerrero and Won Pat, who visited the Institute office soon after their arrival in Washington, the postponement was certainly a disappointment. But they made good use of their unexpected free time.

During the first few days, they went to Capitol Hill and talked with Congressmen Peterson and Crawford. They also spoke with Mills Astin, clerk of the Senate Interior and Insular Affairs Committee. All assured the island delegates that the need for organic legislation for the Pacific islands, particularly Guam, had finally been recognized by those who would be voting on the bills. The bills would pass.

In the executive branch of the government, they met with Interior Department officials, including James P. Davis, director of the Division of Territories and Island Possessions; Emil J. Sady, chief of the Pacific Branch; Gordon MacGregor, also of the Pacific Branch, and Irwin W. Silverman, chief counsel of the Division of Territories. They also met with Captain Ralph B. Randolph, who had succeeded Captain Peter G. Hale as chief of the Island Government Division in the Navy Department.

Through interviews with various press representatives, the delegates presented the case for Guam's organic act to a broad readership. Some writers reported that Mr. Leon Guerrero had been working for such legislation since before 1937, when he first came to Washington to testify before the Senate on citizenship for Guam.

During this time, the Interior Department arranged for the two men to take advantage of a unique opportunity to visit Puerto Rico and the Virgin Islands. "You should come to our island to see what we have been able to accomplish since we have had an organic act," said Jesus T. Pinero, former governor of Puerto Rico, in issuing his invitation. Pinero was then working in the Interior Department in Washington.[2] Like Guam, Puerto Rico had become a United States possession under the terms of the Treaty of Paris after the Spanish-American War in 1898. Its organic legislation, including U.S. citizenship for inhabitants of the island, was part of the Jones Act passed by the U.S. Congress in 1917. The Guamanians visited Puerto Rico on March 23 and March 24. Won Pat then accompanied numerous Puerto Rican officials to the Virgin Islands to witness the inauguration of the first native of that island to be named governor — Morris F. DeCastro.

Back in Washington, Leon Guerrero and Won Pat had a most unusual opportunity. Governor Carlton Skinner had come to Washington with a petition signed by 1,700 Guamanians urging passage of the organic act. He invited the Guam congressmen to accompany him to the White House, where he presented the petition to President Truman on April 17, 1950. It read, in part:

> As we enter the second half-century period of unquestioning allegiance to the United States of America since the signing of the Treaty of Peace between the United States and Spain at Paris on December 10, 1898, providing therein that "The Civil Rights and Political Status of the Native Inhabitants of the Territories Hereby Ceded to the United States Shall be Determined by the

Congress," we, the undersigned native inhabitants of Guam of legal age, and presently residing in Guam, M.I., do hereby memorialize the Congress of the United States to determine our civil rights and political status by the passage of an organic act providing, among other things, the establishment of the Territory of Guam, and the government thereof, and conferring U.S. citizenship upon certain of the inhabitants thereof.[3]

Two days later, on April 19, the Senate Interior and Insular Affairs Subcommittee, under the chairmanship of Clinton P. Anderson (D., N.Mex.), held hearings on S. 1892, which was the same as H.R. 7273. Witnesses included William Warne, Assistant Secretary of the Interior, who read a statement from Secretary Oscar L. Chapman; Guam Governor Carlton Skinner; and Irwin Silverman, counsel of Interior's Division of Territories and Islands. Pedro M. Ada and V. P. Palomo, Guam businessmen who just happened to be in Washington, were introduced to the subcommittee, as was Lieutenant General Henry Larson, a former military governor of Guam. William Hotz, an attorney from Omaha, Nebraska, who had handled legal cases on Guam, flew in to go on record as completely supporting the principles of the bill. R. P. S. McDonnell, a Washington attorney, outlined various objections to specific portions of the bill. He did not question the general desirability of the legislation.

Secretary Chapman's statement outlined the background leading up to the proposed legislation: the obligation imposed by the Treaty of Paris in 1898; the recommendations of War, State, Navy, and Interior Departments in 1945; and ultimately, the September 7, 1949, executive order signed by President Truman directing transfer of Guam administration to the Interior Department effective July 1, 1950.

Chapman's statement was followed by Governor Skinner's, which was described by the press as concise and persuasive. The question of whether Guam would ever qualify for statehood loomed so large that Skinner chose to address it early in his remarks. Here are excerpts printed in the May 15, 1950, *Guam Echo:*

Enactment of an organic law for Guam is justified and required for three principal reasons. First, the American way of life calls for it. Our nation was founded on the principles of self-government. As each territory of the United States has developed and become populated with mature, responsible, educated people, it has been granted rights of self-government. At this point I wish to state unequivocally that the people of Guam do not envision or desire statehood at any future time. The legislation under consideration contains no promise, direct or implied, of statehood.

With citizenship and the addition of Guam to the United States as an unincorporated territory with powers of government defined by the United States Congress, they will be happy and contented as to their political ambitions. They will have the foundation for fulfilling their own destinies economically, politically and socially.[4]

In retrospect, this denial of future political ambitions was probably going a little far. Later statements by various Guam leaders have indicated a yearning for more self-government. But Governor Skinner undoubtedly was facing reality. Questions regarding the relationship of Guam to Alaska and Hawai'i, whose bills for statehood were then awaiting Senate action, had been raised in March when Leon Guerrero and Won Pat met informally with U.S. congressmen. They found it necessary to tell the *Guam Echo* for publication on page one of the March 31, 1950, issue, "There appears to be some misunderstanding on The Hill and a tendency to connect our Guam bill with the entirely unrelated statehood bills."[5] Both Leon Guerrero and Won Pat emphasized that there was no provision in organic legislation that promised Guam statehood at any time. The bill declared Guam to be an "unincorporated territory" of the United States. By contrast, both Alaska and Hawai'i were declared to be "incorporated territories" by acts of the U.S. Congress in 1912 and 1900. That question was still so much in the air that Senator Joseph C. O'Mahoney, chairman of the Senate Interior and Insular Affairs Committee, had made known that he wanted to study the bill carefully and see that it contained no implied promises of statehood for Guam before passing it out of committee for approval by the Senate and President Truman.

Knowing that contemplation of statehood for a territory populated by less than thirty thousand indigenous residents could kill the bill, Governor Skinner therefore found it necessary to say what he did. He went on:

Second, self-government is essential to the growth of a self-reliant and self-supporting population. Self-government will provide the greatest possible stimulus to acceptance of responsibility by Island residents for their own government and their own affairs and responsibility for the support of their community and private activities. Government from Washington by executive action has never provided satisfactory local handling of local problems in the states of this nation. For distant territories it is no better. With local solutions of local problems, there comes local acceptance of responsibility. Responsible self-government will be far more economical for the treasury than government imposed from Washington with final decisions based on considerations in Washington instead of the territory.

Third, self-government will stimulate commercial, agricultural and industrial growth. With a responsible legislature, with an executive branch with clear but limited powers, and with a Federal and local court system officially established as part of the great system of American courts which protect private rights and private property as well as the public interest, the island can become an economic asset to the United States as well as a strategic base of great value. With the best harbor in the western Pacific and with fine airfields and a transpacific cable station, Guam is already a commercial, transportation and communications center. With the foundation provided by an organic act, it can become a vital link in our economic lifeline to southeast Asia and to Japan. A substantial growth of business can be expected if this act is passed to provide political stability for the community. . . .

At this period of crisis in the Far East, thinking people will want to consider the effect of granting self-government to the people who inhabit a strategic naval, military and air base near the Orient. Granting self-government and citizenship can only act to strengthen the island and the base. A self-reliant civilian community frees the military forces of a heavy responsibility. It will assist and help to support the military forces through provision of many business and recreational facilities, government services and the maintenance of law and order, all of which would otherwise be a constant concern of the military forces.

Also, the granting of citizenship and self-government in itself will be a powerful psychological and political weapon in our dealings with the dependent peoples of the Far East. They are watching closely to see if Uncle Sam's professions of democratic ideals are borne out in his treatment of a people who have been under the American flag for over half a century and have demonstrated their intense devotion to that flag in peace and war.

Much of the legislation which is presented to the Congress asks for protection of some kind. The people of Guam have had enough paternalistic protection. They want emancipation. This bill would let them stand on their own feet and do things for themselves. Much of the legislation presented to the Congress asks for authorization for future Federal spending. This bill is an authorization for future Federal savings.

On behalf of the people of Guam, I earnestly plead for enactment of a law which will benefit both the United States and Guam, which will satisfy our American ideals, strengthen our country and bring happiness to many thousands of loyal Americans.

When Governor Skinner finished his testimony, the Guam Organic Act Committee of two had a chance to speak. Both Leon Guerrero and Won Pat expressed their gratitude for the opportunity to appear before the Senate Committee. They said their mission to Washington was to assure the United States Congress of the long-standing desire of the people of Guam for organic legislation and U.S. citizenship. They told their small audience that they and their fellow islanders were ready and able to take on the new responsibilities, and they demonstrated their readiness by answering all questions.[6]

Mr. A. T. Bordallo, president of the Guam Chamber of Commerce, just happened to be in Washington that day. He testified on the economic possibilities of Guam and indicated that the various businesses, civic organizations, and growing enterprises would make Guam a typical American community.

Senator Anderson then posed a series of questions. He said the salaries provided in the bill for the governor and lieutenant governor seemed somewhat excessive. So it was agreed that compensation should be in line with the President's Executive Pay Act. The size of the present two-house Guam Congress also seemed out of proportion, so a unicameral legislature of fifteen members was suggested. Wording was changed to make certain that the executive, legislative, and judicial functions on Guam would be separate and not under the supervision of one central agency or head, as it had been under the Navy.

The subcommittee approved those and other amendments during the first week of May. Before bringing the amended bill before the whole Interior and Insular Affairs Committee, Senator O'Mahoney, chairman, satisfied himself that Guam was neither seeking nor desiring the promises of statehood. In time for the May 15, 1950, *Guam Echo,* members of the Senate Committee staff were able to assure the Institute that the bill would be reported favorably and that the Senate would pass it since it had such strong support.

A few days after the hearing, on May 23, 1950, the House did indeed approve H.R. 7273. More than a month later, on July 26, the Senate followed

Senator Joseph C. O'Mahoney (D., Wyo.) was head of the Senate Interior and Insular Affairs Committee when the Organic Act of Guam was passed in 1950 and had his name on the Senate bill.

suit by approving S. 1892. The bills were identical. But the Senate report on S. 1892 noted that Guam remained under the doctrine of the 1901 *Insular Cases* (described in Chapter 1) without any possibility of statehood.

The legislation that Chamorros had been waiting for more than fifty years was passed with little fanfare. As far as I know, there was no celebration in Washington when it was enacted by Congress. Its passage was not even known to those of us in the Institute of Ethnic Affairs who had worked so hard for it! Why, oh why? How did that happen?

Well, unaware that the big day had finally come, John Collier and Laura Thompson were in New York teaching sociology and anthropology. I was working on Inter-American Indian affairs in the Department of the Interior. Betty was at home with her one-year-old daughter before assuming employment in the office of Senator Gale McGee (D., Wyo.), my college debate coach. The former office of the Institute of Ethnic Affairs on 18th Street in Washington, D.C., was closed.

But the victory had really been won more than a year before, when the Navy, War, State, and Interior Departments had agreed on civilian

This is the historic picture of President Harry S. Truman signing the Organic Act of Guam on August 1, 1950. *Standing left to right:* Senator Joseph O'Mahoney (D., Wyo.); Representative J. Hardin Peterson (D., Fla.); Guam Assemblyman Carlos Taitano; Harold Seidman, U.S. Bureau of the Budget; Frances P. Matthews, Secretary of the Navy; Representative Clinton P. Anderson (D., N. Mex.); Oscar L. Chapman, Secretary of the Interior; and Senator Hugh A. Butler (R., Nebr.).

administration and President Truman in September of 1949 had set a date for the transfer to Interior.

After the congressional action in May and July, all that remained to be done in the summer of 1950 was the ceremonial signing. That took place at the White House six days after the Senate approval. Presumably, there was a bit of celebrating then. Representatives of the executive and legislative branches of the U.S. government and Guam Assemblyman Carlos Taitano are clustered around President Truman in the picture on this book's cover, and they are all smiling.

Young Taitano is the only Guamanian in that famous photo. Shortly afterward, he entered Georgetown University Law School.

Although President Truman signed H.R. 7273 into law on August 1, 1950, the Organic Act of Guam was made effective as of July 21, 1950, the sixth anniversary of Guam Liberation Day.

Fifty-two years lay between the end of the Spanish-American War in

1898 and 1950 when Congress decided Guam's political status as the Treaty of Paris had promised. Certainly the last five years were the hardest in terms of working for the necessary legislation. Those five years did indeed involve fighting the Navy and throwing off the shackles of military government. But no one I know regrets one hour of involvement in that struggle.

History will record that an invisible crowd was behind those in the photograph taken that day. They include the hundreds of Guamanians who petitioned long and hard for self-government, but particularly, B. J. Bordallo, F. B. Leon Guerrero, Antonio Won Pat, Simon Sanchez, Agueda Johnston, and Concepcion (Connie) Barrett. Those who should also be included are John Collier and Laura Thompson, founders of the Institute of Ethnic Affairs; Harold Ickes, former Secretary of the Interior, the articulate spokesman and newspaper columnist who stood fearlessly against military autocracy; Interior Secretary Julius A. Krug; James P. Davis, Director of the Division of Territories and Island Possessions at Interior, together with Roy E. James and Emil J. Sady of the Pacific Division; Carlton Skinner, Interior spokesman who became Guam's first civilian governor; Navy Secretary John Sullivan, Navy Under Secretary W. John Kenney, and Commander Peter G. Hale, who saw the light and brought the Navy Department around; U.S. Senator Guy Cordon (R., Ore.); U.S. Representative Fred L. Crawford (R., Mich.); Representative Norris Poulson (R., Calif.); Representative John E. Miles (D., N.Mex.); Delegate Joseph R. Farrington (R., Hawai'i); the Hopkins Committee — Dr. Ernest Hopkins, Dr. Knowles Ryerson, and Maurice Tobin; newspaper editors, especially Riley Allen of the *Honolulu Star-Bulletin* and Foster Hailey of the *New York Times;* the board of the Institute of Ethnic Affairs, and — yes — even its two-person staff — Betty Winquest Cooper and myself — who wrote, edited, published, and disseminated the thirty monthly Ethnic Institute *News Letters* and the thirty-seven monthly *Guam Echo*s, which over that five-year period kept readers informed.

It was the will of the Guamanian people that brought the Organic Act of Guam about, but without John Collier and Harold L. Ickes starting the ball rolling in 1946 passage might never have happened. Only they had the vision, clout, integrity, and stamina necessary to see the legislation through from beginning to end. It was Collier and Laura Thompson who established the Institute of Ethnic Affairs in 1945 and chose to focus its primary attention on the Pacific islands. Together, through the Institute and direct contact with the people of Guam, they never once in those five years let public interest in the civil rights of the islanders lag. Nor did they slight the people of American Samoa and the Trust Territory. It was Collier who insisted on civilian over military government and who knew that democracy must come from the grass roots up, that it could never be imposed from the top down. That's why he encouraged Guamanian participation every inch of the way. It took all of us to bring the legislation about. It was a war of ideas, a war of words, a bloodless war that brought victory without violence.

John Collier never had the good fortune to visit Guam. He was sixty-six when the Organic Act was passed in 1950 and eighty-four when he died in 1968. Someday, I would like to see in the Office of the Governor of Guam a bronze plaque naming him, president of the Institute of Ethnic Affairs, as a member of the Ancient Order of the Chamorri. I am sure Laura Thompson received acclaim from the people of Guam when she returned to the island in the late 1980s while writing her autobiography, *Beyond the Dream: A Search for Meaning*. But still one other deserves recognition. While you're at it, Mr. Governor, please print a wall certificate like mine for Betty Winquest Cooper.

Chapter 16

Mission Accomplished

As described in Chapter 1 of this book, I had the pleasure of visiting Guam in June 1951 as Pacific Area Assistant in the Office of Territories, United States Department of the Interior. Beginning on January 1, 1951, I was transferred from the Office of the Secretary of the Interior to the Office of Territories, and within six months arrangements were made by my boss, Emil J. Sady, for me to accompany the U.S. Navy on an inspection trip through the Trust Territory of the Pacific Islands.

I flew alone via United Airlines to Hawai'i, where I spent several days with Leonard Mason and other anthropologists at the University of Hawai'i, then on to Guam via Pan American Airways, where I was greeted at the airport by B. J. Bordallo, Simon Sanchez, and Agueda Johnston. The next day I joined four male officers for the trip by a Navy PBY to Tinian, Saipan, Yap, Koror, Truk, Ponape, Majuro, and Kwajalein. They introduced me to all of the top indigenous government officials and encouraged me to meet as many local people as our week-long journey permitted. Upon our return to Guam, I was housed in a Quonset hut as the guest of Rae Moulton, administrative assistant to Carlton Skinner, governor of Guam, and I spent three weeks getting reacquainted with Guamanians who had come to Washington and meeting dozens of others, some of whom were island government employees.

For the next four years, I worked in the Office of Territories in Washington, D.C., as liaison between government officials in Guam and the Trust Territory and federal agency officials in Washington. Our mission was to extend to the islands such federal programs as were believed appropriate. During this time, I also helped to establish the Guam Territorial Society, which sponsored a Cherry Blossom Queen candidate from Guam each spring.

The First Guam Legislature honored me in 1950 with a citation for my work as editor of the *Guam Echo*. And five years later, when my husband

As Pacific Area Assistant in the Department of the Interior in 1951, Doloris Coulter Cogan departs for Guam and inspection of the Trust Territory with the Navy.

Tom and I left government service and Washington to raise our family in Connecticut, I was given a silver medal along with a written Citation for Meritorious Service by the Secretary of the Interior, Douglas McKay. It just happened to reach me by mail on my thirty-first birthday, July 28, 1955. I have always been proud to know it was the Democrats who brought me into Interior and the Republicans who honored my work there (see Appendix 24).

My next connection with Guam took place in the year 2000, when I was invited by Governor Carl T. C. Gutierrez to participate in the 50th Anniversary of the Organic Act of Guam. I was asked to speak of my recollections, along with Governor Carlton Skinner and others, at a day-long seminar on the history of the island held at the University of Guam. Besides accommodations at the Guam Hilton Hotel, I was given a car, a driver (Steve Munoz), and an escort (Grace Garces), and for a week we visited Guam from one end to the other. What a pleasure it was for me to find the Government of Guam and leading businesses staffed from the top down by Guamanians — many of them sons and daughters of members of the

Photo of Betty Winquest Cooper *(left)* and Doloris Coulter Cogan *(right)* taken in Washington, D.C., in the 1980s. They and their families have remained lifelong friends.

Institute of Ethnic Affairs. What I had only dreamed of in the late 1940s had actually come about! What a marvelous example of democracy at work for the rest of the world to see.

On August 1, 2000, in Governor Gutierrez's office, I was made a member of the Ancient Order of the Chamorri and given a framed certificate that now hangs in the family room of my home in Elkhart, Indiana.

Of particular interest to me on that trip was the Micronesian Area Research Center at the University of Guam. I met Maggi Taitano, wife of the founder, Richard F. Taitano, then deceased; Hiro Kurashina, director; Dirk Anthony Ballendorf, Marjorie G. Driver, Robert F. Rogers, and other historians. About a year later, Lee D. Carter, historian, asked me to write a chapter about my experience with Guam for publication in an anticipated second volume of *Guam History: Perspectives.* Instead of a chapter, what he received was the first draft of this book.

Appendixes

Appendix 1
President Roosevelt's Letter to John Collier

January 22, 1945

My dear Commissioner Collier:

It is with particular regret that I have received your resignation of January 19 as Commissioner of Indian Affairs. I understand your deep interest in the American Indians and if you feel that you can serve their cause better from outside of the Government, I do not feel that I have any option except to accept your resignation. This I do as of the date of the qualification of your successor.

I cannot let you go, however, without saying that you have done an outstanding job in one of the most important and difficult offices in the Federal Government. One achievement of my administration in which I shall always take the deepest pride has been the progress that has been made in connection with our first Americans. I hope that the selfish exploitation of the Indians is now definitely a thing of the past over which we may be permitted to draw a veil of silence.

During the last twelve years, more than ever before, we have tried to impress upon the Indians that we are indeed Christians; that we not only avow but practice the qualities of freedom and liberty and opportunity that are explicit in our institutions. We have come to treat the Indian as a human being, as one who possesses the dignity and commands the respect of fellow human beings. In encouraging him to pursue his own life and revive and continue his own culture, we have added to his worth and dignity. We have protected the Indian in his property rights while enlarging them. We have opened the window of his mind to the extent that we have had money with which to do it. We have improved his medical service, we have enlarged his intellectual program. We have protected him in his religion and we have added greatly to his political stature.

All of these things have been done under your leadership because of your wisdom and courage. It has not been an easy task and you might have been subject to far less criticism than has been yours if you had been content merely to mark time within the limits that custom had built up in periods when the feeling was that we should not do too much for the Indians but rather as little as possible. If the Indians generally have come to possess greater self-respect and a stronger feeling of solidarity as members of the political state to which they belong, it is because as Commissioner, you have really believed in the Sermon on the Mount, the Declaration of Independence and the Constitution, and have done what you have to make these symbols by which to live.

Your contribution to the progress and welfare of the American Indians will never be forgotten. Your services as an important member of this administration since 1933 will be an inspiration to those who will follow you. You have my warmest congratulations upon a task well done and my hope, that in the future as in the past, even before you became a member of the administration, you will continue to achieve lasting benefits for the descendants of those misunderstood and misused human beings who originally possessed this great land of ours and who were displaced involuntarily, all too often with a selfish disregard of their right to live their own lives in their own way.

Sincerely yours,
(signed) Franklin D. Roosevelt

Appendix 2
Founders of the Institute of Ethnic Affairs

Some of the most important founders of the Ethnic Institute were Dr. Laura Thompson, Collier's wife; Felix Cohen, associate solicitor of the Interior Department; Rene d'Harnoncourt, chief curator at the Museum of Modern Art; Dr. Clyde Kluckhohn, a Harvard anthropologist; and Dr. Dorothea Leighton, a psychiatrist, all of whom were named directors.

Other people chosen as directors included Louis Adamic, author of *My Native Land;* Dr. John M. Cooper, chairman of the anthropology department at the Catholic University of America; John H. Provinse, Assistant Commissioner of Indian Affairs; Dr. Kurt Lewin, director of the Research Center for Group Dynamics at the Massachusetts Institute of Technology; Dr. Harold Lasswell, law professor at Yale University; Dr. Ronald Lippitt, professor of psychology at the University of Michigan; and Huston Thompson, chairman of the Federal Trade Commission.

Still other directors were Evans Carlson, a retired brigadier general of the Marine Corps known as commander of Carlson's Raiders, who had become an outstanding organizer for peace; Dr. Alexander H. Leighton, an anthropologist who had done research on Japanese Americans relocated during World War II; D'Arcy McNickle, a Flathead Indian who was an author and Assistant Commissioner of Indian Affairs; Carey McWilliams, a liberal author; Dr. Philleo Nash, an anthropologist on the staff of the White House; Dr. Henry A. Murray, distinguished professor of psychology at Harvard; Paul Fejos, a director of the Viking Fund; and Dr. Saul Padover, historian.

The first officers were John Collier, president; Dr. Kurt Lewin, Louis Adamic, and John H. Provinse, vice presidents; Huston Thompson, treasurer; and Allan Harper, secretary.

Appendix 3
Harold L. Ickes' Speech

Our Pacific Dependencies and the Peace Crisis: Navy Rule

Tonight I want to introduce the United States Navy to those whose democracy it is supposed to serve. I do not mean the Navy rushing forth gallantly to meet the enemy. I do not mean the Navy on parade, all dressed up with flags and pennants and bunting, with sailors and marines standing smartly at attention and with chested officers proudly wearing the funny looking hats adorned with ostrich plumes. The Navy that I want to introduce to this audience is the Navy that governs, in the name of a supposedly democratic America, in atolls lying in the Far Pacific. I believe that you will discover, as I have, that this is a different Navy than you have ever imagined.

These islands, small and scattered though they be, are not the concern of the American Navy alone, nor is the manner in which they are governed the sole interest of the Navy, or even of the United States. The way that these islands are governed concerns the United States in its relations with the other nations of the world.

At San Francisco and at London the United States spoke out boldly on the subject of what every other nation should do, without delay, for vast areas of the earth's population. We demanded the doing of those things which the United States is not doing for its own present and its prospective dependencies.

Let me show you how the Navy is involved.

We conquered the Marshalls, the Carolines, and the Marianas, which had been mandated to Japan under the League of Nations.

Last Autumn, the Preparatory Commission of The United Nations brought pressure on all nations holding mandated areas, to declare their intention to trustee them under The United Nations, without delay.

Last February, in the Assembly of The United Nations at London, five of the seven nations holding mandated areas formally declared their intention to enter into trusteeship agreements to the United Nations. They were the United Kingdom, New Zealand, Australia, Belgium and France.

Two nations held out — just two. One was the Union of South Africa. The other was the United States. Yet our obligation is equal to that of the other great powers which received their mandates from the League of Nations. We are morally and legally obligated to trustee our mandated areas as the others are being trusteed.

It was not a pleasant prospect — that one at London — of the United States hiding under a blanket with the Union of South Africa in an effort to escape an obligation which the other nations were accepting.

Of course, our Nation cannot maintain such a position permanently. It is too damaging to our leadership and good name. However, there is a larger and greater danger that we will be intransigent long enough to divest ourselves of moral leadership.

I am convinced that American opinion backs up the Charter to which we subscribed. Why then has our performance, as in London, been so negative? Is it due to our own confusion on policy and methods of administration of American territories? How can we put forward a policy when there is no coordination on territorial matters between State, War, Navy and Interior? I can illustrate this lack of coordination. Last October, President Truman recognized the need for a single United States policy for administration of the Pacific islands. He appointed the Secretaries of State, War, Navy and Interior as a committee to give him a recommendation on this subject without delay. Since there was nothing secret about that directive in October, and since I was not unconnected with the matter prior to February 15, I can tell you that that Committee had not met, at least up to that date, and to my knowledge it never has met in the seven months of its existence. The President's directive in October was to the effect that he wanted a recommendation "satisfactory to all four departments . . . without delay." You can see how completely the Army and Navy can block even the fulfillment of a clear Presidential directive. And, as usual, the State Department fails to take the leadership in insisting upon a unified policy. Its representatives content themselves with polite efforts to secure a compromise — but only if the interested parties are willing to compromise.

If we were to make, now, an unequivocal announcement of our intention to trustee these islands, just as other nations are doing, and if we were to come forward with a workable trusteeship agreement, the moral effect would be worldwide.

The United States should take the lead in establishing trusteeships on sound lines. We are not bound by the hampering traditions of a colonial service. And we can take pride in some of the achievements of our overseas areas under civilian rule. Despite mistakes, as in our economic neglect of the Philippines, we have a flexible and liberal territorial policy. We have recognized the principle of self-determination and we have tolerated a variety of political forms. We have promoted independence for the Philippines. The President has proposed independence for Puerto Rico. We are assisting Hawai'i and Alaska in their progress toward self-governing statehood. Hawai'i is an example of what can be done by an admixture of races which have attained prosperity and democratic unity within the framework of the American system.

It is time that the State Department ceased to be beguiled by the pleasant tinkle of brass and the lustre of gold braid, for it is the Navy which has largely been responsible for our moral failure to date as to our dependencies.

The official pressure to designate the Japanese mandated and other islands as "strategic areas" in their entirety or to annex them outright emanates from the Navy and is motivated in good measure by the Navy's desire to have exclusive responsibility for governing the populations of these areas. The Navy does not want to govern when it is subject to inspection, criticism and publicity. The Navy wants its administration of dependent peoples to be a "top secret."

Furthermore, the Naval governments of Guam and Samoa have become a naval tradition and it is partly in defiant defense of this tradition and without regard to security considerations that the Navy seeks to govern the other Pacific islands. The Navy is well aware that the Federal Government agency which shall be given civil jurisdiction over the formerly mandated islands would also be made responsible for Guam and Samoa. Any other administrative solution would be unthinkable.

Therefore, the Navy is intent upon jurisdiction over the Japanese mandated islands under conditions which will allow it to extend its present tyranny in Guam to an area comprising 3,000,000 square miles of the Pacific.

The history of American Samoa and Guam furnishes one answer to the mystery of our delay in the matter of trusteeships. The Navy's ambitious preparations to rule permanently, by naval absolutism, the civilian populations of the Pacific islands, furnishes another. The Navy is bent upon ruling these island peoples and it is determined that they shall not have those rights which the Charter of the The United Nations guarantees: that they shall not have self-government or democracy or racial equality. My charge is grounded upon the undeviating record of naval words and naval deeds in the government of Guam and American Samoa for the past forty-seven years.

We took Guam from Spain in 1898. By the Treaty of Paris we obligated ourselves to establish, by Act of Congress, "the civil rights and political status" of the people of Guam. With words of great promise, President McKinley launched the naval government of the island. That government, President McKinley proclaimed, would "insure that full measure of individual rights and liberties which is the heritage of free peoples"; it would prove to the Guamanians "that the mission of the United States is one of benevolent assimilation, substituting mild sway of justice and right for arbitrary rule."

Within one year of the date of this pious utterance of President McKinley's the naval government had abolished all of the very considerable home rule which Guam had enjoyed under Spain. Although the Guamanians had been Roman Catholics for centuries, the Navy had exited from the island all of the Roman Catholic priests except one, who happened to be a native Guamanian; it had enacted a law prohibiting Roman Catholic religious processions; it had denied entry to the Island to the Apostolic Delegate, an American charged with the oversight of Roman Catholic interests in that part of the world.

Successive naval governors, with a turnover of one every eighteen months, added such choice items of liberty and human rights as the following: A command forbidding the ringing of the church bells in the mornings. An executive order prohibiting the Guamanians from whistling on the streets in the vicinity of the Naval Governor's palace. A prohibition of the use of the Chamorro language in the government or in the schools.

The naval government gathered up and burned the dictionaries of the Chamorro language. The Guamanian native police were replaced by Marines.

Segregated schools were established for the Guamanians. Heavy taxation — taxation without representation — was levied by the naval governor on Guamanians but not on Navy personnel.

By the year 1902, the Guamanians were petitioning for those "civil rights" and that Congressionally defined "political status" which the Treaty of Paris had promised them. They are petitioning still, after nearly half a century. A year or two before the war these people, out of their own meager resources, sent two representatives to Washington to beg our "democratic" government to lift the dictatorial hand of the American Navy from off of Guam and to place its jurisdiction within the Department of the Interior.

Forty-five years ago these subjects of American oppression began to petition to have their municipal water supply chlorinated, because annually hundreds were made ill and many died from dysentery. The cost of the job was five thousand dollars. The naval government waited forty years before doing this.

Now, let us glance at the record in American Samoa. The Samoans came voluntarily under United States control in 1899, on the basis of an express understanding that they would be given civil status and a rule of law.

From 1899, to and including today, Samoan life has been lived under naval absolutism. There, as in Guam, the naval governor is legislature, executive and court. Again and again the governors have proved themselves to be ignorant or bigoted petty tyrants. Their ordinances have snowballed into a body of codified laws too fantastic to be readily believed, but they exist, in print and in practice.

Let me illustrate: The Samoans are sociable people. They like to visit from village to village, going in little parties for games, feasts, marriages, funerals. Such visitations by the people of one village to another are called *"malagas."*

Here is the Law of March 8, 1927, decreed by his illustrious highness, H. F. Bryan, Naval Governor of Samoa. I quote from Section 6: "In view of the fact that so much time has been wasted since the beginning of this year in cricket games between villages (some of which were played without authority), no permission will be granted for *malaga*s without further notice.

"Section 7. No *malaga* will be made, at any time, for any purpose, without the approval of the governor.

"Section 8. Any disobedience to this order will be considered a violation of Section 10, Offenses Against the Government and the Civil Rights of Citizens . . . and dealt with accordingly."

Section 98 of the Naval code for Samoa reads: "There shall be levied annually on the 15th day of December upon every male Samoan, who shall have reached the height of 5 feet and 1 inch, a general personal tax, which shall be known as the poll tax, the amount of which shall be fixed by the governor."

Among Samoans, as among many peoples, it is a solemn religious custom, after a death, to hold a funeral feast. The Naval code for Samoa prohibits such feasts. I quote Section 3: "From and after the coming into effect of this regulation, the giving of, or the holding of, the participation in, the attendance at, and the furnishing of any or all food for, the 'death feast' by any person whomsoever in the Manu's group of islands, is hereby prohibited."

E. S. Kellogg, another exalted Naval governor, decreed that both a fine and imprisonment could be evoked for violation of this provision.

The Samoans are a less patient folk than the Guamanians, and in the early 1920s their petitions for their denied rights became an uproar, though without physical violence. Thereupon, their leaders were seized by the naval government and charged with "conspiracy." They were thrown in jail and kept there for a number of years. But murmurings of the outburst reached Washington, and in 1930 President Hoover, pursuant to a resolution of Congress, appointed a Joint Commission to study the Samoan situation. The Commission was headed by Senator Hiram Bingham of Connecticut and it went to Samoa to do its work on the ground.

The Commission unanimously concluded that the Samoans ought to be given American citizenship, a bill of rights and an organic act. It announced its conclusion to the assembled Samoans, came home, and pressed for the promised legislation. The Senate passed it and the Navy (backed, I regret to have to say, by the Department of State) had it killed in the House. Through successive Congresses this has been the record.

Grotesque, inefficient, tyrannical, not wantonly cruel, but faithless to pledges given — such has been naval rule over subject peoples as proved by the unvarying record of long years in Guam and Samoa. Such a result is inevitable from naval administration. It is no accident, no mere circumstance which might change. Such is the nature of naval dominance when applied to civilian populations. I quote from Captain A. T. Mahan, the naval prophet whose writings have influenced the strategical thinking of the world.

"Naval administration is very clearly and sharply differentiated by the presence of an element which is foreign to almost all other activities of life in countries like Great Britain and the United States. The military factor is to it not merely incidental but fundamental."

What Captain Mahan meant is that naval organization, training and thinking relate entirely to the tasks of war. They have no relationship to the complicated problems of civilian populations. Every modern government except the United States knows this fact and has acted accordingly. England, France, Holland, Belgium, New Zealand, Australia and Russia rule their dependencies through civilian, not military governments. The American Navy controls its subject populations by direct and autocratic methods which it frankly labels "dictatorship." In scores of Congressional hearings the testimony of naval officers follows the same pattern: the natives are ignorant, lazy, slothful, immoral children. An island is a battleship and is run as such. The civilian population happens to be on the island and cannot be got rid of. It must be endured like other tropical inconveniences. Automatically and with finality, the rules by which the Navy governs itself are clamped down on the civilian population. The result is a rule of authority, color distinction, and the ignoring of the problems of and strivings toward democratic living.

I have cited the record of naval government on our islands during the forty years before Pearl Harbor. I now give you some of today's facts about the Navy's "beneficent" rule over the Guamanians. One would suppose that the Admirals, when seeking, as they recently have been and are doing, the establishment, by Executive Order, of the "pre-Pearl Harbor" system of naval government for the islands of Micronesia, would try to lift the face of naval autocracy on Guam. But this would be a violent assumption.

The Navy is still arguing that the Guamanians are not qualified to assume the duties and responsibilities of citizenship. The Navy persists in this stand although not a single Guamanian out of 23,000 has been convicted of disloyalty to the United States during their years under the Japanese.

Last Autumn, Congress voted and made immediately available funds to compensate the Guamanians for death and personal injury and loss of personal property caused by the Naval bombardment or confiscated by the Navy. To this hour the Navy has not settled the claims of these people first rendered destitute by the Japanese and then deprived by the Navy of two-thirds of the good land of their small island.

Large numbers of the 23,000 Guamanians subsist now as mere squatters in shacks and hovels built from dunnage lumber, packing cases, canvas and salvaged sheet metal. Their homes have been destroyed, they have been ousted from their lands, and they are not permitted to return even today, many months after the end of the war. Meanwhile, on a hill almost directly overlooking these shanty towns, the Navy is building for its class-conscious officers an 18-hole, 6,000-yard golf course with water hazards and sand traps.

Wage discrimination has become greatly intensified in Guam, even as compared with pre-Pearl Harbor naval practices. A Guamanian carpenter gets 43 cents an hour, a Continental American citizen who starts his employment when in Guam, $1.36 an hour, while the Continental American citizen transferred to Guam receives $1.66 an hour. Often the three classes of carpenters are working side by side at the same work.

As for Guamanian laborers, they get 20 cents per hour, a 4 percent increase from the Navy's pre-Pearl Harbor rate for Guamanian labor. Perhaps such wages would not be amiss if prices were correspondingly low, but a pair of shoes costs $7.10, a pound of corned beef 53 cents, etc.

The discrimination goes even farther. The Guamanians and the "Continental American" workers are alike paid from Federal funds. The "Continental Americans" get annual and sick leave with pay. If the Guamanian takes such leave it is without pay. The "Continental American" worker gets time and a half for overtime for all time in excess of 40 hours a week, the Guamanian worker gets only straight time, no matter how long he may work.

Naval absolutism sneers at every Constitutional guarantee. It permits the inhabitants of Guam to be subject to arrest, trial and sentence for any offense up to and including a capital one, without presentment or indictment by a grand jury, without jury trial, in a rump "Naval courts and Boards" court. The houses of the dependent people can be entered and searched without a warrant, their property seized at will by a police officer, and they can be — and are — ordered from their houses and lands at any hour of the day or night. They exist under a perpetual curfew law. It is unlawful for a Guamanian to ride in a government vehicle and he would be punished for so doing, by fine or imprisonment or both, even when invited by the driver. Such is the "benevolent" rule of which the Navy boasts.

A final affront to the Guamanian, as well as to the American sense of justice, is the recent announcement by the Navy that "Naval military rule" is being ended at Guam and "Naval civil rule" substituted. Under Naval Military rule the Guamanians had the slight advantage of at least some forms of law. When convicted on serious charges, they had a right of appeal. The Naval Military courts operated under rules not of their own making, which they could not abrogate at will. Under cavalier Naval Civil rule, the Governor, an admiral, makes the law and the rules, and changes them at will. He is the court, and from his civil or criminal judgment there is no appeal. It is into this system of one-man absolutism that the Guamanians are passing.

I sum up this record and the facts as of today. The Navy in Guam and Samoa, for nearly half a century, has prevented the fulfillment of national pledges made and accepted in good faith. It has arrogantly overruled the Government of the United States. It has refused to grant on its own motion, and its effective lobby has prevented Congress from granting any vestige of a bill of rights to its subject peoples. In its own unrestrained conduct of civilian affairs it has violated, willfully and persistently, many of the tenets of the American bill of rights. It has scorned every concept of due process of law and almost every principle of democracy. It has ignored the economic problems of the Islanders and has given them inferior education in segregated schools. It has trampled upon, with complete abandon, the standards of social policy of the International Labor Office for dependent areas. Its absolutism has been maintained as a result of effective lobbying in Congress.

There is no sign that the Navy proposes to depart from its pre-war methods in Guam and Samoa. The natives are its "wards"; and by wardship, apparently, is meant a policy of segregation — isolation from mainland culture, from modern education and denial of the protection of our Constitution. There is not one full-fledged lawyer on the Island. And certainly it is not to the Navy's credit, after nearly 50 years of its rule, and there is not a single Guamanian dentist, engineer or native teacher who has had training in the United States.

Now the Navy proposes to extend these abuses into the newly acquired Pacific islands. The Navy wishes that our national moral obligation to trustee the Carolines, the Marshalls, and the Marianas, to the Assembly of the United Nations shall not be fulfilled, and this despite the fact that Australia and New Zealand have already declared their intention of trusteeing nearby islands which also have international status.

Nor would the Navy, if it had its will, be satisfied with maintaining dictatorships over people of other than American strains. I have not yet recovered from the shock that I received after Pearl Harbor when my friend, the late Secretary Frank Knox, to whom I had a personal attachment, declared in my office that Hawai'i should be under Naval rule. As if it was the civilian administration that had been responsible for our fleet being huddled like pinioned ducks in a harbor! I disputed this theory then and I oppose it today. If necessary I would be willing for the retirement pay of our superannuated admirals to be increased. But I am not willing that more soft berths should be created for them in the governments of dependent peoples in violation of every concept of democracy and the guarantees of the Bill of Rights.

The record shows that the Navy cannot be trusted to rule civilian populations. The Navy is arbitrary, dictatorial and totally disregardful of civilian rights. I submit that it is not necessary in the interest of military security to make a mock of human welfare and the civilian rights of the peoples of such areas as we have been considering. If there is any merit in the claim of the Navy that it be permitted to keep and put fetters upon the civilian populations of such islands as Guam, Samoa, and the mandated Island of Japan; if the Navy is to be permitted to block as it is secretly doing, statehood for Hawai'i, then by a parity of reasoning, civilian rights should be struck down in such areas as Alaska, the Aleutian Islands, Puerto Rico and the Virgin Islands. Moreover, if we require Naval absolutism for purposes of military security in such places as these, then there would be no logical reason why we should not hand over to its benign rule such vital continental areas as Boston, New York Harbor, Charleston, San Diego, San Francisco and Seattle.

Democracy, as we have understood it in this country, will be entering upon its swift decline if we do not firmly adhere to the principle that our armed forces are for defense in times of war and not for civilian administration in times of peace.

Democracy and human rights and hope for peace in the entire world will suffer if we continue to withhold our national leadership in the vital matter of trusteeships under the United Nations. Our leadership can only be regained and maintained by action, not by mere words. The action needed is the enactment of Representative Biemiller's bill which would take jurisdiction over Guam and Samoa away from the Navy and give it to the Department of the Interior, and the announcement that we are going to trustee the former Japanese islands under the Assembly of the United Nations.

Appendix 4
Telegram to President Truman, August 30, 1946

The President
White House
Washington, D.C.

We urge that you make clear to the world that the United States intends to place the Japanese mandated islands under United Nations trusteeship and to govern them, as administering authority, through a civilian agency of government.

Indefinite contradictory announcements in press August 29 and 30 by spokesmen in whom final authority does not rest have the effect of increasing the confusion in American and world mind.

The General Assembly of the United Nations at its first session adopted a resolution inviting States administering territories now held under mandate to undertake practical steps for implementation of trusteeship chapters of Charter in order to submit trusteeship agreements for approval not later than the General Assembly session next September. Australia, Belgium, France, New Zealand and United Kingdom have responded affirmatively to this resolution and to the Charter provisions. The failure of the United States to make clear that it intends to trustee the mandated area which it, as military occupant, administers is injurious to development of United Nations trusteeship system and to traditional position of world leadership by this country in promoting the interests of dependent peoples.

In addition to placing these islands under trusteeship, they should be placed under civilian administration. Government of people by military agencies except in times of national emergency is contrary to American principles of democracy, justice, and freedom and obstructs fulfillment of present and possible future obligations of the United States set forth in Chapters XI, XII, and XIII of Charter. Military requirements can be fully met through trusteeship under Assembly of United Nations and without subjecting inhabitants of these islands to permanent naval rule.

Therefore, we join our fellow citizens in urging that you declare unequivocally United States intentions, and take the needed steps, to trustee the Japanese mandated islands under the Assembly of the United Nations, with the United States as administering authority, and to place these islands, along with Guam, Samoa and other United States Pacific Island possessions, under the administration of a civilian agency of the government.

John Collier, President, Institute of Ethnic Affairs
Richard Wood, President, National Peace Conference
Justice Owen J. Roberts, President, UN Council of Philadelphia
Norman Thomas, Chairman, Post War World Council
Mrs. William H. Davis, President, Women's National Democratic Club
Mrs. Edgerton Parsons, American Section, Pan-Pacific Women's Assn.
Dorothy Kenyon
Harry Laidlar
Friends Committee on National Legislation
National Council of Jewish Women
Union for Democratic Action
Council Against Intolerance
Workers Defense League
Council for Democracy
Friends General Conference

United States Student Assembly
Council for Social Action
Catholic War Veterans

[It was this telegram, allegedly cited by Forrestal's former employee then in the Treasury Department, that resulted in rejection by the Internal Revenue Service of the Institute's application for tax-free status. None of the other signers (organizations) suffered the same treatment.]

Appendix 5
How the Military Sways Foreign Policy

When the military institution makes foreign policy, foreign policy makes toward war. . . . The Army and Navy (majority members and veto-endowed members of SWNCC) handle their own predominating part of the SWNCC job in the characteristic military fashion. That fashion is to assume that an Army or Navy officer holding a certain rank is automatically, without specific training, experience or interest, fully competent to do and to judge anything in the universe that the Army and Navy deem to be within the scope of a certain rank. Therefore the units within the Army and Navy consist of only a handful of officers, men with little training in international matters, or none at all, who dispose of their business through snap-judgment or bias — an isolationist bias which does not work for peace.

One day these men may be dealing with Pacific island matters, the next with oil in the Near East, the next with peace conference issues. The State Department technicians, adequate in numbers and often adequate in technical knowledge, confront the military snap-judgment and prejudice; and again and again, to procure action at all, they find themselves accepting compromises or worse, to the grave and cumulative injury of the United States and world peace.

[—John Collier, *News Letter of the Institute of Ethnic Affairs, Inc.*, November 1946]

Appendix 6
Bills Introduced in the 80th Congress

H.R. 6858, introduced by Rep. Andrew J. Biemiller (D., Wisc.), would transfer administration of the Pacific Islands to the Department of the Interior and enact separate organic acts for Guam and American Samoa.

H.J. Res. 80, introduced by Rep. Henry M. Jackson (D., Wash.), provided for civilian administration under the Secretary of the Interior over the Caroline,

Marshall, and Marianas Islands as well as Guam and American Samoa. Any unexpended balance of funds allocated for expenditure by the Navy Department in the administration of native affairs was to be made transferable to the Department of the Interior.

S.J. Res. 51, introduced by Sen. Hugh A. Butler (R., Nebr.), was identical to the Jackson Resolution. Butler was then chairman of the full Committee on Public Lands in the Senate, a key position.

H.R. 874, introduced by Sen. Willis W. Bradley (R., Calif.), former Navy Governor of Guam, would confer U.S. citizenship upon the inhabitants of Guam.

H.R. 1417, introduced by Delegate Joseph R. Farrington (R., Hawai'i), would also give Guamanians U.S. citizenship. It had first been introduced in the 79th Congress.

H.R. 64, introduced by Robert A. Grant (R., Ind.), would provide citizenship and an organic act for Guam. It allowed the President to appoint as Governor of Guam someone who remained in the Navy or other military service and included a salary scale for administrators that Guamanians probably could not afford.

Appendix 7
Senate and House Subcommittees in 1947

Senate Subcommittee on Territorial and Insular Affairs
    Guy Cordon (R., Ore.), chairman
    Hugh A. Butler (R., Nebr.)
    A. Willis Robertson (R., Wyo.)
    Sheridan Downey (D., Calif.)
    Ernest W. McFarland (D., Ariz.)

House Subcommittee on Territorial and Insular Affairs
    Fred Crawford (R., Mich.), chairman
    William Lemke (R., N. Dak.)
    Karl M. LeCompte (R., Iowa)
    Norris Poulson (R., Calif.)
    Dean P. Taylor (R., N.Y.)
    Jay LeFevre (R., N.Y.)
    A. L. Miller (R., Nebr.)
    Charles H. Russell (R., Nev.)
    John Sanborn (R., Idaho)
    Edward H. Jenison (R., Ill.)
    William A. Dawson (R., Utah)
    Joseph R. Farrington (R., Hawai'i)

Names added to House Subcommittee in March 1947
  C. Jasper Bell (D., Mo.)
  Clair Engle (D., Calif.)
  E. H. Hendrick (D., W.Va.)
  P. E. Peden (D., Okla.)
  M. M. Redden (D., N.C.)
  Antonio Fernandez (D., N.Mex.)
  E. L. Bartlett (Alaska)
  Antonio Fernos-Isern (Puerto Rico)

Senator Butler (R., Nebr.) was chairman of the full Senate Committee on Public
Lands, and Richard J. Welch (R., Calif.) was chairman of the House Committee
on Public Lands.

Appendix 8
What Guamanians Told the Hopkins Committee

Letter from a Leading Guamanian to the Institute of Ethnic Affairs

The Dr. Ernest M. Hopkins Commission will be a success . . . if the Commission
will recommend what they heard from the crowd that met them at the Guam
Congress Hall.

No war damage claims over $5,000 have yet been paid.

Present business methods are embarrassing. Our claims have no significance
or value to the bank to be used as collateral. Even the lands with clear titles are
not accepted as collateral. Our collaterals before the war were our houses, lands
and merchandise. The former are in ashes and both the former and the latter are
in figures in the office of the Land and Claims Commission. As far as we know
only $5,000 claims will be payable in Guam and the rest have to be given further
treatment. Who knows what is the ultimate destiny?

The government owns or has the whole say of our lands or our whereabouts.
Such a condition creates discontent. The business of shoving around must be
stopped. Units at times occupying our properties won't let us come to such
properties. Most Units display the signs, "RESTRICTED AREA. KEEP AWAY." The
products of the lands—such as mangoes, oranges, etc.—are, as a rule, denied
us. Unsettled people cannot work in harmony.

Prices of food are in the upward swing. Because we are short of agricultural
land, we have to live on our pay as laborers. Guam citizens' labor pay cannot
meet with the prices of foods. The lands question must be settled so the people
can come back to the farms and make up the difference in their salaries.

The discrimination of pay between the people of Guam and the imported
labor gives us another headache. Salaries for imported labor run about four
times higher than natives' salaries for the same kind and amount of work.

Salaries must be based on the ability of the individual and not on nationality, color or creed.

There is a shortage of essentials, even of kerosene for lamps.

There should be a representative of the Veterans Bureau here in Guam to take care of the destitute veterans and dependents.

Civil rights are not being enjoyed as practiced or preached in our Mother Country. During the Japanese occupation our wild radio revealed that the Mother Country promised us or already had made us citizens. We want now the reality. We want American ideals for our children as taught in our schools and not the old Spanish ways of life. We think, do, eat and act American. Our money, stamps and language are all American. What is left is admitted to be a part of the great American nation that we helped defend, regardless of the consequences during the two great wars. The sons of Guam shared with other Americans hardships and even death during the two wars. But civil rights enjoyed by Americans are not shared. As soon as the Guam Congress reconvened in January, 1947, it passed a resolution asking the United States Congress for citizenship and an organic act. Almost all the people of all the towns approved it. This is now our great aspiration.

[From the *News Letter of the Institute of Ethnic Affairs,* March 1947, 7]

Appendix 9
Witnesses at the House Hearings in 1947

May 27
Rep. Robert A. Grant, sponsor of H.R. 3044
Sen. Hugh A. Butler, sponsor of S. 1078
John Wiig, Honolulu attorney who was Chief of Police in
    Military Government on Guam during the war

May 28
Interior Secretary Julius A. Krug
Navy Under Secretary John L. Sullivan
Assistant Secretary of State John H. Hilldring
Rep. Willis W. Bradley, Jr., former naval Governor of Guam
Maurice J. Tobin, member of the Hopkins Committee
Richard H. Wels, New York attorney who had served with
    the Navy on Guam during the war
Laura Thompson, Ph.D., author of *Guam and Its People*

June 2
Former Interior Secretary Harold L. Ickes
Assistant Secretary of State John H. Hilldring

Appendix 10
New U.S. Policy in the Pacific Islands

June 18, 1947
The President
The White House

Dear Mr. President:

Pursuant to your request, the Secretaries of State, War, Navy and Interior have held several meetings and have agreed upon the following course of action:

1. Separate organic legislation for Guam to provide civil government and to grant citizenship, a bill of rights, and legislative powers to Guamanians should be enacted this session. . . .
2. Organic legislation for American Samoa . . . should be prepared by the Navy and Interior Departments and presented to the next session of Congress.
3. Suggestions for organic legislation for those Pacific islands placed under United States trusteeship are in preparation by the Department of State for presentation to Congress, provided favorable congressional action is taken on the trusteeship agreement to be shortly presented for approval.
4. The Navy Department should continue to have administrative responsibility for Guam and American Samoa on an interim basis pending the transfer to a civilian agency of the Government at the earliest practicable date, such date to be determined by the President. With respect to the trust territory, a similar transfer should be effected by the President at the earliest practicable date.
5. Provided Congress acts favorably on the trusteeship agreement, an Executive Order should be issued when the agreement enters into force terminating military government in the trust territory and delegating civil administration to the Navy Department on an interim basis, subject to the conditions set forth in paragraph 4.

Faithfully yours,
G. C. Marshall

[In transmitting this letter to Congress on June 19, 1947, President Truman wrote: "It has long been my view that the inhabitants of Guam and Samoa should enjoy those fundamental human rights and that democratic form of government which are the rich heritage of the people of the United States."]

Appendix 11
Ickes' Column on the Nuclear Bomb Test in Bikini

September 26, 1947

Bikini Natives

Apparently it has not yet penetrated the Navy mind that every case of arrogant injustice to a native people has become an international question. This is due to the fact that America can be so outraged by the oppression of a minority group by any other nation. We can become highly self-righteous when we think of what is happening to the Indonesians or to the Jews who are seeking asylum in Palestine, in accordance with the promises in the Balfour Declaration. But the Navy cannot see the mote in its own eye.

On July 1, 1946, at 9:00 A.M., a Nagasaki-type atomic bomb was dropped at Bikini Island from the Superfortress "Dave's Dream." A fleet of 73 vessels was anchored off the Bikini atoll. Five were sunk, including two transports, two destroyers and a Japanese cruiser. Nine were heavily damaged, among them, the battleship U.S.S. *Arkansas* and the Japanese cruiser *Sakawa*. Ninety percent of the experimental animals (goats, pigs, sheep, rats and mice) survived the explosion. Now, more than a year later, additional and more serious casualty figures, involving human beings, may be revealed.

Bikini Island comprises approximately 1,500 square acres, and had been inhabited for no one knows how many hundreds of years by people who lived contentedly on an adequate island economy. Breadfruit was plentiful, and coconut palms graced the island, in abundance. To set the stage for the bomb test, the benevolent U.S. Navy persuaded the 160 natives of Bikini to move to neighboring Rongerik Island "as their contribution to the advancement of science." The Navy generously provided free transportation, and newsreel cameramen were on hand for moving day. . . .

Unfortunately, Rongerik Island has only slightly more than 400 square acres, as compared with almost 1,500 square acres which the Bikini Islanders gave up at the request of the benevolent Navy. Moreover, the soil is poor — so poor that never in history had it been inhabited. It cannot grow food successfully. People had never attempted to live there because numerous exploring parties composed of nearby natives, discovered that the island was too barren to support human beings. . . .

Now comes word that the natives are actually and literally dying of starvation. As late as a month ago, the Rongerik Islanders, late of Bikini, were in the last stages of dire want. Neither chickens nor pigs exist on Rongerik. Those who know report that domesticated animal life on the island is restricted to one old dog so under-nourished that it has developed rickets. The desperate people have been reduced to cutting down their few coconut trees in order to eat their hearts.

The Deputy High Commissioner of the Trust Territories, who has responsibility for the government and welfare of these people (under a mandate of the

United Nations to the United States) is Rear Admiral Carleton H. Wright. He is the humane brass hat who wrote the recent article in *The Saturday Evening Post* entitled "Let's Not Civilize These Happy People." I suspect that even a little food would persuade these unhappy people to adopt unanimously a resolution declaring that, not for the world, would they substitute civilian for Navy rule. This is the way it has worked in Guam. . . .

Appendix 12
Joint Congressional Committee in 1948

House Public Lands

Fred L. Crawford (R., Mich.)
William Lemke (R., N.Dak.)
Antonio M. Fernandez (D., N.Mex.)

House Foreign Affairs

James G. Fulton (R., Pa.)
Donald L. Jackson (R., Calif.)
Joseph L. Pfeifer (R., N.Y.)

Senate Interior and Insular Affairs

Guy Cordon (R., Ore.)
George W. Malone (R., Nev.)
Joseph C. O'Mahoney (D., Wyo.)

Senate Foreign Relations

Alexander Wiley (R., Wisc.)
H. Alexander Smith (R., N.J.)
Alben W. Barkley (D., Ky.)

Appendix 13
Senate Committee in 1949

Joseph C. O'Mahoney (D., Wyo.), Chairman
James E. Murray (D., Mont.)
Sheridan Downey (D., Calif.)
Ernest W. McFarland (D., Ariz.)
Clinton P. Anderson (D., N.Mex.)
Bert H. Miller (D., Idaho)
Robert S. Kerr (D., Okla.)
Hugh Butler (R., Nebr.)
Eugene D. Millikin (R., Colo.)
Guy Cordon (R., Ore.)
Zales N. Ecton (R., Mont.)
George W. Malone (R., Nev.)
Arthur V. Watkins (R., Utah)

Mills Astin, of Wyoming, was named chief clerk of the committee, replacing Hugh Brown of Nebraska. Mr. Astin had been an administrative assistant to Senator O'Mahoney for fifteen years and was conversant with the problems of offshore territories.

The group decided not to establish standing subcommittees, as had been the custom in the past, but to act as a unit. Special subcommittees would be appointed by the chairman as required.

Appendix 14
Institute News Release on Guam Assembly Walkout

FOR RELEASE TO P.M. PAPERS
March 8, 1949

Guam Assembly Walkout

"I hope that Congress and the American people will understand the significance of the walkout by the Guam Assembly at their meeting on March 5," John Collier, president of the Institute of Ethnic Affairs, stated today.

"That walkout, staged in protest against naval administration, dramatically indicates their desire for an organic act and civilian government.

"It should prompt the Navy and Interior Departments immediately to forward to Congress the organic acts they have had under consideration for many months.

"It should stimulate Congress to take action in defining the political status of Guamanians, a treaty obligation which has been neglected for 50 years.

"December 23, 1948 marked the 50th anniversary of military law in Guam," he continued. "For half a century Guamanians have been subjected to the arbitrary rule of naval governors, few of whom have stayed longer than two years. They have no Constitution. They have no court appeal beyond the Secretary of the Navy.

"Until the last two years, the Guam Congress has had advisory power only. Though the full facts are not yet available here, it has been learned that the present walkout was in protest to what Guamanians said was an attempt by the Navy to curtail their legislative authority.

"It is significant that the last act by the adjourning Assembly was unanimous approval of enactment by the United States Congress of organic legislation and civil rule. It is equally significant that the Guamanians feel they must go on strike to get the United States Congress to take an interest in their needs."

Citizenship, organic legislation, and civilian administration were recommended for Guam by an agreement of the Secretaries of State, War, Navy, and Interior, communicated to Congress on June 18, 1947 by the President.

On February 11, 1949 President Truman addressed a letter to each of the four Secretaries, stating his intention, upon enactment of organic acts, to designate the Department of the Interior as the civilian agency responsible for the administration of Guam.

On March 3, 1949 Interior Secretary J. A. Krug stated that in his opinion a target date ought to be set for a transfer of administration on Guam.

[Institute of Ethnic Affairs news release, "Guam Assembly Walkout," March 8, 1949]

Appendix 15
News Letter Story of the Guam Assembly Walkout

GUAM

What has been described as "Guam's Boston Tea Party" took place at Agana, the capital of Guam, in March. The lower house of the native Congress had been investigating possible violations of the Naval Government's economic policy, which is designed to prevent exploitation of local business by outsiders with large capital. They found that despite this policy numerous businessmen from Hawaii and the mainland, using Guamanians as "front men" had been licensed to operate in Guam. On Feb. 3 they subpoenaed one Abe Goldstein, a federal civil service employee who allegedly had a financial interest in the Guam Style Center, to appear before the investigating committee. He appeared but refused to testify, respectfully questioning the authority of the Guam Congress to conduct such an investigation. Advised that the Congress was so empowered, he still refused to testify. So the Assembly on Feb. 5 voted to charge the man with contempt of Congress and have him arrested. Prior to this vote they had been advised by the Attorney General of Guam, a naval officer appointed by the Governor, that such action was in order. But when the warrant of arrest was being served, the Governor intervened, thus contradicting the advice of the Attorney General and in effect making Goldstein immune to the laws of Guam. The Assemblymen considered this interference to constitute curtailment of the legislative authority granted them by order of Navy Secretary John L. Sullivan in 1947. On Mar. 5 they voted to adjourn in protest. A letter from the Speaker of the Assembly to the Governor dated Mar. 9 emphasized that the adjournment was not based on any single incident but upon a series of incidents which had made it impossible for the Guam Congress to know when it was performing its mission and when it was not. He said the Assemblymen preferred not to attempt to discharge their duties until their powers are defined by act of the U.S. Congress. The lower house did not meet for the regularly scheduled session, Mar. 12, though the Governor had announced that he would deliver a message on the state of Guam on that day. Following this the Governor declared the seats of the adjourned Assemblymen vacated and announced that he would appoint new legislators to their places. This brought mass meetings throughout the island at which villagers voted unanimously to stand behind their elected representatives.

In the face of this opposition to an appointed Assembly, Navy Secretary Sullivan advised Governor Pownall that he should invite the elected Assemblymen back, or, failing their return, call a special election. On Apr. 1 the 34 recessed Assemblymen were told by Governor C. A. Pownall that they could resume their seats if they returned for the regular session Apr. 1 and if they would personally register at the bar of the House of Assembly "for consideration by the Governor." Irked that they, elected representatives, should be asked to "come a-begging at the bar," the Assemblymen steadfastly maintained that their seats had never been vacated, that they were performing the will of the people. At an informal meeting on Apr. 2, the adjourned Assemblymen agreed that they would reconvene the next day, not in answer to the Governor's call but to demonstrate that their seats were not in fact vacated. Though they refused to register, the Governor accepted this meeting as sufficient fulfillment of his call to reconvene, and accordingly went through the motions of reinstating them.

Meanwhile, the Council, the upper house, took further steps to nullify the Governor's action in calling the adjourned Assemblymen's seats vacated. At informal meetings of Assemblymen and Councilmen it was agreed that the Guam Congress should invoke as its own a provision in the United States Constitution stating that neither house of the U.S. Congress can remain in adjournment more than three days without consent of the other. In carrying this out, the Council on Apr. 2 voted not to consent to the Assembly's adjournment. (Only one meeting date actually had been skipped by the Assembly, Mar. 12. The Guam Congress meets regularly on the first and second Saturday of each month.) This vote of the Council has been explained in various press releases as condemnation by the Council of the Assembly's action. But according to a letter received by the Institute of Ethnic Affairs from Councilman F. B. Leon Guerrero, speaking for the Council, it was strictly a device to circumvent the Governor's action and retain the elected Assembly. He said, "We did not then [on Apr. 2] and do not now disapprove of the motive of or the result in adjournment of the other house. Our action was for support of the status quo." Had a special election been called, Guamanians write the Institute, there is no doubt that the adjourned Assemblymen would have been re-elected.

More intensified than ever as a result of events of the past month is the feeling on Guam that not until the United States Congress acts on organic legislation granting Guam civilian government will the legislative and other rights of Guam's 26,000 native people be guaranteed. On Mar. 5 both houses of the Guam Congress approved a proposed organic act which they voted to forward to the U.S. Congress. By Mar. 22 the Institute of Ethnic Affairs had received a mimeographed, signed copy. As of the middle of April, Congress has not yet received this act of the Guam people. Presumably it is still working its way through Navy Department channels.

[From the *News Letter of the Institute of Ethnic Affairs,* March–April 1949, 6–7]

Appendix 16
Washington Post Guest Column about the Walkout

Guam Rebels at New Navy "Rule"

Four years after Agana, the capital of Guam, was reduced to ruins in the Pacific war, the Guam Congress Building emerged from the rubble, built by the Navy with American taxpayers' dollars.

Dedication of this building by Gov. Charles A. Pownall last July marked what Guamanians hoped would be a new epoch in their history. Eleven months before, Admiral Pownall had appeared before the Congress, meeting in a Quonset hut, to proclaim its authority increased from advisory to legislative status, as decreed by Navy Secretary John L. Sullivan.

Now less than a year since that building went into use, the lower house has considered its legislative powers so curtailed by the same Governor who proclaimed them that the members have voted to adjourn until the United States clarifies Guam's political status and protects their rights by act of Congress.

The Assembly adjournment March 5 was precipitated by Pownall's refusal to permit the arrest of a recalcitrant witness in an economic inquiry.

Behind the Scenes

Since the war the naval government has sought to protect Guamanian business by preventing "the unrestricted admission to Guam of outside business interests until such time as the Guamanian economy has been rehabilitated." Guamanian congressmen contend that business has been exploited not by business interests in Hawai'i and the mainland alone, but by former naval officers and Navy civil service personnel in Guam, using Guamanians as "front men."

Last November, the Guam Assembly delegated the commerce and trade committee to investigate the matter.

On February 3, Abe Goldstein, a civil service employee alleged to have a financial interest in the Guam Style Center, a women's clothing store, was subpoenaed by the committee. He repeatedly declined to submit to questioning, saying, "I hereby respectfully question the authority and jurisdiction of this committee and of the Guam Congress to inquire into the matter."

On February 5, at a regular meeting of the Congress, assemblymen emphasized that they did not wish to prejudge Goldstein. They did, however, consider him guilty of contempt of Congress. A motion to issue a warrant for his arrest was carried by a large majority. Assemblyman Joaquin C. Perez advised the

Assembly that the attorney general of Guam had informed him informally that such action was in order and that he would honor such a warrant. [Guamanians since have informed this writer that the attorney general was notified before every move the Assembly made and that he "granted permission with his blessings."]

At the next regular meeting, February 12, the speaker of the Assembly reported that he had signed the warrant for arrest, but to his knowledge it had not been served.

Commerce and Trade Committee Chairman Jesus C. Okiyama, in an applauded speech, observed:

"The Governor of Guam, as I understand, has already intervened in this case. . . . The Governor has no right to intervene until such time as Goldstein is brought before the Island Court. . . . If that warrant of arrest is not honored and Goldstein is made immune to the laws of Guam, gentlemen, we might as well dissolve this Guam Congress."

The Governor continued to object to the arrest. Early news reports of his reasons for doing so were exceedingly vague. The Navy Department recently explained to this writer that the Governor considered the Congress to be exceeding its legislative authority in attempting to arrest and perhaps imprison an uncooperative witness. Officials said that to their knowledge the issue was not whether the power of subpoena extended over military personnel and Federal civil service employees on Guam, as has been suggested by some sources, but whether the Congress, by assuming judicial authority and ordering the arrest, might place the government of Guam in an untenable position.

Whatever the reason, Governor Pownall stayed the order to commit Goldstein. This resulted in the walkout of the Assembly March 5.

Four days later, Antonio B. Won Pat, speaker of the House of Assembly, wrote the Governor of Guam:

"It must be emphasized that the Assembly's action was not based upon any single incident, but upon a series of actions which have occurred with increasing frequency since the issuance of the proclamation of August 4, 1947 [which granted the Guam Congress legislative powers]. Definition of the scope of its powers has become, in the opinion of the Assembly, a matter of interpretation of individual actions of the Congress by the executive branch of the government without observance of any uniform rule. This has created an atmosphere of uncertainty as a result of which the Assembly does not feel that it can determine when it is performing its mission and when it is not, when it is being repudiated and when it is not, and when it is being circumvented and when it is not . . . .

"The members of the House of Assembly consider that the powers of the three branches of the government must be defined. . . . Until such time as they are permitted to play their proper role in the government of Guam, they prefer not to attempt to discharge their duties as members of the House of Assembly, Guam Congress."

Backed by Legal Ruling

The assemblymen then declined to attend a special session of the Congress called by Governor Pownall for March 12. As a result of these actions, the attorney general ruled the adjourned assemblymen's seats vacated and informed the Governor that he was empowered to appoint new members.

On March 19 Pownall announced that he would "form a new House of Assembly at the earliest practical moment and clothe it with identical power to that of the defaulted House of Assembly." He asked each village commissioner to submit names of three candidates from his district.

At mass meetings since in 12 of the 19 village districts, the Governor's action has been opposed. Villages have voted unanimously to retain their elected representatives and have indorsed messages to Governor Pownall saying they "have no intention of recognizing appointed representatives."

Carlos Taitano, an ousted assemblyman, told the press March 23 that while this incident was the last straw, the political revolt grew out of three major long-standing grievances: "(l) Arbitrary rule by naval government; (2) lack of a constitution or documents anywhere guaranteeing civil rights; (3) lack of a court of appeal beyond the Secretary of the Navy." He said Guam feels this sort of government is fit only for conquered peoples, not nationals who have been loyal to the American flag for 50 years.

The issue is so explosive that it is regarded in some quarters as likely to bring to a head the transfer of administration of Guam to a civilian agency.

Variable "Self-Rule"

Since it was ceded to the United States by Spain in 1898 Guam has been under control of the Navy Department. Its self-government has been proportionate to the liberality of the presiding naval officer.

No native Assembly existed until 1917. Until 1931 the Guam Congress was not elective. It remained purely advisory until 1947. Then the 15-member council and 36-member Assembly jointly requested the power to enact law. "Interim" legislative authority was granted by the Navy Secretary in August 1947, pending enactment by Congress of organic legislation embodying law-making rights.

Two months before, President Truman had recommended to Congress that organic legislation for Guam be adopted and that jurisdiction of the island be transferred to a civilian agency at the earliest practicable date. He was supported in this recommendation by the Secretaries of Navy, Army, State, and Interior.

The final act of the Assembly before its protest adjournment March 5 was to vote unanimous approval of a proposed organic act introduced in the Eighty-first Congress by Representative Norris Poulson (R., Calif.). This bill would give Guamanians United States citizenship, a bill of rights, a resident commissioner, a two-house Legislature with power, among other things, "to institute and conduct investigations, issue subpoenas to witnesses and other parties concerned and administer oaths," a Federal court system, and extension of miscellaneous

Federal services to Guam. It would vest administrative authority for Guam under supervision of a civilian agency.

[Doloris Cogan, guest column in the *Washington Post,* April 3, 1949]

Appendix 17
Letter to the *New York Times* about the Walkout

**Forgotten Guam: Investigation by Our Legislators
Is Urged, or Enactment of Legislation**

Since 1901 the people of Guam have been petitioning the United States Congress for definition of their political status. The most recent of such petitions was personally presented by Guam Assemblywoman Concepcion Barrett to the House Subcommittee on Territories and Insular Possessions at an open hearing on May 5. A few of our Congressmen are keenly aware of the need for answering that petition with enactment of an organic act. But for the most part, as you state in your editorial of May 16, "Congress has not yet come to grips with the need for adopting an organic act for Guam." This is an anomaly to the 26,000 Guamanians.

For years civilian administration, as would be provided under all organic acts now pending, was actively opposed by the Navy, which since 1898 has governed Guam. But since the war, agreement has been reached between the Departments of Navy, War (this was before unification of the armed forces), State and Interior to transfer the administration of Pacific island peoples to a civilian agency. Testifying before the House subcommittee on May 5, Capt. P. G. Hale, chief of the Office of Island Governments, supported organic legislation which would do exactly that. No one opposed the legislation, at least in principle.

The committee, however, seems reluctant to act until it sees things for itself. There is no indication that action, favorable or otherwise, will be taken until after a trip is made.

A joint investigation of Guam, Samoa, and the Trust Territory was planned by the House and Senate last year. Plans were all set for the committee to depart Nov. 9. Then, suddenly, a week before [the] election, the trip was called off. In view of this experience Guamanians are wondering what assurance they have ever of being visited by United States legislators. Resolutions for separate investigations by the House and Senate have been introduced in the Eighty-first Congress. To date they have not been heard by either side. If an investigation is all that Congress can promise Guam this year, then that investigation should be set up and secured beyond doubt. If busy legislators are lukewarm to a 9,000-mile trip to spend a few hours on an island, then it might be suggested that organic legislation for Guam, to which there is no known opposition, be enacted without further delay. Guamanians, tired of waiting for Congress to come to them, now are considering a resolution that would appropriate $10,000 for two delegates to go to Washington. This should indicate how the people feel about their island, which *The New York Times* three years ago called "forgotten Guam."

Doloris Coulter,
Editor, *Guam Echo*
Washington, May 23, 1949

Appendix 18
Washington Officials Called On by Connie Barrett

Rep. Monroe M. Redden (D., N.C.), Rep. Fred L. Crawford (R., Mich.), Del. Joseph R. Farrington (R., Hawai'i), Rep. Reva Beck Bosone (D., Utah), all members of the Subcommittee on Territorial and Insular Possessions; Rep. Norris Poulson (R., Calif.), author of H.R. 2987 to provide civil government for Guam; Mrs. Mary Louise Steele, clerk of the House Public Lands Committee

Sen. Hugh A. Butler (R., Nebr.), author of S. 185 to provide a civil government for Guam; Sen. Margaret Chase Smith (R., Maine), United States' only woman senator at that time, and her Republican colleague from Maine, Sen. Owen Brewster. Mills Astin, clerk of the Senate Interior and Insular Affairs Committee

Rep. Robert Hale (R., Maine); Rep. Robert T. Secrest (D., Ohio), who served in the Pacific during the war and knew some Guamanians; Rep. Helen Gahagan Douglas (D., Calif.)

Oscar Chapman, Interior Department Under Secretary; James P. Davis, director of the Division of Territories and Island Possessions; Rex Lee, assistant director of the Division; Emil J. Sady, chief of the Pacific Branch; Irwin W. Silverman, chief counsel of the Division

John T. Koehler, Assistant Secretary of the Navy; Capt. Peter G. Hale, chief of the Office of Island Governments; R. Adm. H. L. Pugh, who was in the medical corps of Guam from 1935 to 1937

Philleo Nash, of the White House staff; Roger W. Jones, assistant to the director of the Bureau of the Budget; Harold Seidman and Scott Moore, administrative analysts in the Division of Administrative Management, Budget Bureau

William Yeomans, in the Dependent Areas Affairs Division of the State Department; Roy E. James, former chief of the Pacific Branch, Interior Department, then in the office of the Assistant Secretary of the Army; Frank Pollak in the Justice Department

Congressional Women's Club

Appendix 19
Truman's Letter to Interior

May 14, 1949

The Honorable
The Secretary of the Interior

My dear Mr. Secretary:

I have today informed the Director of the Bureau of the Budget that the drafts of organic legislation for Guam and American Samoa, prepared by the Department of the Interior, have my approval. The Department of the Interior will have the responsibility of presenting the measures to the Congress. I have asked the Secretary of the Navy to assist you and I enclose a copy of my letter to him.

I indicated in my letter of February 11, 1948, to the Secretaries of State, Navy and the Interior, that it was my intention, upon approval of organic acts for the Pacific Islands, to designate the Department of the Interior as the civilian agency with general supervision over civil administration of these islands. While I state again that such a designation would be without prejudice to future consideration based upon further study of long-range plans for administration of United States territories and possessions, it is my desire that realistic planning be undertaken immediately to effectuate orderly transfer of the aforementioned islands from naval to civilian administration. Accordingly, I request that you take the lead, in cooperation with the Secretary of the Navy, in developing a specific time schedule within which the desired transfers may be effected, regardless of the status of pending legislation. Preferably, under such a schedule, the Island of Guam should be transferred to civilian administration within the next year, and American Samoa and the Trust Territories within the next two to three years. Plans devised under these time arrangements can then be integrated with whatever legislative proposals are ultimately enacted.

I further request that you advise me by September 1, 1949, of the plans recommended under the aforementioned procedure.

It is the announced aim of this Government to accord civil government and a full measure of civil rights to the inhabitants of its Pacific territories. The accomplishment of this objective will be furthered by the transfer of these territories to civilian administration and the enactment of organic legislation at the earliest practicable date.

A copy of this letter is being sent to the Secretary of the Navy.

Sincerely yours,
(Sgd.) Harry S. Truman

Appendix 20
Memorandum of Understanding

1. The President should designate the future civilian Governor of Guam as soon as possible. Interior's selection for civilian Governor should be nominated by the Secretary of the Navy through the Secretary of Defense.
2. The civilian Governor should assume office on or about September 1, 1949, and from that date until the transfer date should be responsible to the Secretary of the Navy.
3. The civilian Governor, with Interior's assistance, should immediately after this designation commence recruiting civilians to replace naval personnel. The Navy Department will process the appointments and arrange for the transportation of civilian replacements.
4. Responsibility for the government of Guam should be transferred from Navy to Interior on July 1, 1950, and from that date forward the Governor should be responsible to the Secretary of the Interior.
5. Naval military personnel on duty with the Guam government will, except as otherwise agreed upon in individual cases, be detached from that duty on the transfer date, or earlier if requested by the Governor, provided that the foregoing shall not affect normal rotation of duty in individual cases. If any services are required to be performed by naval units to the Guam government after July 1, 1950, such services will be the subject of separate agreements.
6. Naval civilian personnel whom the Governor does not wish to retain will, by July 1, 1950, be reassigned to other duty or dismissed, as the Navy determines.
7. Specific arrangements with respect to the transfer of property now owned by the United States and used by the naval government of Guam will be the subject of separate agreements. These arrangements will be consistent with policies relating to property transfer set forth in the draft organic act for Guam recommended by the Interior and Navy Departments to the Eighty-first Congress.
8. Interior will submit a supplemental budget request for fiscal 1950 to cover salaries and transportation of civilian replacements of naval personnel and other costs incidental to the transfer.
9. The two Departments will cooperate closely with each other at each stage of the transfer process, making available to one another information, facilities, and personal and other services to the fullest extent practicable in order to insure an orderly transfer.

Appendix 21
House Committee in 1949 (a.k.a. Miles Committee)

John E. Miles (D., N.Mex.), Chairman
Fred L. Crawford (R., Mich.)
William Lemke (R., N.Dak.)
George P. Miller (D., Calif.)
Edward H. Jenison (R., Ill.)
Joseph R. Farrington, Delegate, Hawai'i

Accompanying them to the Pacific Islands were:
Captain Peter G. Hale, Assistant Chief of Naval Operations for Island
Governments
Irwin W. Silverman, Chief Counsel of the Division of Territories and Island
Possessions, Department of the Interior
William I. Cargo, Assistant Chief of the Division of Dependent Area Affairs
of the Department of State

Appendix 22
Institute Board Members Elected in 1949

President

John Collier

Honorary Vice Presidents

Dr. Manuel Gamio, Mexico
Dr. A. Grenfell Price, Australia
Dr. Richard C. Thurnwald, Germany
Mrs. Eleanor Roosevelt, U.S.A.

Treasurer

Huston Thompson

Directors

Burt W. Aginsky
Roger Baldwin
Warren Brown
Elliot Cohen
Felix S. Cohen
John Collier
Albert Deutsch
René d'Harnoncourt

Henrietta Durham
Paul Fejos
Charles S. Johnson
Clyde Kluckhohn
Harold Lasswell
Alexander Leighton
Ronald Lippitt
Carey McWilliams
Henry A. Murray
Jay B. Nash
Clarence Senior
Huston Thompson
Laura Thompson
John Useem
F. B. Leon Guerrero, Guam

Executive Secretary

Betty Winquest Cooper

Editor

Doloris Coulter Cogan

Appendix 23
Miles Committee Recommendations

The committee recommends:

1. That H.R. 4499, organic legislation for Guam, be passed by the House of
   Representatives as reported by the Public Lands Committee (Rept. No.
   1365) and as further amended in accordance with this report, and that it be
   passed by the Senate at this session.
2. That H.R. 4500, organic legislation for American Samoa, be promptly and
   favorably reported by the House of Representatives with the amendments
   proposed by this report, and that it be passed by the House and the Senate
   at this session.
3. That organic legislation for the Trust Territory along the lines indicated by
   this report be given early consideration by the Public Lands Committee,
   and that it be enacted by the Congress at this session.
4. That the Maritime Commission make small boats available to local government agencies, trading corporations, or to individuals in the Trust Territory, for the purpose of building up a local shipping industry, and that
   other interested Federal agencies give such assistance as may be necessary.
5. That consideration be given to the necessity of developing an intraterrito-

rial air transportation service, to connect the islands of the Trust Territory on regular schedules, fanning out from Truk and Guam.

6. That every effort be made by interested Federal agencies to encourage the establishment of locally owned and operated commercial enterprises in the Trust Territory, such as the Truk Trading Co.

7. That consideration be given by the Congress to pending legislation reorganizing the Island Trading Company of Micronesia along the lines of the Virgin Islands Corporation, to provide a source of capital and to engage in development work in the Trust Territory.

8. That the possibility of reviving markets in the Orient for products of the Trust Territory be promptly explored and that a staff be assigned to work out plans for enabling the islands to become as economically self-sufficient as possible.

9. That agricultural extension-grant legislation be extended to the Trust Territory, and that the Trust Territory be exempted from the taxes on processing of coconut oil levied by the Internal Revenue Code.

10. That the occupation authorities in Japan be asked to consider the possibility of admitting Japanese and Okinawan fishermen to the Trust Territory for the purpose of restoring the fishing industry there.

11. That every effort be made to settle promptly the outstanding war damage and land claims in the Trust Territory, Guam, and American Samoa.

12. That efforts be made to have the local communities in the Trust Territory assume as much of the cost of their school systems and health services as possible.

13. That the possibility of arranging for a floating hospital ship to visit outlying parts of the Trust Territory regularly to provide medical services to the inhabitants be explored.

14. That the armed forces immediately resurvey their military needs for lands throughout the Trust Territory, and in Guam and American Samoa, so that all land not absolutely required for military purposes may be returned to private ownership and use.

15. That the administering agency explore the possibilities of common administrative arrangements for Saipan, Tinian, Rota, and Guam, with a view to meeting the needs and the desires of the inhabitants of these areas.

16. That investigations be made to work out some plans whereby the destructive consequences of phosphate mining on Anguar may be avoided.

17. That the Department of State explore with the United Kingdom Government possible solutions to the problem of joint administration of Canton and Enderbury, and to settle the question of ownership as quickly as possible.

18. That an appropriate but inexpensive war memorial be established on Wake Island in memory of the United States soldiers who lost their lives there.

19. That appropriate amendments be made to the Nationality Act to enable

persons of American Samoan ancestry living in Hawai'i to become naturalized citizens.

20. That the rehabilitation program on Okinawa be completed as rapidly as possible.
21. That the Department of State explore the possibility of a union of American Samoa and Western Samoa.
22. That consideration be given to the establishment of a coconut-oil processing plant on Guam.
23. That pending the establishment of the Commissions provided for by the
organic legislation, the Department of State, Navy, and Interior recommend to the Congress what Federal legislation, particularly grant-in-aid
acts, should be extended immediately to Guam, American Samoa, and the
Trust Territory, and upon what basis.

[From the Report on the Pacific Islands to the Public Lands Committee of the
House of Representatives]

Appendix 24
Citation for Meritorious Service Awarded
to Doloris C. Cogan in 1955

The Secretary of the Interior
Washington
Citation for Meritorious Service
Doloris C. Cogan
In recognition of superior service in handling
territorial matters relating to Guam.

Mrs. Cogan was employed by the Office of the Secretary of the Interior and
by the Bureau of Indian Affairs approximately a year before she was detailed to
the Office of Territories in 1950. She was appointed Pacific Area Assistant four
months later, and it was from this position that she resigned on February 17,
1955. In this capacity she performed various services, including membership
on inter-departmental committees operating in connection with international
matters, particularly with relation to affairs of the Pacific islands. Mrs. Cogan's
primary responsibility was the handling of territorial matters relating to Guam.
The superior manner in which she performed her duties led to the successful
solution of a number of problems arising from the establishment of the Guamanian Government under the Organic Act in 1950 and the simultaneous transfer
of administrative responsibility for Guam from the Department of the Navy
to the Department of the Interior. She also took a personal interest in Guamanian affairs and devoted considerable time and effort to activities of the Guam

Territorial Society of Washington, D.C., and added immeasurably to the creation of a beneficial relationship between the people of Guam and the Federal Government. In recognition of this superior service the Department of the Interior bestows upon Mrs. Cogan its Meritorious Service award.

(signed) Douglas McKay
Secretary of the Interior

Notes

Chapter 1: Welcome to Guam

1. Arnold H. Liebowitz, *Defining Status* (Amsterdam: Martinus Nijhoff Publishers, 1984), 484. Based on Davidson, "Archaeology in Micronesia since 1965: Past Achievements and Future Prospects," paper prepared for Micronesian Archaeology Conference, September 1987 (National Museum of New Zealand, 1987).

2. Robert F. Rogers, *Destiny's Landfall* (Honolulu: University of Hawai'i Press, 1995), 1–40.

3. Marjorie G. Driver, *The Spanish Governors of the Mariana Islands and the Saga of the Palacio* (Hagatna: University of Guam, 2005). Much of what follows in this chapter is derived from this source.

4. Rogers, *Destiny's Landfall,* 108.

5. Ibid., 112.

6. Ibid., 113.

7. Ibid., 114.

8. Ibid.

9. Ibid., 117–123.

10. Ruth G. Van Cleve, *The Office of Territorial Affairs* (New York and Washington, D.C.: Praeger Publishers, 1974).

11. Rogers, *Destiny's Landfall,* 125–126.

12. Ibid., 196.

13. Ibid., 113. Article IX of the Treaty of Paris.

Chapter 2: The Institute of Ethnic Affairs

1. Graham D. Taylor, *The New Deal and American Indian Tribalism* (Lincoln: University of Nebraska Press, 1990), 150. Kenneth R. Philip, *John Collier's Crusade for Indian Reform 1920–1954* (Tucson: University of Arizona Press, 1977). John Collier, *From Every Zenith* (Denver: Sage Books, 1963). Lawrence C. Kelly, *The Assault on Assimilation: John Collier and the Origins of Indian Policy Reform* (Albuquerque: University of New Mexico Press, 1983). Lawrence C. Kelly, *Federal Indian Policy* (London: Chelsea House Publishers,1990).

2. H. A. C. Dobbs, *Operational Research and Action Research,* foreword to monograph published by the Institute of Ethnic Affairs, Washington, D.C., 1949. Dobbs was a lecturer on colonial administration at Oxford University in England who had independently developed "operational research" along the same lines as Collier's "action research."

3. John Collier's paper filled thirty-eight pages of the September 1945 issue of *Social Research: An International Quarterly of Political and Social Science* and was distributed to members of the Ethnic Institute as a backgrounder on what he hoped might be done for dependent peoples worldwide.

4. John Collier, "What Is Cooperative Action-Research?" *News Letter of the Institute of Ethnic Affairs,* February 1946, 5–6.

Chapter 3: Collier and Ickes Kick Off the Battle

1. On January 10, 1946, Betty made the first entry in her Institute of Ethnic Affairs ledger of $115 "for 23 residents of Guam" at $5.00 each. No specific names were attached. In July, four more Guamanians became members. They were Felix M. Camacho, Jose C. Duenas, Antonio Perez, and Jesus C. Santos. Then, in the fall, came the first avalanche of Guam members. The earliest entries among the forty-one who responded after the Ickes speech were for Edward T. Calvo, Ismael T. Calvo, Vincente Camacho, Francisco Flores, Francisco B. Leon Guerrero, William L. Lujan, Jose C. Manibusan, Juan Muna, Vincente C. Reyes, Juan Roberto, Simon A. Sanchez, and Shimizu. A ledger entry for them was made early in October. A week or two later, a larger batch of donors was recorded: Herman T. Ada, Joseph T. Ada, Rose T. Aguigui, Joaquin T. Aguon, Francisco D. Alacantara, Jesus C. Artero, Antonio C. Blaz, Pedro M. Camacho, Pedro S. Camacho, Felix T. Carbullido, Manuel T. Charfauros, Enemecio S. N. Diego, Antonio S. N. Duenas, Juan C. Flores, Juan B. Guerrero, Paciano G. Gumatantas, Cristobal Hines, Agueda I. Johnston, Segundo P. Leon Guerrero, Joaquin A. Limtiaco, E. C. Sablan, Ramon M. Sablan, Enrique S. San Nicholas, Francisco Q. Sanchez, Joaquin S. Santos, Mariano B. Santos, Joaquin T. Shimizu, and Vincente C. Tydingco. More and more Guamanians kept joining after that. I don't have all their names, but the list grew to 500 before the Organic Act of Guam was passed in 1950.

2. "Current Developments in the Institute's Sphere of Action," *News Letter of the Institute of Ethnic Affairs,* September 1946, 10.

Chapter 4: To Be or Not to Be a Strategic Trusteeship

1. "Micronesia and Trusteeship: Test for America and Crucial Need for the World," *News Letter of the Institute of Ethnic Affairs,* September 1946, 2–9.

2. Ibid., 5.

3. "Urgency of the Issues," *News Letter of the Institute of Ethnic Affairs,* September 1946, 2.

4. "The Job that Lies Ahead," *News Letter of the Institute of Ethnic Affairs,* September 1946, 10.

5. "Notes on the Pacific," *News Letter of the Institute of Ethnic Affairs,* November 1946, 7.

6. Ibid.

7. Ibid.

8. Ibid.

9. "U.S. Trusteeship Draft: Analysis and Recommendation," *News Letter of the Institute of Ethnic Affairs,* December 1946, 1.

10. Ibid., 2.

11. "How the Military Sways Foreign Policy," *News Letter to the Institute of Ethnic Affairs,* November 1946, 6.

12. "U.S. Trusteeship Draft: Analysis and Recommendation," *News Letter of the Institute of Ethnic Affairs,* December 1946, 2.

13. "Institute to Publish Newspaper for Guamanians," *News Letter of the Institute of Ethnic Affairs,* December 1946, 7.

Chapter 5: The *Guam Echo*

1. *Guam Echo,* February 1947, 2.

2. "Ickes Plays Peacemaker," by Drew Pearson, from the *Washington Merry-Go-Round,* in January 26, 1947, newspapers; reprinted in *Guam Echo,* February 1947, 3.

3. *Guam Echo,* February 1947, 4.

4. "Guam Looks to the 80th Congress," *News Letter of the Institute of Ethnic Affairs,* January 1947, 1.

5. Ibid., reprint of part of article by Lloyd Norman, of the Chicago Tribune Press Service, November 4, 1946, 1.

6. Ibid., reprint of part of article by John G. Norris in the *Washington Post,* November 24, 1946, 2.

7. Ibid., reprint of part of article by Roland Sawyer in *The Christian Science Monitor,* December 5, 1946, 2.

8. Ibid., reprint of part of article by Roland Sawyer in *The Christian Science Monitor,* December 17, 1946, 2.

9. Ibid., reprint of part of article by Eugene Rachlis in the *New Republic,* December 9, 1946, 2.

10. Ibid., 3.

11. Ibid., 4.

12. "Krug Favors Citizenship for Guam," *Guam Echo,* February 27, 1947, 1.

13. "Congressmen Express Views on Pacific Islands Government," *Guam Echo,* February 27, 1947, 2.

Chapter 6: The Fight for Civilian Government

1. "Civilian Administration: 'The Next Step,'" *News Letter of the Institute of Ethnic Affairs,* March 1947, 6.

2. Ibid.

3. John Collier letter to the *New York Times,* dated March 3, 1947; reprinted in the *News Letter of the Institute of Ethnic Affairs,* March 1947, 4.

4. Ibid., 5.

5. Robert F. Rogers, *Destiny's Landfall* (Honolulu: University of Hawai'i Press), 206–207.

6. "Secretary Krug: 'A Friend of Guam,'" *Guam Echo,* March 20, 1947, 1.

7. Ibid.

8. Ibid.

9. Ibid.

10. Reprint from *The Honolulu Advertiser*, in the *Guam Echo*, March 20, 1947, 2.

11. "Letter-to-the-Editor," *Guam Echo*, March 20, 1947, 4.

12. "Civilian Administration: 'The Next Step,'" *News Letter of the Institute of Ethnic Affairs*, March 1946, 7.

13. "Forrestal and Poulson Clash over Guam Resolution," *Guam Echo*, April 15, 1947, 1.

14. Ibid., 2.

15. Ibid., 2.

16. Syndicated "Man to Man" column, Harold L. Ickes, April 9, 1947.

17. "New Bills for Guam," *Guam Echo*, April 15, 1947, 4.

18. "The Hopkins Report," *Guam Echo*, May 15, 1947, 1.

19. Ibid., 3.

20. "Time Only Can Tell . . . ," *News Letter of the Institute of Ethnic Affairs*, May 1947, 5–8.

21. "Navy Department Receives Hopkins Committee Recommendations: Supports U.S. Citizenship and Organic Act for Guam and American Samoa," *Guam Echo*, May 15, 1947, 1–5.

22. "House Committee Holds Hearings on Guam Bills," *Guam Echo*, June 4, 1947, 1.

23. Ibid.

24. Ibid. Poulson accuses Krug of compromising his principles, 2.

25. Ibid. Hilldring likes civilian administration, 2.

26. Ibid.

27. Ibid. Laura Thompson brings up land claims, 3.

28. Ibid. Third edition of "Guam and Its People," by Laura Thompson, is distributed, 3.

29. Ibid. Representative William Lemke challenges State Secretary Hilldring, 3.

30. Ibid. Representative Fred Crawford presses for civilian administration now, 3.

31. Ibid. Richard Wels suggests bringing Guamanians to Washington to testify, 3.

Chapter 7: The Press Weighs In

1. "Congress Delays Action on Guam Bills until January," *Guam Echo*, July 1, 1947, 1.

2. "Congress Looks to Guam," *News Letter of the Institute of Ethnic Affairs*, June–July 1947, 4.

3. Ibid., 2.

4. "Truman Policy," *Guam Echo,* July 1, 1947, 2.

5. "Congress Looks to Guam," *News Letter of the Institute of Ethnic Affairs,* June–July 1947, 1.

6. Senator Poulson's letter had appeared in the *New York Times* for June 22, 1947. The Bradley and A Guamanian letters were printed in the *New York Times* of June 23 and July 8, respectively. Large portions, if not all, of the latter two were reprinted in the *Guam Echo,* August 12, 1947, 3–5.

7. "An American Samoan Speaks," *News Letter of the Institute of Ethnic Affairs,* August–September 1947, 6–8.

8. Ibid., 5.

9. "Guam Resolution for Retention of Naval Administration Disappoints Advocates of Civilian Government," *Guam Echo,* September 26, 1947, 1.

10. Ibid.

11. Ibid.

12. Ibid., 2.

13. Reprint, "Battle over the Islands" by Mary Van Rensselaer Thayer in the Aug. 14, 1947, *Washington Post; Guam Echo,* September 26, 1947, 4.

14. "Guam Students Reach the U.S.," *Guam Echo,* September 26, 1947, 2. The students, their intended fields of studies, and their colleges were Segundo Aguon and Jose Guerrero, public accounting, at Aquinas College at Grand Rapids, Michigan; Vincente Blaz, medicine, and Juan Salas, electrical engineering, at the University of Notre Dame at South Bend, Indiana; Serafina Pangelinan, music, at Rosemont College, Rosemont, Pennsylvania; Albert Rios, civil engineering, and Jose Salas, medicine, at Manhattan College, New York City.

15. "Civilian Judge Departs for Guam," *Guam Echo,* September 26, 1947, 3.

16. Reprint of "The Bikini Natives," syndicated newspaper column by Harold L. Ickes, in *Guam Echo,* September 26, 1947, 5.

17. "The Bikini Story," *Guam Echo,* December 26, 1947, 4.

Chapter 8: The Navy versus the Guamanians

1. "Governor Pownall Holds Washington Press Conference," *Guam Echo,* October 31, 1947, 1.

2. Ibid.

3. Ibid.

4. Ibid., 4

5. "Civil Rights for Guam Urged by President's Committee," *Guam Echo,* October 31, 1947, 1, 3.

6. "Samoa Passes Resolution to Retain Naval Government," *Guam Echo,* October 31, 1947, 3.

7. "Armed Forces Committee Recommends Decentralizing Pacific Forces," *Guam Echo,* November 28, 1947, 2–3.

8. "Crawford Expresses Concern over Armed Forces Recommendation," *Guam Echo,* November 28, 1947, 3.

9. Ibid.

10. Ibid., 3. *Honolulu Star-Bulletin* editorial, November 12, 1947; reprinted in the *Guam Echo,* November 28, 1947, 3.

11. "Our Responsibility," from the November 13, 1947, *Omaha World Herald,* reprinted in the *Guam Echo,* November 28, 1947, 4.

12. "A Tug of War with Guam in the Middle," from the November 8, 1947, *Baltimore Sun;* reprinted in the *Guam Echo,* November 28, 1947, 4.

13. "Civil Rights on Guam and Samoa," from the November 14, 1947, *Honolulu Star-Bulletin;* reprinted in the *Guam Echo,* November 28, 1947, 4.

14. "U.S., Debt to Guam," from the October 28, 1947, *Honolulu Advertiser;* reprinted in the *Guam Echo,* November 28, 1947, 4.

15. "VFW Ask Citizenship and Civilian Government for Guamanians," *Guam Echo,* November 28, 2947, 3.

16. Letter from John Collier dated July 17, 1947, *Guam Echo,* July 17, 1947, 5.

Chapter 9: Rehabilitation of Guam Begins

1. "Senate Approves $106,714,500 for Guam Construction," *Guam Echo,* January 30, 1948, 1.

2. "Guam Construction Costs," *Guam Echo,* December 26, 1947, 2.

3. Reprint, "Guam Corporation Making History," by Doug Lovelace, in the *Honolulu Star-Bulletin,* January 14, 1948; *Guam Echo,* January 30, 1948, 2.

4. "Guam's Educational Problems," *Guam Echo,* January 30, 1948, 2.

5. "The 1948 Outlook on Guam Legislation," *Guam Echo,* January 30, 1948, 3.

6. "Congress Receives 29 War Damage Claims," *Guam Echo,* February 28, 1948, 1.

7. "Truman Visits Puerto Rico and Virgin Islands," *Guam Echo,* February 28, 1948, 2.

8. "Action Lags on Guam Bills," *Guam Echo,* February 28, 1948, 3.

9. Ibid.

10. "James to Run for Congress," *Guam Echo,* February 28, 1948, 3.

11. "Editor's Note," Harold L. Ickes' comment, *Guam Echo,* January 30, 1948, 5.

12. Willis W. Bradley comment, Ibid.

13. Jerry Tallmer comment, Ibid.

14. Henry A. Murray comment, Ibid.

15. "Jenison Expresses Legislative Interest in Guam," *Guam Echo,* February 28, 1948, 3.

16. "Samoans Ask That Action on Samoan Bills Be Tabled '10 Years or More,'" *Guam Echo,* March 31, 1948, 1.

17. Ibid.

18. John Collier letter to the *New York Times,* April 19, 1948.

19. "Crawford Seeks Impartial Survey," *Guam Echo,* June 30, 1948, 2.

20. "Congressmen Hear Arguments for Civilian Administration of Pacific Islands at Hearings in July," *Guam Echo,* July 31, 1948, 1–2.

21. Ibid., 2.

22. "The Tumon Beach Controversy," *Guam Echo,* June 30, 1948, 4–5.

23. "Samoan Chief Rejects Equality," *Guam Echo,* July 31, 1948, 4–5.

24. Ibid., 5.

25. "The Navy and 'Trust Territory,'" *Guam Echo,* July 31, 1948, 4.

Chapter 10: F. B. Leon Guerrero Goes to Washington

1. Statement of F. B. Leon Guerrero in a letter to Foster Hailey, an editorial writer for the *New York Times,* August 26, 1948, from Doloris Coulter.

2. Institute of Ethnic Affairs news release, "Navy Will Support Civilian Administration of Pacific Islands, Guamanian Is Assured," August 29, 1948.

3. "More Delay on Guam?" editorial in the *New York Times,* October 31, 1948, reprinted in the *Guam Echo,* October 31, 1948, 5.

4. "Crawford Deplores Postponement of Trip," *Guam Echo,* November 30, 1948, 2.

5. Book Review, *Guam Echo,* December–January 1949, 5.

6. Ibid.

7. Ibid.

8. "Guam Petition," *Guam Echo,* December–January 1949, 1.

9. Reprint of Emil J. Sady statement to the *Honolulu Star-Bulletin,* January 6, 1949; reprinted in *Guam Echo,* December–January 1949, 2.

Chapter 11: Guam Assembly Walkout Spurs Congress

1. "Navy Action Protested by Guam Assembly," *Washington Post,* March 5, 1949.

2. Institute of Ethnic Affairs news release, "Guam Assembly Walkout," March 8, 1949.

3. Robert F. Rogers, *Destiny's Landfall* (Honolulu: University of Hawai'i Press, 1995), 220.

4. Ibid., 213.

5. "Motion for Adjournment," *Guam Echo,* March 15, 1949, 1.

6. "Guam Congress Walkout Spurs Action on Pacific Affairs," *Guam Echo,* March 15, 1949, 1.

7. Ibid., Representative Crawford statement, 2.

8. "Sec. Krug States Intention of Taking Over Pacific Islands," *Guam Echo,* March 15, 1949, 2.

9. "Guamanians Double Support of *Guam Echo*," *Guam Echo,* March 15, 1949, 5.

10. "Shot heard round the world," *The Dictionary of Cultural Literacy,* ed. E. D. Hirsch, Jr., Joseph F. Kett, James Trefil (Boston: Houghton Mifflin Company, 1988), 253.

11. Carlos P. Taitano's chapter, "Status Tensions between Guam and the United States: Participant-Observer Accounts," in *Guam History: Perspectives,* vol. 1,

Agana, Guam (Micronesian Area Research Center at the University of Guam, 1998), 260.

12. Rogers, *Destiny's Landfall*, 219–220.

Chapter 12: Connie Barrett Goes to Washington

1. "Housing on Guam," *Guam Echo*, March 15, 1949, 3.

2. "Needed: New Guam High School," *Guam Echo*, March 15, 1949, 3 and 5.

3. "U.S Naval Air Station," *Guam Echo*, December–January 1949, 3.

4. Ibid.

5. Ibid., 4.

6. "Navy, Interior, Mrs. Barrett Ask Congress for Organic Act for Guam," *Guam Echo*, May 6, 1949, 1.

7. Ibid.

8. Ibid., 2.

9. Ibid., 3.

10. Ibid., 3.

Chapter 13: Truman Decides by Decree

1. "Truman Directs Civilian Government for Pacific Islands," *Guam Echo*, May 27, 1949, 1.

2. "Papers Indifferent to President's May 14 Letter," *Guam Echo*, May 27, 1949, 4.

3. "Guam Thanks Truman," *Guam Echo*, May 27, 1949, 2.

4. "Rep. Redden States Intention to Visit Guam," *Guam Echo*, May 27, 1949, 3.

5. Reprint of "Pacific Rule," *Washington Post* editorial, June 14, 1949; reprinted in *Guam Echo*, July 30, 1949, 4.

6. "Navy and Interior Reach Transfer Schedule Agreement," *Guam Echo*, July 30, 1949, 1.

7. "House Rejects Transfer Funds," *Guam Echo*, August 31, 1949, 1, 2, and 3.

8. Ibid., 2.

9. Ibid., 3

10. John Collier editorial, *Guam Echo*, August 31, 1949, 4–5.

11. *Washington Post* editorial, September 4, 1949; reprinted in *Guam Echo*, September 15, 1949, 5.

12. Executive Order No. 10,077, *Guam Echo*, September 4, 1949, 2.

Chapter 14: Skinner Becomes First Civilian Governor

1. "Carlton Skinner Appointed First Civilian Governor of Guam," *Guam Echo*, September 15, 1949, 1.

2. "We Want to . . . Talk with the People in the Villages," *Guam Echo*, October 31, 1949, 1.

3. "Mrs. Johnston Leaves for Guam After Full Schedule Here," *Guam Echo*, October 31, 1949, 4.

4. Excerpts of "The Ethnic Institute's Effort in the Pacific: Accomplishment and Outlook," Dr. Laura Thompson, *News Letter of the Institute of Ethnic Affairs,* November 1949, 4.

5. "Mrs. Johnston Speaks for Guam at Ethnic Institute Meeting," *Guam Echo,* October 31, 1949, 3.

6. Ibid. Telegram from Guam Members, 5.

7. "House Committee Returns from the Pacific Prepared to Recommend Enactment Organic Acts," *Guam Echo,* December 15, 1949, 1, 2, and 4.

8. "Governor Skinner Attends Budget Conferences in Washington," *Guam Echo,* December 15, 1949, 2.

9. Ibid., 1.

10. "Typhoon Damage Reported," *Guam Echo,* November 15, 1949, 4.

11. Ibid. "Governor Skinner Attends Budget Conferences in Washington," *Guam Echo,* December 15, 1949, 4.

12. Ibid., 3.

13. "Committee Report Calls for Guam Organic Act," *Guam Echo,* January 30, 1950, 1, 2, and 3.

14. Ibid., 2.

15. "The Annual Meeting," *News Letter of the Institute of Ethnic Affairs,* November 1949, 1.

16. "Opportunity Fellowships," *News Letter of the Institute of Ethnic Affairs,* May–June, 1950, 8.

Chapter 15: The Organic Act Becomes Law

1. "Attention Focused on Guam Organic Act as U.S. Congress Slates Action and Members of Guam Congress Organic Act Committee Arrive in Washington," *Guam Echo,* March 31, 1950, 1, 2, and 5.

2. "Guam Committeemen Visit Puerto Rico and the Virgin Islands," *Guam Echo,* March 31, 1950, 4.

3. "Truman Reaffirms Support," *Guam Echo,* May 15, 1950, 1.

4. "Governor Skinner's Statement Persuasive," *Guam Echo,* May 15, 1950, 4–5.

5. "No Relation to Statehood Bills," *Guam Echo,* March 31, 1950, 1.

6. "Senate Subcommittee Hears Witnesses Approve Proposed Guam Bill," *Guam Echo,* May 15, 1950, 2.

Map and Photo Credits

Maps and photos courtesy of:

Elizabeth Barrett Anderson: p. 147

Michael Bordallo: p. 155

Doloris Coulter Cogan: pp. 47, 58, 116, 144, 188

Betty Winquest Cooper: pp. 32, 41, 189

Guam Public Library, Agana, Guam: p. 18

Library of Congress: pp. 67, 75, 78, 86, 107, 118, 149, 157, 168, 183

Micronesian Area Research Center, Mangilao, Guam: pp. 11, 13, 22, 23, 26, 33, 35, 43, 72, 124, 139, 177, 184

Robert F. Rogers, *Destiny's Landfall: A History of Guam* (Honolulu: University of Hawai'i Press, 1995): pp. viii, 4, 5, 6, 8

Nathan Sady: p. 121

Time and Life Pictures/Getty Images: p. 40

Carlos Taitano: p. 137

U.S. Department of the Interior Museum: pp. 70, 114

U.S. National Archives: pp. 27, 49, 95, 98, 120, 125, 156

Index

About the Author

Doloris Coulter Cogan received an M.S. from the Columbia University Graduate School of Journalism in 1946. Upon graduation, she was named editor of publications for the new Institute of Ethnic Affairs in Washington, D.C. In 1951, she was appointed Pacific Islands Assistant in the Department of the Interior, where she worked until 1955. From 1965 to 1988 she was director of corporate communications for Fortune 500 companies. She is retired and lives in Indiana.

Production Notes for Cogan | WE FOUGHT THE NAVY AND WON
Cover and interior design by April Leidig-Higgins in MinionPro,
    with display type in The Serif.
Composition by Copperline Book Services, Inc.
Printing and binding by The Maple-Vail Book Manufacturing Group
Printed on 60# Text White Opaque, 426 ppi